THE
GOLEM
TRIPTYCH

OTHER PLAYS BY ERIC BASSO

Smorfia (1977)
The Villain (1978)
Nighlight (1979) ⎫ the
The Lecture (1980) ⎬ *Enigmas*
Gentlemen of the Old School (1981) ⎭ trilogy
Business from Porlock (1981)
The Armoire (1982)
Adèle Pierre (1982)
Under the House (1984)
The Habsburg Chin (1984)
Simon the Magician (1984)
The Sabattier Effect (1985)
The Sword and the Mask (1985)
The Footsteps (1985)
Dragon Hand (1986)
The Cult of the Gods (1986) ⎫ the
Theodora (1986) ⎬ *Byzantium*
Naked in Byzantium (1987) ⎭ trilogy

SCREENPLAY

The Golden Hour (1988)

THE GOLEM TRIPTYCH

♣ A DRAMATIC TRILOGY ♣

BY

ERIC BASSO

*with incidental music
composed & arranged
by the author*

SANTA MARIA | ASYLUM ARTS | 1994

Copyright © 1994 by Eric Basso

Dates of copyright as unpublished works: *Middle Distance* (American version) Copyright © 1980 by Eric Basso; *Joseph in the Underground* (American version) Copyright © 1981 by Eric Basso; *Middle Distance* (British version), *Joseph in the Underground* (British version) and *The Fall of Prague* as *The Golem Triptych* Copyright © 1983 by Eric Basso.

Cover illustration *Golem* (1978) by the author.

Special thanks to Charles R. Boyd, who set the musical score for this book.

CAUTION: Professionals and amateurs are hereby warned that the plays in this volume are fully protected under the copyright laws of the United States of America, the British Empire, the Dominion of Canada, and are thereby subject to royalty arrangements. All performance rights, including professional, amateur, motion picture, recitation, lecturing, public reading, and radio and television broadcasting, and the rights of translation into foreign languages, are strictly reserved. Permission for performances and readings must be secured from the author in writing. All inquiries concerning these rights should be addressed to Eric Basso, c/o Asylum Arts, P. O. Box 6203, Santa Maria, CA 93456, U.S.A.

ISBN 1-878580-15-9 (cloth)
ISBN 1-878580-16-7 (paper)
Library of Congress Catalogue Number: 93-70300

       Basso, Eric, 1947-
       The Golem Triptych

          1. Golem - Drama. 2. Golem and Rabbi Judah Loew - Mythology.
          3. Rabbi Judah Loew, Tycho Brahe, Rudolf II - History.
          4. Divination - Magic. 5. Golem - Religion.

                               FIRST EDITION

Author's Note

The dialogue is written in British. All stage directions *left* and *right* are from the actor's point of view.

in memoriam
ERNANO BASSO
1917-1990
my father

I.
Middle Distance

I'anatomise maintenant les testes de diuers animaux, pour expliquer en quoy consistent l'imagination, la memoire, &c.

—Descartes

DRAMATIS PERSONÆ

JOSEPH, *a man of eighty*

LUBA, *a brunette in her twenties*

1ST GUARD
JOSH } *a man in his middle thirties*
RAPITRONE

2ND GUARD
JAKE } *a man in his late twenties*
CORBY

JUNE
LYLA } *a blonde in her twenties*
PEG

SPAHDA
CHESTER
SHEM } *a man in his forties*
VOICE

ACT ONE

Scene 1

Darkness. Then a shaft of moonlight falls across the L-shaped stair from an oval window on the landing, the stair at centre stage.

JOSEPH (*unseen beyond the top of the stair, longingly or like a dying man*): Luba.

    Pause.

Luba!

    Pause.
    LUBA *silently mounts the stair, her nude figure rising from utter darkness, through the ellipse of moonlight, into the upper shadows.*
    Fade to black.

Scene 2

An old house parlour, twilight. Up centre, the L-shaped stair can be seen in the dimness of the hall through the parlour archway; at the right end of the hall, out of view, the front door. The parlour furniture is almost antique, but in good repair. Bookshelves along the right wall, a window, and a desk; a typewriter on the desk, a litter of papers, etc. In the left wall, the door to SPAHDA's *bedroom.*

    Down centre, slumped in a chair facing the audience, JOSEPH *appears to be sleeping: his head is thrown back; an open newspaper lies on his face, covering the top front of his striped pyjamas; his emaciated hands hang limply over the padded armrests. He is barefoot, lighted by the floor lamp beside his chair. None of the other lamps are on.*

    Long pause.

    The front door opens then slams as the 1ST *and* 2ND GUARD *rush in from the hall in the midst of a heated argument.*

1ST GUARD: Don't give me that! You must have done something to set him off —

2ND GUARD: I swear, I didn't do anything —

1ST GUARD: You expect me to believe that after —

2ND GUARD: Look, just have a look at him! You'll see.

> *They prop their rifles against the nearby sofa and begin to scrutinise* JOSEPH; *neither moves to touch him.*
> *Pause.*

Well? You see?

1ST GUARD: I can't tell anything yet. What's the paper for?

2ND GUARD: Well, I thought —

1ST GUARD: He looks like he's asleep.

2ND GUARD: Yeh, I thought—

1ST GUARD: Sssh!

> *He puts his ear to the newspaper.*
> *Pause.*

You're right. He's not breathing. You're sure you didn't —

2ND GUARD: I told you already —

1ST GUARD: Because I know you. I know what you're like. You know how important this is; if you've done anything, I'll have to —

2ND GUARD: Listen, you've got to believe me; I —

1ST GUARD: All right, all right. Let me think. (*Brief pause*) Did you talk to him at all? I mean, did you try to question him?

2ND GUARD: Look, what's that got to do with it —

1ST GUARD: Just tell me!

ACT ONE 13

2ND GUARD: Well, yes.

1ST GUARD: Good! Then it isn't a total loss. What did he say?

2ND GUARD: He must have been delirious, I don't know.

1ST GUARD: What do you mean? Come on.

2ND GUARD: He kept saying, If I could remember, if only I could remember.

1ST GUARD: Nothing else?

2ND GUARD: Not much.

1ST GUARD: Well? What else did he say?

2ND GUARD: A name. I can't remember.

1ST GUARD: What? Think. You've got to —

2ND GUARD: Give me a bit of time, it'll come back to me.

1ST GUARD: Where was Captain Spahda during all this?

2ND GUARD (*indicating the bedroom*): In his room.

1ST GUARD: And Corporal Odradek?

2ND GUARD: Haven't seen her all day. I don't know where she is.

1ST GUARD: Hmph, strange. *You'll* have to tell Spahda. It was your fault.

2ND GUARD (*swallows hard*): He'll have me shot. You don't think — do you think we can make something up? I mean, we could give him a story, make up a story about how the old man talked just before he died; you know, something that fits in with what —

1ST GUARD: It's no good. This is too important. You know how important this is for the Captain to interrupt his schedule like this just to question him, to question him personally. You know how unusual that is. It must mean that —

2ND GUARD (*nodding*): Yes —

1ST GUARD: That large movements of troops have already begun to sweep across the border.

2ND GUARD: It's hard to believe.

1ST GUARD (*nodding*): Hmph. Who'd have thought it would come to this? It doesn't make sense, when you think about it. Something's wrong. It just doesn't make sense.

He goes to the window and peers out through the blinds.

Looks like being snow. What do you think, you think it'll snow?

2ND GUARD: It's cold enough.

1ST GUARD: Wssh, it's hot in *here*.

He unbuckles his gun belt and removes his greatcoat, tossing them on to a nearby chair as he talks; the 2ND GUARD *follows suit.*

Anyhow, if it's all up, if we *are* pulling back from the border, the snow'll slow things down a bit, give us time. It'll work to our advantage.

2ND GUARD: But if that *is* the case, if the guerrillas *have* broken through and we're in retreat, we should have been told something by now.

1ST GUARD: Not necessarily. You know the army.

2ND GUARD: You're forgetting the procedure —

1ST GUARD: Ah, that —

2ND GUARD: In the event of a general retreat, we're to round up the villagers and—

1ST GUARD: No, I didn't forget. I just don't like to think about it. Here, have a look.

The 2ND GUARD *peers through the blinds.*

See anything? There, against the bushes. It's starting to come down. No, don't look at the sky, you won't see anything.

ACT ONE 15

2ND GUARD: I don't know.

1ST GUARD: What?

2ND GUARD: I can't tell.

1ST GUARD (*raising the blind*): Here.

2ND GUARD: Hmmm.

1ST GUARD: Look at the bushes.

2ND GUARD: I am.

1ST GUARD: You have to look at them in a certain way to see it. It's very fine. It's not begun to lay.

2ND GUARD: Uuuh. I don't see anything.

The 1ST GUARD *takes another long look.*
Pause.

1ST GUARD: It's stopped. Look at the sky. Like lead —

2ND GUARD: Mmmm.

1ST GUARD: When I was posted in the North, in the camp they had there years ago—

2ND GUARD: Mmmm —

1ST GUARD: It isn't there now.

2ND GUARD: I remember.

1ST GUARD: Were you ever there?

2ND GUARD: No, but everyone knows the things that went on up there —

1ST GUARD: Hah! Everyone knows. You can't imagine what the prisoners were like there. They were like mad dogs! I thought I would go mad myself. No one stayed there long, you know; it was a very brief tour of duty. I was there in the winter. It was like . . . Huh, it was like guarding a pit, a white pit full of . . . monsters. I mean, they weren't — they weren't human, none of them. Not by then. You couldn't keep them inside. You'd think concentration camp duty would be worse, but *this* . . . The sickness —

2ND GUARD (*nodding*): Ah.

Pause.

1ST GUARD: I don't know what they called it, I can't remember. I'd sit up there on the catwalk, my legs dangling over the side, looking down at the snow littered with bones and excrement, and them walking there duing the day like normal people, until the shadow fell across the ditch. It was a kind of amnesia they had. Huh, we would've done better to kill them right off — men, women, children, the whole lot — but, you know, because they were our own people . . . Whenever anyone acted strangely, whenever anyone began to forget things, they were rounded up, herded into a boxcar and taken north to the camp.

2ND GUARD: North to mystery.

1ST GUARD: You remember. Yeh, that's what they used to say. No one really knew what went on there until after it was all over. Oh, there were rumours, but nothing ever really got out; nothing certain, that is. The army kept the lid on.

Pause.

It was a huge ditch they were in, over half a mile long, but narrow enough across for us to see the watchmen on the other catwalk through our field glasses. Most of the watchmen were old men; don't ask me why, I never sorted it out. Perhaps somebody thought old men would prove more reliable for the work. It wasn't so. I mean, we had nothing to do all day; it was bloody boring. I think most of the older watchmen were senile and tried not to let on.

2ND GUARD: Huh?

1ST GUARD: Yeh. Most of them had to be led by the hand to their post, especially at night. Well, at night everyone went a bit barmy. It didn't half make your flesh crawl to hear the weeping, that groaning, and none of it human. Worst of all was at dusk, like it is now; everything grey, the prisoners changing form.

2ND GUARD: What do you mean?

1ST GUARD: It's hard to explain what it was actually like. The other watchmen and

ACT ONE

I, we passed a cigarette from hand to hand and tried not to look down — anything to keep us occupied during that period of metamorphosis — it was always so unsettling. You could accustom yourself to anything but that. We could forget about them down there during the day; they were all right then, never kicked up a fuss, chatted quietly amongst themselves, yeh, and never seemed to notice they were living in a ditch where the next snowfall buried the filth they made along with the bones of the animals they'd eaten, the animals we threw down to them at night — animals to the animals.

2ND GUARD: Are you telling me these people — these amnesiacs — could change themselves, physically, into animals, like a werewolf or something?

1ST GUARD: It wasn't like that. They weren't in control of themselves. No, I suppose if you think about it, except for the voices there was no physical change; but—

2ND GUARD: Only their voices, then.

1ST GUARD: Yeh, their voices. Christ, I can't even describe it. The moonless nights were almost unbearable, and we weren't allowed to plug our ears either. We had to keep our ears open because the lights didn't reach far. With no moon, the middle distance was black as pitch; you couldn't see a thing. They all gathered there, those that hadn't been eaten alive by the others and still had the strength to carry themselves out of range of the lights. The noise, it makes me sick just thinking about it.

2ND GUARD: It sounds so unreal.

1ST GUARD: Hmmm. I can scarcely believe it myself, even now with the image fixed in my mind as clearly as on that first night of the watch. Sometimes I think I imagined it all, that it couldn't have happened, that I dreamt it all and forgot it was a dream.

2ND GUARD: A nightmare, more like.

1ST GUARD: Yes, I have my doubts. If I could see some of the others who were up there with me. Never saw any of them again. Most are probably dead of old age or killed off in the war. Until I can talk to one of the other watchmen again, I'll always have my doubts. They say some of them — some of the prisoners, I mean — actually got better, were sent home, and behaved as though nothing had happened. That's what really bothers me. It nags at me — you know? — like something horrible, something horrible you remember doing as a child that everyone tells you never happened; people who would know tell you you only imagined it. That's what I can't get out of my head.

2ND GUARD: Perhaps Spahda can help you locate one of the ones who was with you on the catwalk watch.

1ST GUARD: Hah! You can forget about that now his prize turkey's copped it.

He lowers the blind.

2ND GUARD: Cor, don't remind me.

They return to JOSEPH, *prowling about his chair, aimlessly scrutinising him as they talk; neither moves to touch him.*

1ST GUARD: Well, we can't put it off for ever. He'll be coming out soon. So, what about that name?

2ND GUARD: What?

1ST GUARD: The name he mentioned just before he popped off.

2ND GUARD: I'm still working on it.

Sound of the front door opening, closing. Enter JUNE, *after a pause, in military skirt, blouse, tie, etc.*

JUNE: You. What's all this? (*Suddenly eyeing their greatcoats*) Don't you lot know enough to hang your coats in the hall?

2ND GUARD: We were in a hurry.

JUNE (*eyeing* JOSEPH): What are you letting him sleep in *here* for?

1ST GUARD: Captain Spahda's orders. He's here for questioning.

JUNE: Well, you might at least wake him up. (*To* JOSEPH) Here, you!

She lifts off the newspaper and casts it aside; the 2ND GUARD *snatches it nervously out of the air.* JOSEPH's *face is revealed: sunken jaws, blue with stubble; a gaping, toothless mouth; closed eyes; a shaved head. His 'pyjama' top bears three large numerals above the breast pocket: 432.*

(*Nudging* JOSEPH) Up you get! You can't sleep here.

1ST GUARD (*restraining her*): What's the matter with you? Look at him.

Pause.

JUNE: Oh.

1ST GUARD: Yes.

JUNE: Well, what's he doing in Captain Spahda's office if he's dead?

2ND GUARD: He wasn't when we brought him in.

JUNE: Where's the Captain, then?

1ST GUARD: In his room.

JUNE: Oh, yes. Of course, but —

2ND GUARD: He doesn't know yet.

JUNE: That, uh, 432 is dead.

2ND GUARD: Right.

JUNE: Well, don't you think you'd best go in and tell him?

2ND GUARD: We've been trying to get up the nerve.

JUNE: Ah, he was that important.

1ST GUARD: Who knows? Only, what with all the unrest lately . . .

JUNE: Ah, yes.

2ND GUARD: The guerrillas, they've broken through all along the border —

1ST GUARD: Shut up!

JUNE: Where did you hear that?

1ST GUARD (*to* 2ND GUARD): You imbecile!

JUNE: Well, it's news to me.

She exits into SPAHDA's *room.*

1ST GUARD: Bloody hell! When are you going to learn to keep your mouth shut?

2ND GUARD: Well, I thought that, being Spadha's secretary and all, she might —

1ST GUARD: Oh, never mind, never mind. If you know what's good for you you'll come up with that name, and quick. She's probably in there giving him the lowdown on our friend here right now. He'll be fit to be tied.

Enter SPAHDA *brusquely,* JUNE *trailing behind.* SPAHDA, *clad in his vest, jodhpurs (braces down)* and riding boots, is wiping shaving cream from the unshaven half of his face with a towel, which he quickly tosses to the* 2ND GUARD.

SPAHDA: The maps! Get out the maps!

1ST GUARD (*saluting*): Yes, Commandant!

He runs to the couch and drops to his knees, extracting several rolled maps from beneath.

SPAHDA: What's the prisoner doing in my chair? For God's sake, put him on the floor!

2ND GUARD (*saluting*): Yes, Commandant!

The 1ST *and* 2ND GUARD *scramble, lifting* JOSEPH *out of the armchair, half dropping him to the floor in their haste.*

SPAHDA: Look inside his mouth!

He collapses into the vacated chair.

1ST GUARD: Commandant —

SPAHDA: Under the tongue. Quick! Look under the tongue, you imbeciles!

---

* vest = undershirt; braces = suspenders

The 2ND GUARD *holds* JOSEPH's *mouth open while the* 1ST GUARD *peers into it with the aid of a torch.*

Well? Well?

1ST GUARD: Nothing.

SPAHDA: Nothing. You're sure?

1ST GUARD: Yes, Commandant.

SPAHDA: Nothing on or under the tongue?

1ST GUARD: It's difficult to see under —

SPAHDA (*to* JUNE): Corporal Odradek, look into the prisoner's mouth.

JUNE: But Captain, I —

SPAHDA (*uneasily*): Don't be afraid. It's perfectly normal. Just have a look.

Reluctantly, she kneels beside JOSEPH *and peers into his mouth, lit by the beam of the* 1ST GUARD's *torch.*

Well? Anything?

Pause.

JUNE: I can't see anything. He hasn't got a single tooth in his head.

SPAHDA: Put your finger under the tongue.

JUNE: What?

SPAHDA: It's all right. Just put your finger in and tell me if there's anything.

Even more reluctantly, she slips her finger into JOSEPH's *mouth.*

(*Staring straight ahead*) Well? Have you got it in?

JUNE (*squeamishly*): Yes.

SPAHDA: Under the tongue?

JUNE: Wait.

    Pause.

SPAHDA (*always staring ahead*): Don't worry. There's nothing to be ashamed of —

JUNE: Yes.

SPAHDA: Feel anything?

JUNE: Only the tongue.

SPAHDA: Ah.

JUNE: It's dry, like sandpaper.

SPAHDA: Nothing else? You're sure?

JUNE: Nothing.

    She takes her finger out and wipes it off on the towel. The 2ND GUARD *withdraws his hands from* JOSEPH*'s lips, which continue to gape.*

SPAHDA: Who is he?

2ND GUARD: 432.

SPAHDA: I can see that!

    The 1ST GUARD *hands him a clipboard. He glances at the manifest without emotion.*

So, Joseph Golem is dead. (*Suddenly blasé*) Take him away.

2ND GUARD (*at attention*): Commandant, it was my fault.

SPAHDA: No matter. You oughtn't to have put him in my chair, is all.

    The 1ST *and* 2ND GUARD *move toward* JOSEPH. SPAHDA *grabs the sleeve of the* 2ND GUARD.

No. You stay here. He can handle it well enough.

The 1ST GUARD *puts on his greatcoat, extracts a cudgel from his belt, lifts* JOSEPH'*s head and places the cudgel, horizontally, against the nape of the dead man's neck, forcing the head back upon it by gripping* JOSEPH *under the chin with his free hand. Thus he exits, dragging* JOSEPH'*s body toward the hall.*

(*To* JUNE) Go open the door for him.

She exits into the hall.

2ND GUARD: He said very little, Commandant.

SPAHDA: It's of no consequence.

2ND GUARD: It was his memory. Even if he'd survived for the interrogation we'd have got nothing out of him.

SPAHDA: *What* about his memory?

2ND GUARD: He kept saying, If I could remember, if only I could remember. Or something to that effect.

SPAHDA (*firmly*): Yes.

2ND GUARD: And a name.

SPAHDA: Ah, the name. I suppose he forgot his name.

2ND GUARD: No, sir. I mean . . . What I mean is, he kept repeating —

SPAHDA: So, he remembered it then. Nothing unusual in that.

2ND GUARD: The name of another.

SPAHDA: What?

2ND GUARD: Someone else's name.

SPAHDA: Whose? What name? Was it my name?

2ND GUARD: One syllable.

SPAHDA: Ah. It wasn't my name, then.

2ND GUARD: No, sir.

The front door closes.

SPAHDA (*rising*): Well. That's something, at least.

2ND GUARD: Yes, Commandant.

JUNE *returns.*

SPAHDA: And the syllable?

2ND GUARD: What? Oh, it's slipped my mind. I nearly had it a minute ago.

SPAHDA: Never mind. It'll come to you. Don't try to force it, it'll come. How many times did he say it?

JUNE: Is this important?

SPAHDA: You never know.

2ND GUARD: Let me think.

Pause.
He shrugs his shoulders.

SPAHDA: Well, just give it time. You're new, aren't you?

2ND GUARD: Yes, sir.

SPAHDA: Just give it time. It's probably nothing, nothing at all.

2ND GUARD: He must have been delirious, sir.

SPAHDA: Yes, that's it. He must have been delirious.

2ND GUARD: Huh, that's brought it back! I remember now.

SPAHDA: Ah.

2ND GUARD: Faust!

SPAHDA: Faust. You're sure?

2ND GUARD: Yes, Commandant. Faust.

> *Pause.*
>
> Just before he stopped breathing. He said he was Faust.

SPAHDA: He told you he was Faust, or he called the name?

2ND GUARD: No, that's what made me remember — his being delirious. He didn't ... I mean he called, Faust! Faust! at first, then told me he was Faust, or that he believed he might be Faust. He didn't sound at all sure about it.

SPAHDA (*pondering*): Mmmm.

> *Pause.*
>
> What about the other guard, was he with you?

2ND GUARD: No, sir.

SPAHDA: So, you were alone with the old man when he died; you were the only one to hear this.

2ND GUARD: Yes, Commandant.

SPAHDA: I see.

> *Pause.*
>
> All right, you're dismissed. I may want to question you later.

2ND GUARD (*snaps to salute*): Commandant!

> *He gathers up his things and exits via the hall. The front door slams.* SPAHDA *is momentarily lost in thought.*

JUNE: Captain?

SPAHDA: Uh, what?

JUNE: You think it might have been cyanide?

SPAHDA: What?

JUNE: The prisoner —

SPAHDA: No —

JUNE: That the prisoner had a cyanide capsule in his mouth and —

SPAHDA: No, no. Without teeth? You saw for yourself. How could he break the capsule open?

JUNE: With his hands, they weren't tied. He could have slipped the powder into his mouth.

SPAHDA: Possible. Did you smell anything —

JUNE: I . . . No. I mean, I didn't get close to him —

SPAHDA: Let me see your finger.

He takes her hand, sniffs the extended finger, then thrusts it into his mouth, sucking it.

JUNE: Captain Spahda!

She yanks her finger out of his mouth, snatching up the towel, and wipes it dry.

SPAHDA: It's all right. Nothing to be ashamed of —

JUNE: Ugh —

SPAHDA: It wasn't cyanide, that's for sure. Give me the towel. (*Sniffing the towel*) Uh, mmm. Not a trace. Didn't think it was cyanide, but it never hurts to be sure.

He goes to the window.

You can never be too sure.

He raises the blind.

It's snowing, look. I didn't realise.

JUNE: Ah, well. And about time, too.

She joins him at the window.

SPAHDA: Look, it's begun to settle.

JUNE: Mmmm. Looks like being a blizzard.

SPAHDA: What's the weather report?

JUNE: Snow throughout the night, ending late tomorrow.

SPAHDA: Ah.

Pause.

(*To himself*) Faust.

JUNE: Mmmm?

SPAHDA: The prisoner. Faust —

JUNE: Oh.

SPAHDA: Strange.

JUNE: What?

SPAHDA: The snow. It just reminded me of something. Of course, the prisoner was delirious . . .

JUNE: Mmmm. What were you going to say?

SPAHDA: Suppose Faust had the Devil and a lap dog in to tea?

JUNE (*chuckling*): What? The Devil and a —

SPAHDA: Faust one evening under the snows. You never heard that?

JUNE: No.

SPAHDA: Ah, well. Faust one evening under the snows had the Devil and a lap dog in to tea. You understand?

> *Pause.*

JUNE: No.

SPAHDA: It's simple.

JUNE: I don't understand it.

SPAHDA: Well. What if it was only a lap dog and not Mephistopheles at all?

JUNE: Hmmm?

SPAHDA: Don't you see? If the lap dog was a *real* dog, and not the Devil in disguise—

JUNE: Mmmm —

SPAHDA: Then all the wonders worked by Faust, all the tricks and miracles that brought him fame and riches, were of his own devising, not a gift to him in exchange for his soul, an eternal damnation. You see? Faust would then have been a true magician, a magus instead of a charlatan, the Devil's stooge.

JUNE: Yes. I see what you're getting at. It's a pretty conceit.

SPAHDA: Mmmm. The snow made me think of it. Whenever it snows, I . . .

> *Pause.*
>
> I don't know, there's something, something . . . an image — I can't explain it. Gives me a queer feeling, the snow. It makes me . . . uneasy.

JUNE: Mmmm.

SPAHDA: You don't know what I'm talking about, do you?

JUNE: Well . . .

SPAHDA: I don't know, myself, sometimes.

JUNE: Do you believe in the Devil?

SPAHDA: Huh! What a question. We're not living in the Middle Ages. (*Watching the snow*) Look, it's really coming down. Under the lamps.

JUNE: Mmmm —

SPAHDA: What did you find out?

JUNE: Hmmm?

SPAHDA: Luba. What did you find out about her?

JUNE: Not much. Not much at all.

SPAHDA: Uh —

JUNE: Very little to go on.

SPAHDA: Ah. I was afraid of that. Well, tell me everything.

JUNE: But there *are* certain things... You know how it is, none of us is to know any more than he should about the others involved. It's for our own protection.

SPAHDA: But who decides?

JUNE: Orders.

SPAHDA (*pacing, excitedly*): Orders! We must have orders before we can proceed with anything. What orders brought me here? How did I come to be here? I was perfectly content to be where I was. (*Faltering*) Where I was.

   She embraces him.

JUNE: Calm yourself.

SPAHDA (*absently*): What?

   He returns her embrace as they collapse into the armchair, JUNE *straddling* SPAHDA's *lap. They kiss. His hands wander absentmindedly over her hips and buttocks.*

   That's better.

JUNE: Ummm, yes?

SPAHDA: Yes.

JUNE: Ouch! (*Pressing her face to his clean-shaven cheek*) Ah, that's more like it. (*Stroking his stubbled cheek*) Mmmm. Feels rough, like the prisoner's tongue.

SPAHDA: Yes.

JUNE (*nuzzling*): Ummm, yes?

SPAHDA: Yes.

JUNE (*softly*): Yes.

She rises, straightens her skirt, etc., and begins to rummage amongst the papers on the desk.

Hmmm, it's getting dark.

She switches on the desk lamp, sits, and continues to leaf through the papers.

Ah, now I can see what I'm about.

SPAHDA (*calmly*): You'd better pull the blind.

She swivels her chair, lowers the blind, and returns to the scattered papers, putting a small sheet in the typewriter. She types.

(*Staring straight ahead*) June?

She continues to type.

June?

She stops.

JUNE: Yes, Captain?

SPAHDA: What about that other business?

JUNE: What business?

SPAHDA: The maps. I nearly forgot. *What* did he say?

JUNE: Who?

SPAHDA: The guard. The new one. What's his name?

JUNE: I forgot.

SPAHDA: I want to have a look at the maps. Ring him up. Get both of them back here.

JUNE: It's getting late.

SPAHDA: What time is it?

JUNE (*glancing at her watch*): Hmm, getting on for half past five.

SPAHDA: Hmmm.

> *She picks up the phone.*

Never mind. They'll have gone off by now.

JUNE (*hanging up the receiver*): Shouldn't you be getting ready?

SPAHDA (*nodding*): Mmmm —

JUNE: You still have to finish shaving.

SPAHDA: What is it, half past five, did you say?

JUNE: Mmmm.

SPAHDA: I've still got time.

JUNE: What about the snow?

SPAHDA: It isn't far, two blocks; maybe three, I don't remember. It isn't far. I'm walking.

JUNE: Ah, of course. You can't take one of the civilian cars.

SPAHDA: I doubt if any of them is still in working order after all this time. As for the jeep . . . Well —

JUNE: Mmmm. Yes, out of the question.

SPAHDA: I think she's already beginning to suspect.

JUNE: Who, the nurse?

SPAHDA: Mmmm, if that's what she is.

JUNE: Where are you taking her?

SPAHDA: Nowhere.

JUNE: Oh?

SPAHDA: No. It's dinner for two at her digs. (*Rubbing his hands*) I don't mind.

JUNE (*chuckling*): Hah.

SPAHDA: What about my curfew pass, Corporal?

She types the last line and pulls the sheet from the typewriter.

JUNE (*waving the pass*): Waiting to be authorised by Captain Spahda.

They chuckle. SPAHDA *rises, goes to the desk, and signs the pass.*

SPAHDA: Check the date.

JUNE: It's all right.

She stamps the pass.

(*Handing it over*) Well. There you are . . . Chester.

Conspiratorial chuckles.
Exit SPAHDA *into his room.*
JUNE *hoods the typewriter, tidies up the desk, then rises. She loosens her tie, unbuttons her collar, stretches, and yawns as she walks into the hall. Silently, she mounts the stairs.*
Fade to black.

ACT TWO

A drab bed-sitting room, night. Along the rear wall, from right to left: an oval mirror above the liquor cabinet; a door giving on the outer hall; a curtained window. Beneath the window, an old brass bed, its headboard flush with the left wall. A night table, lamp and phone beside the bed, down left. Down right, the kitchen doorway; up right, the bathroom door lies directly opposite the foot of the bed. Down centre, the table is set for an intimate candlelight supper, a chair at either end. A light from the kitchen dimly illuminates the room.

LUBA, *in her nurse's uniform, lights the centrepiece candle with a long kitchen match, stares at the match-flame for a few seconds more, then blows it out.* JOSEPH *lies motionless on the bed, his head protruding above the sheets, hidden in the darkness.*

LUBA (*glancing at her watch*): Hmmm.

> *She goes into the kitchen and reënters with two red linen napkins, folding them into cones, standing each on a plate to the left and right of the centrepiece. She takes in the overall effect, straightening one or two pieces of cutlery.*

(*With satisfaction*) Ah.

> *She goes to the window, parts the curtains, and raises the shade on a view of falling snow, thus revealing* JOSEPH's *silhouette on the bed.*
> *Pause.*
> *She lowers the shade, draws the curtains to darkness.*

(*Murmuring, slowly*) Joseph.

> *Pause.*

Joooseph.

> *Sound of* JOSEPH's *laboured breathing.*
> *Pause.*

JOSEPH (*in a gasping whisper*): Naaah . . . Luh —

LUBA: Joooseph —

JOSEPH: Luuu . . .

> *Gasps. Laboured breathing.*
> *Pause.*
> *The breathing stops.*
> LUBA *switches on the night-table lamp and sits on the bed. She leans over* JOSEPH'*s upturned face, places her hand over his heart.*
> *Pause.*

LUBA: There's still a heartbeat, Joseph. Very faint, but I can feel it. Don't try to fool *me*, I always know when you're faking. (*Brief pause*) What's going through that subtle brain of yours, old man, eh?

> *Her lips to his ear, she murmurs . . .*

Old Man Joseph. (*Seductively*) Joseph, Joooseph.

> *He gasps, and begins to breathe again.*
> *Pause.*

(*Whispering*) Joooooseph.

> *He sighs.*

JOSEPH (*whispering*): Uuuuuuuh . . .

LUBA (*still at his ear*): Joseph. It's snowing, Joseph.

> *Pause.*

JOSEPH: Luhh . . .

LUBA: I'm coming, Joseph. Yes —

JOSEPH: Luuuu —

LUBA: I'm coming. Old Man Joseph.

JOSEPH: Luuuba.

ACT TWO

>*He gasps.*

Luba.

LUBA (*whispering*): I'm coming.

>*Long pause.*
>JOSEPH'*s breathing becomes gradually more regular.*
>LUBA *raises her head.*

(*Murmuring*) Joseph.

>*Pause.*

Joooseph. I've had a troubling dream, Joseph. All your brothers, Joseph. Lying in the drifts. Your brothers who betrayed you.

>*Pause.*

Listen, Joseph. (*Seductively*) Joooseph. My husband's away, Joseph. Gone away. He won't be back tonight. You know the story, old as it is. Older than you, Joseph. Old Joseph, old man. How does it end? Tell me the ending.

>*Pause.*

What's going through that brain of yours? What are you thinking? What can you be thinking, eh? Have you relinquished *all* the old beliefs, Joseph?

>*Pause.*

Ah. You're stubborn. Like the lid of a tomb. Like the snow. Joseph, it's snowing. Come to the window, I'll hold you up; you can put your arm round my waist. Come with me to the window. The snow's falling, Joseph. Falling. The snow's falling. Catch the pattern in each flake with a jeweller's loupe before they turn to water. Water, Joseph. Melting geometries. Death by water, water. By water they die. You must be dry, bone dry. Your throat. Your tongue. Like sandpaper. You want to drink. Come, Joseph, don't play coy with *me*; you haven't crossed the threshold *yet*, I know you're playing possum. There's water in the bathroom tap, it isn't far. You're parched. You want to drink. Cool water. Cool.

>*Pause.*

You can't walk away as easily as that, Joseph. Old Joseph. I'm coming. You can't hear me, but I'm coming, getting nearer every minute. Where are you? Joseph, where are you? Speak to me from the top of the stair. The dark stair. You can't see me, but I'm coming. You're the one, Joseph. You're the one, old man. Yes. No one else but you. None but Joseph. Yes. You're breathing more easily. You'll be coming back. Back from the dead, eh? Almost. Back to snow. To memory. Remember, Joseph. Try to remember. Who am I? I'm coming. Who am I? Silently, on tiptoe, I come into your room. Who am I? Come down out of the attic, Joseph. Who am I?

    Pause.

JOSEPH (*cadaverously*): Luba.

LUBA: That's better. One for the hawkers, eh Joseph? Hawkers in the drifts. See them now, the sellers? The sellers are hawking their wares to your dead brothers. The sellers. The cellars of Prague, cold and dank. It's cold, Joseph. Button your coat. Where's your coat, old man? What have they done with your coat? Left it for dead, eh? What's wrong with it? What's wrong with it, can you tell me? (*Brief pause*) Think. Think, Joseph. What's wrong with it? Who has the coat? Which of them is Joseph now? What's wrong with it? Think. Add them up. How many colours? Are they all there? Are the colours there? Are they there?

    JOSEPH *gasps.*
    Pause.

(*Nodding*) Ah, so *that's* it. Cat got your tongue? (*Seductively*) Joseph, Joooseph.

    JOSEPH *gasps.*
    Pause.

Talk to me, Joseph. Talk to me. Come on. A few words, you can manage it. Talk. Say whatever comes into your mind. What are you thinking? Are you thinking of me? Are you thinking —

JOSEPH (*gasping*): Luba!

LUBA: It's Luba, Joseph. Luba's here. Luba, coming on tiptoe. Come near the door; open the door, Joseph. Find the knob; it's dark, I know it's so dark in the attic. Find the knob. Turn the knob and walk to the head of the stair. No, don't look down. You can't see a thing. Find your way by touch to the door. I'm coming. I'm coming, Joseph. Old Man Joseph. Tell me where you're hiding. I've got something for you. Come out of the attic.

ACT TWO

JOSEPH: Luba.

LUBA: Yes, Luba. Luba. Here she is, Joseph, waiting for you to come to the head of the stair. Luba. (*Seductively*) Luba. (*Into his ear*) Luuuba.

> JOSEPH *gasps.*
> *Pause.*

(*Murmuring*) Aw, stubborn. Stubborn Joseph. Luba's waiting. Come, Joseph. Come. Tell Luba you remember. Try. It's snowing, Joseph. Cold, white. Soft, it falls. Cold, white. I've got something for you, Joseph. It's Luba. Feel what I've got. Put out your hand. Feel how warm it is.

> JOSEPH *shudders.*

You oughtn't to have let them take your coat. Remember what I told you? You shouldn't have. You should have listened to *me*.

JOSEPH: Lies.

LUBA: Yes.

JOSEPH: Lies!

LUBA: Yes, Joseph. Lies, all lies.

> JOSEPH *opens his eyes, his gaze fixed upon the ceiling.*

Ah, can you see me?

JOSEPH: Lies. Another Joseph.

LUBA: Joseph, look at me —

JOSEPH: Lies —

LUBA: Yes. Now, look me in the eyes —

JOSEPH: Another one. Another Joseph —

LUBA: Yes —

JOSEPH: Not me.

LUBA: Yes.

JOSEPH: Only . . . the snow.

LUBA: The snow. You can see the snow. Another Joseph.

   JOSEPH continues to stare upward. His gaze remains fixed throughout.

  It's snowing —

JOSEPH: The sky, grey.

LUBA: Yes.

JOSEPH: The earth, white.

LUBA: Yes, Joseph.

JOSEPH: Another Joseph.

LUBA: Yes.

JOSEPH: Dead trees, thin in the distance. I've been buried. They buried me.

LUBA: Where, Joseph?

JOSEPH: There.

LUBA: They buried you —

JOSEPH: Buried me there. In white.

LUBA: White.

JOSEPH: In grey. The face, as well. All to arrest . . .

  Pause.

LUBA: All to arrest —

JOSEPH: They keep me there in grey. All grey. Even the trees. All to . . .

Pause.

LUBA: Tell Luba.

JOSEPH: All to arrest . . .

LUBA: Yes?

JOSEPH: The progress of decay.

LUBA: Yes?

Pause.

Joseph.

JOSEPH: Another Joseph.

LUBA: No, Joseph!

JOSEPH: Lies!

LUBA: No lies!

JOSEPH (*gasping*): No lies.

Pause.

LUBA: Old man. Old Man Joseph. The Old Grey Man.

JOSEPH (*murmuring*): Old Grey Man.

LUBA: Old Joseph under the snow.

JOSEPH: Grey. Clay. The Old Clay Man.

LUBA: No.

JOSEPH (*exhausted*): No.

Pause.

I'm dying.

LUBA: Quite the reverse. (*Brief pause*) Come downstairs to me and we'll watch the snow.

JOSEPH: Snow. The sky, grey —

LUBA: Through the window, you and I —

JOSEPH: I, they buried me —

LUBA: I'll hold you up. Nothing to fear —

JOSEPH: Left me for dead —

LUBA: Just put your arm round my waist —

JOSEPH: Cold, white —

LUBA: You won't fall.

JOSEPH: Clay.

LUBA: You won't fall.

JOSEPH: Trees fall —

LUBA: If you fall —

JOSEPH: Thin in the distance.

LUBA: You'll fall on me.

JOSEPH: Yes.

LUBA: Yes, Joseph —

JOSEPH: Yes —

LUBA: On me you'd like to, eh?

JOSEPH: Eh —

LUBA: You'd like to.

    Pause.

    Who am I, then?

JOSEPH: Then —

LUBA: Who, Joseph?

JOSEPH: I'd like —

LUBA: Who?

JOSEPH: I'd like to —

LUBA: Who would you like to —

JOSEPH: Sit up.

LUBA: Lie still.

JOSEPH: Sit up.

LUBA: I'm sitting up. I'm going to lie down.

JOSEPH: Who?

LUBA: Who?

JOSEPH: Luba.

LUBA: Beside you, Joseph —

JOSEPH: Luba —

LUBA: I'm going to lie down beside you, old man.

    JOSEPH *mechanically sits up, dressed as in Act One. His prisoner's number is gone. A red monogram, 'J. G.,' adorns his pyjama pocket.*

Ah. *Very* good. Now, Joseph . . .

Pause.

She passes her hand before his eyes.

Here, you've got to look now, Joseph.

Pause.

Look at me.

He continues to stare ahead, simple-mindedly.

What do you see?

JOSEPH: Nothing.

LUBA: *I'll* give you something to look at —

JOSEPH: No light.

LUBA: You're in bed, Joseph.

JOSEPH: Dark —

LUBA: You're not in the attic any more. You've come down out of the attic —

JOSEPH: No light —

LUBA: Yes! The light's on. You only have to see it.

JOSEPH: I don't believe it —

LUBA: You don't have to believe anything now. Just look.

Pause.

What do you see?

JOSEPH: Yes —

LUBA: What do you see?

ACT TWO   43

JOSEPH: All right, yes.

LUBA: The light. Is the light on?

JOSEPH: Yes.

LUBA: You're not trying to *fool* me?

JOSEPH (*smiling, vaguely*): You don't have to believe anything.

LUBA: Ah, now we're getting somewhere, Joseph. Are you thirsty?

JOSEPH: No.

LUBA: Hungry?

JOSEPH: No.

    LUBA nods, biting her underlip.
    Pause.

LUBA: Uh, Joseph . . .

    She clasps his head, pressing his face to her bosom.

Recognise anything?

    JOSEPH's answer is smothered.
    Pause.

Hmmm.

    She releases him. He continues to sit, as before.

(*Into his ear*) Joseph. (*Seductively*) Joooseph. I want you to look at me, Joseph. I want you to look at my body.

    She rocks him gently from side to side as he stares ahead.

Don't play coy with me, I know what you're thinking, eh? I know what you're after. It's white, Joseph.

JOSEPH: White, it falls. Cold, white —

LUBA: No, warm. Warm. (*Placing his hand on her midriff*) Here.

    She inhales, sensuously.
    Pause.
    She exhales slowly, releasing her grip on JOSEPH'*s hand, which remains in place.*

Lower.

    Pause.
    His hand is motionless.

(*Murmuring*) Lower, Joseph. Your hand, feel lower down.

    Pause.
    JOSEPH *continues to stare ahead at the bathroom doorway, and does not move his hand.*
    LUBA *climbs off the bed.* JOSEPH'*s hand falls limply to his side.*

A hard case. You're a hard case, old man.

    She takes off her nurse's cap and places it on JOSEPH'*s head. He remains imperturbable.*

Old tree. (*Tapping her head*) Termites, that's your problem, Joseph. Termites!

    She glances at her watch and steps to the foot of the bed, unfastening the top three buttons of her uniform. She lets down her hair.
    JOSEPH *moves mechanically on to his hands and knees. He stares at* LUBA.

(*Ironically*) Umm, His Master's Voice.

    Pause.

Now you look at me, you drooling imbecile. *I* know you.

    Pause.

(*Contemptuously*) Bastard. Cheat. Liar. Filthy old bugger.

    JOSEPH'*s stare becomes more attentive. He remains in position throughout.*

ACT TWO

That's right, stare. It's about all you *can* do, isn't it? (*Removing her white shoes*) Well, here's something to stare at, toothless old sod.

She throws the shoes in his general direction and quickly unfastens the rest of her front buttons, slipping out of the nurse's uniform.

You'll see something now, something *you* haven't seen in a long time, I'll be bound.

She tosses her uniform at his head, strutting back and forth before him, clad in her white underthings: brassière, panties, suspenders*, stockings.

JOSEPH (*murmuring*): Fucking bitch. Dirty fucking bitch.

She plants her right foot on the bed, under JOSEPH's *eyes, and unhooks her suspenders. She rolls her stocking down a bit more with each 'Joseph.'*

LUBA (*mockingly*): Joseph. Joseph. Joseph. Joseph —

JOSEPH (*muttering*): Cunt. Miserable cunt. Dogfuckin' tart.

She bats the nurse's cap off JOSEPH's *head and drapes the white stocking round his neck.*

LUBA (*taunting him*): Kiss my arse.

She plants her left foot on the bed, unfastens her suspenders, and quickly removes her stocking, chucking it in JOSEPH's *face. She takes off her suspenders, pulls the elastic as though aiming a catapult* at* JOSEPH, *and lets them fly.*

(*Cupping him under the chin, breezily*) Just enough time for a quick shower, Joseph. (*Walking toward the bathroom*) I'll have to leave the door open in case the bell rings.

She exits into the bathroom.

You'll call me if it rings, won't you?

Her bra comes sailing toward the bed.

---

* suspenders = garter belt; catapult = slingshot

JOSEPH (*muttering*): Bitch.

> He crawls to the foot of the bed, his eyes riveted on the bathroom throughout.
> LUBA's panties sail toward him. He tries to bat them out of the air, then resumes his dog-like posture, more animated than before.

(*Muttering in the negative*) Huh! Shake your arse at me. (*Louder*) Take off your watch. You forgot your watch!

LUBA (*off*): What time is it?

JOSEPH: Take off your watch, you slut!

LUBA (*off*): What time is it, Joseph?

JOSEPH: Take it off, you whoring slut!

LUBA (*off*): Half past?

JOSEPH: Take it off!

LUBA (*off*): Quarter past —

JOSEPH (*muttering*): Quarter past.

> *Sound of shower running.*

LUBA (*off*): What?

JOSEPH: It's running backwards, take it off!

LUBA (*off*): Can't hear you.

JOSEPH: It'll break down. The crystal.

LUBA (*off*): What?

JOSEPH: Water. The water'll break it down.

LUBA (*off*): Louder, Joseph.

JOSEPH: The crystal!

LUBA (*off*): Ah, thirsty?

JOSEPH: Bint!

LUBA (*off*): Huh? Look, why don't you come and scrub my back?

JOSEPH: Miserable cunt!

LUBA (*off*): With your tongue.

JOSEPH: Trollop!

> *Pause.*

LUBA (*off*): Look, Joseph. I always soap myself all over, first.

> *She giggles.*

JOSEPH (*muttering*): All over —

LUBA (*off, beckoning operatically*): Joseph. Joooseph! I'm starkers!

JOSEPH (*to himself*): Hah! Always the same old game, it never changes. Hmph, wants a licking, she does. Wants to have her tongue lopped off and shoved up her arse to keep her quiet —

LUBA (*off, playfully*): Oooo! Joseph, mmmm —

JOSEPH (*to himself, faintly Yiddish*): So who'd have guessed, with a face like that? Who'd have guessed? A nice girl. She looks like a nice girl, this nurse. So who'd have guessed?

> *Shower off. The patter of* LUBA's *feet on the tiles.*
> *Pause.*

LUBA (*off*): Joseph, you Peeping Tom! Are you still at it?

JOSEPH (*as before*): A nice girl.

LUBA (*off*): You should come in sometime and read the towels. Look at this one.

Pause.
JOSEPH'*s mouth drops open.*

Nice, innit? Just think where it's been, Joseph.

JOSEPH (*to himself, normal accent*): Erotica.

Sounds of LUBA *dressing.*

LUBA (*off*): Oh, you like it, eh? Feeling a bit better, are you? Back in the swing of things? Do you have to pee?

JOSEPH: No.

LUBA (*off*): Good. That's normal.

JOSEPH (*shaking his head, to himself*): I forgot.

LUBA (*off*): You forgot how to pee? It's simple. Look. All you do is —

JOSEPH: I know how to pee! I know how to pee!

LUBA (*off*): Well, then, what are you running on about?

JOSEPH: Something I've got to remember, that's all. Let me think!

LUBA (*off*): Concentrate.

JOSEPH *concentrates, his eyes, as ever, riveted on the bathroom.*
Pause.

JOSEPH: Ach, no use. Too much distraction.

LUBA (*off*): Ah, Joseph. You'll never get anywhere if you can't learn to concentrate.

Sound of toilet flushing.
Pause.

What do you think, Joseph? Which one?

ACT TWO 49

JOSEPH: The red. Definitely, the red.

LUBA (*off*): The red it is.

JOSEPH (*chuckling, to himself*): To match your eyes.

LUBA (*off*): What? Good, you're laughing. That's good. Think of funny things.

JOSEPH: I was thinking about my wife, is all. I didn't give your eyes a second thought.

LUBA (*off*): What did you say? Your wife?

JOSEPH: Nothing.

LUBA (*off*): You're worried about your wife.

JOSEPH: No wife.

LUBA (*off*): Your wife.

JOSEPH: Who?

LUBA (*off*): You're safe.

JOSEPH: Who?

LUBA (*off*): From your wife.

JOSEPH: What did you say?

LUBA (*off*): Nothing.

JOSEPH (*threateningly*): Something.

LUBA (*off*): Nothing.

 The doorbell.

LUBA (*off*): Joseph, get the door.

 Remains on his hands and knees.
 Pause.
 The doorbell.

(*Vexed*) Oh.

 LUBA *enters, clad in a provocative blue evening dress, pulling the bathroom door closed behind her.*

 (*Patting her hair*) Now, remember, Joseph; your best behaviour, now.

 She opens the door.

Chester! Right on time.

 Enter CHESTER, *muffled to the ears, bearing a bouquet of roses, his hat, overcoat and rubbers peppered with snow.* JOSEPH *stares at him.*

CHESTER: I set off early so I wouldn't be late. (*Giving her the bouquet*) For you.

 He catches sight of JOSEPH, *seems puzzled, even shocked, and cannot take his eyes from him.*

LUBA: Ooo, they're beautiful! Wherever did you find them?

 JOSEPH *remains in position throughout, his gaze roving from* CHESTER *to* LUBA *as they speak; his eyes are fixed, he must turn his head like a dog to see them.*
 Pause.

CHESTER: Uh?

LUBA: Oh, this is Old Joseph.

 She pats JOSEPH's *head.*

CHESTER: Eh?

LUBA: Oh, I know he looks a hard case. He's just come round. You should have seen him a while ago.

CHESTER (*to* JOSEPH): H — how do you do?

JOSEPH: Hallo.

LUBA (*on her way to the kitchen*): He's really no trouble at all. Just make yourself

ACT TWO 51

at home, get acquainted while I put these in water.

She exits.
CHESTER, *under the watchful eye of* JOSEPH, *removes hat, gloves, overcoat and rubbers. He wears a tasteless combination of jacket, tie and slacks.*

(*Peering in from the kitchen doorway*) You'd best hang them in the bathroom to dry.

CHESTER: Uh?

LUBA (*pointing*): In there.

CHESTER: Ah.

  CHESTER *to the bathroom with his wet things.*
  Pause.
  Enter LUBA *with roses in a vase. She sets the vase down on the night table.*

LUBA: Ah.

  Enter CHESTER, *unencumbered.*

Well, why don't you fix us a couple of drinks?

  LUBA *to the kitchen.*

I'll have Scotch. God, I could do with one! Been on my feet all day.

  Sundry kitchen noises. CHESTER *busies himself at the liquor cabinet.*
  Enter LUBA *with a paper cup.*

The ice. Frightful night.

CHESTER: Mmmm, wind's really beginning to whip up.

  He drops ice cubes from the cup into three glasses.

LUBA: Huh, that'll mean drifts. Eh, Joseph?

  Pause.

(*To* CHESTER) Joseph isn't thirsty yet. He'll let us know. (*To* JOSEPH) Let us know. Don't forget.

Pause.

CHESTER: Here we are.

LUBA: Ah.

She takes her glass.

Cheers.

They drink

Ah. Just what the doctor ordered. Now, how do you like the table?

CHESTER: Oh, beautiful. Really beautiful. Must have taken you hours.

He glances back at JOSEPH.

I, uh. (*Confidentially*) He's, uh. I mean, is he all right?

LUBA (*chuckling*): What, Joseph? Of course. He's just not used to you. Go pat him on the head.

CHESTER: No, I —

LUBA: No, it's all right.

CHESTER: I — I couldn't. I mean, he's —

LUBA: Nonsense. Take my word for it. Go on.

CHESTER: Well, perhaps later. When I've had a bit more to drink.

LUBA: Oooo. Well, go easy. I want your taste buds in working order. You can drink yourself blind after we eat.

They chuckle. JOSEPH *remains impassive.*

Come on, let's sit down.

They sit down at the table, LUBA *at the right end,* CHESTER *at the left.*

ACT TWO 53

CHESTER (*confidentially*): He's . . . Are those his real pyjamas?

LUBA: Well, they're not mine. Why?

CHESTER: I . . . Nothing, I —

LUBA: Hmmm?

CHESTER: No. I, uh. I've a pair like that at home myself.

LUBA (*suggestively*): Well, I'd like to see them sometime —

CHESTER: I just wondered where he got them.

LUBA: Haven't the foggiest. Why don't you ask him? Not that he'd tell you.

CHESTER: Ah. No. After all, we've got better things to do than talk about the old man's pyjamas, eh?

He chuckles nervously, coughs.

LUBA (*confidentially*): He's quiet. He's calmed down. You should have seen him before.

CHESTER: You know, I really didn't expect to —

LUBA: Oh, I know. I'm sorry. Nothing I could do about it, though. Sometimes, when it's a really hard case like this, I have to stick it twenty-four hours a day.

CHESTER: You mean he's been here all day?

LUBA: Mmmm, just look at him. He's got it bad, you can see that.

CHESTER: What's he doing with that stocking round his neck?

LUBA: It's part of his treatment.

CHESTER: Ah —

LUBA: Here, forget about Old Joseph. He shan't bother us the way he is now. Anyhow, it's good for him to observe things at this point. Just act natural and ignore him. Act as though he weren't there. So. Tell me, how did you manage the roses?

> JOSEPH *fixes his gaze on the bathroom throughout.*

CHESTER: It wasn't —

LUBA: I'll bet you had them frozen from last year.

CHESTER: No. No, I never plan anything that far ahead.

> *They chuckle.*
> *The doorbell.*

LUBA (*rising, peeved*): Oh, now who can that be?

CHESTER: Don't answer it!

LUBA: It's probably just one of the neighbours. I'm not expecting anyone. Go on, finish your drink.

> *She opens the door.*
> *Enter* JAKE, *a disreputable-looking young man, peppered with snow.*

JAKE (*gregariously*): Here, what's this? Looks like I barged in at the wrong time, eh?

> *He waves to* CHESTER.

LUBA: Look here, what do you want?

> CHESTER *waves back in confusion, puzzled, and a bit shocked; he stares at* JAKE, *irritably surprised. He rises.*

JAKE: The hospital sent me over.

LUBA: The hospital? I've never seen you there.

JAKE: I work another shift. (*To* CHESTER, *as he removes his overcoat*) Cor blimey, it's really coming down out there now. Must be four inches at least —

LUBA: Here, what do you think you're —

CHESTER (*to* JAKE): Uh, you wouldn't be the doctor, would you?

JAKE: Uh, that's right! (*Shaking* CHESTER's *hand*) How are you?

He winks conspiratorially at CHESTER.

LUBA (*to* CHESTER): The doctor? I didn't —

CHESTER (*to* JAKE): Here, make it quick.

JAKE *glances at* CHESTER.

JAKE: All in good time, all in good time. (*To* LUBA) I could do with a drink.

LUBA: Scotch all right?

JAKE: Perfect.

LUBA: Why don't you hang your wet things in the bathroom.

JAKE: Right. (*To* CHESTER) Do I know you?

JAKE *to the bathroom.*
LUBA *shrugs helplessly at* CHESTER *and pours the Scotch.*

LUBA (*to* JAKE): Ice?

JAKE (*off*): One cube'll do.

LUBA: Good, because it's all I've left.

JAKE (*off*): I'll take it as it comes, no water.

LUBA (*to* CHESTER): One cube. He doesn't look like a doctor to me. Where's his bag?

CHESTER *shrugs.*
Enter, JAKE, *unencumbered, rubbing his hands.*

JAKE: Where'd you get those towels?

LUBA: Oh, I've always had them.

JAKE (*taking his drink*): Well, down the hatch.

He drains the glass in one gulp and hands it back to her.

Ah, that's the ticket. (*To* LUBA, *patting* JOSEPH'*s head*) How's he doing?

LUBA: He's coming on —

JAKE (*to* JOSEPH): How you doin', old son?

JOSEPH, *still on all fours, continues to stare ahead.*

(*To* LUBA, *petting* JOSEPH) How long's he been like this?

LUBA: Not long. About fifteen minutes, maybe less.

JAKE: Mmmm. Any previous history?

LUBA: Huh?

JAKE: Smallpox, chicken pox, encephalitis, apoplexy?

LUBA: Uh —

JAKE: Afflatus, distemper, Infusoria?

LUBA: No —

JAKE: The mange, the clap?

LUBA: What? No. Look, I don't see —

JAKE: Well, we'll have a good look at him. You can never be too sure.

CHESTER: Here, shouldn't he be in hospital, where he can be properly looked after?

JAKE: Now, don't let's be hasty. Nothing to be hasty about. I'm sure the young lady here has been doin' a proper job on him. (*To* JOSEPH, *chucking him under the chin*) How about it, squire?

CHESTER: Look here, you can't be —

JAKE: Relax. (*Conspiratorially*) Just relax, all right? (*To* LUBA) I'll need a pan of warm water.

ACT TWO 57

    LUBA *to the kitchen.*
    Pause.

CHESTER: Well?

JAKE: What?

CHESTER: What are you here for? If you've got something to say, say it, then clear off as soon as you can.

JAKE: Oh, yeh. Listen, I'm sorry I picked such a rotten time, and all.

CHESTER: Yes?

JAKE: Look, I'll make it as quick as possible, right?

CHESTER: Well? Come on.

JAKE: Yeh, well. The hospital didn't actually send me.

CHESTER: Of course not. (*Sarcastically*) I thought not.

JAKE: Yeh I just said that, you know?

CHESTER: Yes, well?

JAKE: Yeh. Well... I just happened to find myself in the neighbourhood and thought I'd pop in and have a look at the old man. That's all. But keep it quiet, eh? I wouldn't want *her* to think I was here without a good reason. You know how women are, always jumping to the wrong conclusions. I'd rather not make things any more complicated than they are, know what I mean?

CHESTER: But you still haven't —

    Enter LUBA *with the pan of water.*

JAKE: Ssssh! (*To* LUBA) You can set it on the table.

    She complies.

LUBA: Anything else?

JAKE: What's all that on the bed, yours?

LUBA: No, the old man's.

JAKE: Very funny. (*Clapping his hands together and rubbing them*) Right. Might as well begin.

LUBA: Joseph, the doctor's here. The doctor's here, Joseph. Look at the doctor.

> JAKE *kneels on the floor at the foot of the bed, eye to eye with* JOSEPH, *and passes his hand before* JOSEPH'S *face, snapping his fingers once, twice* . . .

JAKE: Joseph. Joseph.

> *He makes a second pass with his hand.* JOSEPH *follows it with his eyes.*

Joseph.

> JAKE *snaps his fingers twice.* JOSEPH, *with quick, bird-like movements of the head, jerks his gaze from* JAKE *to* LUBA *to* CHESTER *to* JAKE.

There's a *good* lad! Good. (*Patting* JOSEPH'S *head*) That's the way, old sport. (*Snapping his fingers above* JOSEPH'S *head*) Up, boy. Sit. Sit. Come on. Sit, Joseph. Come on. Sit.

> JOSEPH *does not move.*

Aha. (*To* CHESTER) We've got a very sick man here. (*To* LUBA) Got a thermometer, luv?

> LUBA *brings a thermometer from the pocket of her uniform on the bed.*

Good. (*To* JOSEPH) Now, open wide.

> *Pause.*

Open. Don't be afraid. It's perfectly normal.

> *Pause.*
> *He forces* JOSEPH'S *mouth open with his hands.*

(*To* LUBA) Stick it in.

LUBA: What?

JAKE: It's all right. Just put it in and tell me if there's anything.

LUBA: Wait.

Then she slips the thermometer into JOSEPH's *yawning mouth.*

JAKE: Well? Have you got it in?

LUBA: Yes.

JAKE: Under the tongue?

LUBA: Wait.

She makes an adjustment.

JAKE: Don't worry. There's nothing to be ashamed of.

LUBA: Right, it's in.

JAKE: Good.

He closes JOSEPH's *mouth, presses his hand under* JOSEPH's *ribs, etc.*

Mmmm. (*Feeling* JOSEPH's *legs as though they belonged to a sick horse*) Aha. (*To* CHESTER) Yes, a very sick man.

He pats JOSEPH's *head, removes the thermometer, glances at it, shakes it down, wipes it on his lapel, and tosses it carelessly on to the bed.*
CHESTER nudges LUBA downstage as JAKE continues his veterinary examination ad libitum.

CHESTER: Here, what do you think?

LUBA: I don't know *what* to think. I mean, he was doing so well up to now. The treatment —

CHESTER: No! I mean what do you think of *him*, the doctor?

JAKE: Cough.

JOSEPH *coughs.*

LUBA: He seems to know his business.

JAKE: Again.

CHESTER: He didn't even wash his hands.

    JOSEPH *coughs.*

    You call that knowing his business?

JAKE: Good boy! How do you feel? Any complaints?

CHESTER: I don't know, he doesn't look right to me. You're supposed to be the nurse—

JAKE (*louder*): Any complaints, Joseph?

JOSEPH: Huh?

JAKE: Complaints! Any complaints!

CHESTER: I mean, you're the nurse. You ought to be able to tell —

JOSEPH (*loudly*): Complaints!

CHESTER: To tell a real doctor from a phoney.

JAKE: Good!

    JAKE *hurries into the bathroom.*

LUBA: His methods are perfectly sound, from what I can see.

CHESTER: You're sure? He seems more like a horse doctor to me.

LUBA: You don't understand. They're trying lots of new techinques today — experimenting, you know — all that sort of thing.

CHESTER: Uh —

JAKE (*off*): Joseph!

JOSEPH: Joseph!

ACT TWO

CHESTER: What's he on about now?

She shrugs.

JAKE (*off*): Pay attention, Joseph. You see this towel?

Pause.

Eh, Joseph? Do you see this towel?

JOSEPH: Uh-huh.

CHESTER: He's daft.

JAKE (*off*): Do you see the letters on this towel, under the picture?

JOSEPH: Ah.

JAKE (*off*): Read them. What does it say?

JOSEPH: Erotica.

CHESTER: This —

LUBA: Ssssh —

JAKE (*off*): No. The letters, Joseph. Read them out.

JOSEPH *squints, reading the letters out to himself, slowly, silently.*

That's right. Good . . . Good . . . Good. Right, got it?

JOSEPH: Chuh-chuh —

JAKE (*off*): Yes?

JOSEPH: Chuh chub —

JAKE (*off*): Come on.

JOSEPH: Chubby Combustibles!

JAKE (*off*): Excellent!

Enter JAKE, *beaming.*

(*Shaking* JOSEPH's *hand*) Congratulations. (*To* CHESTER) You see that? He knows what's going on.

Pause.

Now, Joseph . . .

JOSEPH: Yes.

JAKE: Good.

JOSEPH: Yes.

JAKE: Any complaints?

JOSEPH: I've been out.

JAKE: You're a sick man.

JOSEPH: What is it? I can take it. I'm dying.

JAKE: Quite the reverse.

JOSEPH: Eh?

JAKE: I'll give it to you straight — deoxyribonucleiosis.

JOSEPH: Is it serious?

JAKE: It's hereditary.

JOSEPH (*to himself*): That bad.

Pause.

JAKE (*to* CHESTER): Give me a hand with him, will you? I think he can take some food now. Nothing heavy, though. (*To* LUBA) Just a little soup, if you've got it.

JAKE *and* CHESTER *take* JOSEPH *under the arms as* LUBA *hurries into the kitchen.*

(*To* JOSEPH) Here we go, squire. Up you come. (*On their way to the table*) That's right. (*To* CHESTER) Mind how you go, he's a bit wobbly in the knees. (*To* JOSEPH) Come on, old son. You can make it. Don't give up the ship. That's right. Steady on. Almost there . . .

They seat JOSEPH *at the left end of the table.*

Ah, there. Everything all right?

JOSEPH *flashes 'okay' with thumb and index.*

(*Removing the stocking*) Here. You won't be needing this any longer. (*Tying a napkin round* JOSEPH's *neck*) Here. Try this on for size.

Enter LUBA *with a bowl of soup.*

Ah.

LUBA: You think it's too much?

JAKE: What is it?

LUBA: Chicken broth.

JAKE: Couldn't be better. (*To* JOSEPH) Chicken broth, how's that?

JOSEPH: Yummy. Yummy for the tummy.

JAKE: That's the spirit.

JOSEPH *slurps his soup noisily, ravenously throughout, never raising his eyes from the bowl.*

(*To* LUBA) Look at him. He likes it.

JAKE *dips his hands into the pan of water and wipes them off on the other napkin, dragging* LUBA's *chair round behind the table in order to sit at the right hand of* JOSEPH.

Yeh. Really gives you an appetite — don't it? — to see a man who enjoys his food. Really sets the old taste buds into a frenzy of anticipation. (*To* CHESTER, *sitting*) Why don't you get a few more chairs and sit down. Take a load off your feet.

> LUBA *takes the pan into the kitchen, with* CHESTER *hot at her heels.*

> (*To* JOSEPH) Atta way, squire. Keep it up. You'll be back on your feet in no time.

> *Enter* LUBA *with extra plates, napkins and cutlery. She sets* JAKE'*s place and a place beside him, pushing the centrepiece to the near edge of the table.*

> (*To* LUBA) Look at him. He's the proper article, in't he?

LUBA: Huh, you don't have to tell *me*.

JAKE: The old sod, I'll bet *he's* been round. Seen a lot in his day. Things we couldn't imagine. (*To* JOSEPH) Right, guv?

> *Enter* CHESTER, *puffing, a kitchen chair under each arm; he sets the first at the right end of the table, the second — into which* LUBA *immediately collapses with a sigh — beside* JAKE. *Defeated,* CHESTER *sits in the first chair, facing* JOSEPH *across the length of the table.*

> (*To* CHESTER) What do *you* think?

CHESTER: What? I wasn't listening.

JAKE: The old geezer here. Looks like knowing a lot more than he lets on. What do you think?

CHESTER: I think he'd be a bloody lot better off without all that Chubby Combustibles rot.

JAKE: Here, listen, therapy is therapy! (*To* LUBA) Right, luv?

JOSEPH (*between slurps*): Luba.

JAKE: Eh?

> LUBA *rises, flashing a helpless look at* CHESTER, *and vanishes into the kitchen.*

JOSEPH (*to* JAKE, *as before*): Luba. Show some respect.

JAKE: Yeh. (*Calling after her*) Right, Luba?

ACT TWO   65

Pause.

(*To* CHESTER) So.

Awkward silence, save for the old man's slurping.

Yeh, we've had some success with the new methods — Luba can tell you that. Yeh, when we catch 'em like this — like the old dosser here — there's no problem at all. He'll be fine, just fine. Yeh. Just listen to him. Enough to drive you up the bleedin' wall, innit? But we're trained for these things, Luba and me. Trained to put up with the noise, the puke, the blood. It never gets to us. We're never uneasy, never queasy, always prepared for any emergency. You got to be like that in our line of work, otherwise where would we bloody be, know what I mean? Yeh. I mean, yeh, we have our ups and downs. We lose more than we cure — I admit it, but just between the two of us, you understand; send me up before a commission of enquiry and I'll swear I never seen you before, right? Just so we understand each other. I'm not so hard to get on with, am I? I mean, I think I've got a pretty fair bedside manner. What do you think? You've seen me at it. A lot of the lads — I mean my colleagues — a lot of them are brutal. Not me. I didn't dodge about all this way in the snow just to look in on his nibs here — mind, I'm not interested in the girl at all, you don't have to worry about that. I mean, she's a gorgeous bit o' crumpet, don't get me wrong — and the soup don't smell bad either. Looks as though you got lucky; she's a bleedin' good cook, from what I can see. But I'm not interested; I mean, that's right out. I mean, if you fancied tearin' her clothes off right now and layin' her out on the table, I wouldn't lift a finger. Please yourself, I wouldn't try to stop you. I got feelings, I know how it is, though I couldn't vouch for the old man here. (*Confidentially*) You never know how they're going to react, know what I mean? I mean, I can't answer for what he might do, you can understand that. You seem a pretty reasonable sort. Here, where's the soup? What's taking her so long with the soup? I'm bloody starving. No, like I said, some of the lads are really terrible; hard-boiled, you know? No. No, I could never be like that. You got to have some compassion in my line of work, otherwise where the bloody hell would we be? No, I took one look at the old bugger and my heart just melted away. You can understand that. You can understand that.

CHESTER: I, uh. Of course. I can understand that.

JAKE: Right. It's no picnic, though, the profession. I mean, the patients! Never know who the bloody hell they are, except in their lucid intervals; never know where they are, whether they're a cat, a mouse, or a bleedin' turd. I mean, Christ! Yeh, I know what people say, that we should leave well alone. Yeh, well, it's all right when it's not *your* husband or *your* wife what's gone down with it. People are always —

JOSEPH: Belt up, Jake. (*Calling*) Luba, bring on the next course!

JAKE: Here, what about us? Eh? We're wasting away in here. Right, uh?

CHESTER: Chester —

JOSEPH: Luba!

JAKE: Yeh. Chester —

LUBA (*off*): Hang on, I'm coming! I'm coming! Keep your socks on!

JOSEPH: I in't wearin' any.

> JOSEPH *finishes his last spoonful and, for the first time since he began to eat, looks about, suddenly more aware.*

I finished it all up, Luba! Didn't leave a blessed drop, not a one!

> *Enter* LUBA *with a plate of meat for* JOSEPH.

Ah —

LUBA: You needn't shout. I'm not deaf.

JOSEPH: Meat. What about some wine?

LUBA: Give us a chance, will you? Now, put your spoon in the bowl.

> *He tosses his soup spoon into the bowl.*

Here, watch it! It may not be the best china, but it's china all the same.

> *She sets the meat plate down in front of* JOSEPH *and takes his soup bowl into the kitchen.* JOSEPH *eats with gusto.*

JAKE: Yeh, China. Where they're starving. Here, they're not only starving in China. Can't you hear my stomach? I think the old man's right! I think you

ACT TWO

must be deaf! (*Calling after her*) Here! Who do Chester and I have to shag to get a meal round here, can you tell me that?

    Enter LUBA *with three plates of meat. She sets them down.*

    Is this all? Just meat? What became of the soup? Do you think we're barbarians?

JOSEPH: What about that wine?

LUBA (*to the kitchen*): No soup.

JAKE: Bloody hell!

JOSEPH: The wine —

LUBA (*off*): I'm just getting it.

    JAKE *and* CHESTER *tear into their meat.*
    Enter LUBA *with a bottle of wine.*

JAKE (*his mouth full*): Ah. Want me to open it?

LUBA (*sitting*): No, you just unscrew it.

    JAKE *snatches the bottle out of her hand, opens it, and fills his glass.*

JOSEPH (*to* CHESTER, *chuckling*): Look at the boy. Never could teach him any manners. Jake! Fill her glass and pass the bottle on! What's got into you?

    JAKE *complies, passing the bottle to* CHESTER, *who fills his glass.*

That's more like it. That's it. You'd think you were raised in a pigsty. Don't bolt your food! (*To* CHESTER) How's the wine? Is it all right?

CHESTER: Mmmm.

    JOSEPH *pours himself a glass.*

JOSEPH (*toasting*): Confusion.

    He drinks.

Ah. Not bad, not bad. Tuck in, everyone. Tuck in.

They all tear ravenously into their meat, sometimes speaking with their mouths full.
Pause.

Christ, I feel I haven't eaten in an age!

JAKE (*to* LUBA): Is this it? Is this all?

LUBA: There's dessert.

JAKE: What is it? No, don't tell me. I like surprises.

JOSEPH (*to* CHESTER): Jake is really in his element, you can see that. Just look at him, the pig. Look at the way he eats! Doesn't care aught about where he puts his hands. I tell you, Chester, I don't know what the bloody hell I'm going to do with him.

CHESTER (*nodding*): Mmmm —

JOSEPH: These young people today, pah! Well, it's our own fault, don't think it isn't. We've only ourselves to blame. They're all so bloody spoilt, never thinking of anything but themselves —

JAKE: Puah —

JOSEPH (*sarcastically*): Puahuah. (*To* CHESTER) Well, what can you do? It's always the same. It never changes. You plead with them. You prostate yourself. And where's the good of it? I ask you.

CHESTER (*shrugging*): Hmph.

JOSEPH: It wasn't like that in my day, I can tell you that! People had respect. Not like today, with everyone dodging about like headless chickens. No, I should've stayed in America. Ever been there?

CHESTER: Uh —

JOSEPH (*expansively*): Well, now that was a country. Mind you, it wasn't a paradise; but you could get out of the house and stretch your legs, not like here. Here everybody's got a caper, you can't believe anything. Got to keep your hands in your pockets whenever some bloke opens his mouth for fear he's gonna rob you blind! I'm crackin' it on a lot less sleep these days, I can tell you.

CHESTER: Huh?

JOSEPH: I'm reading Machiavelli. He makes more bloody sense now than anybody. Yeh. Over in America you didn't need Machiavelli, you could get on all right without Machiavelli. And the American women! Very healthy, really something to look at. Must be all that milk. (*To* JAKE) Refill your sister's glass.

JAKE *complies*.

Yeh, that was a country, America. I'll bet you never suspected that's where I'm from, now, did you?

CHESTER: Uh —

JOSEPH: Come on. Be honest.

CHESTER: Well, no. It's actually quite remarkable.

JOSEPH: Yeh. No one ever guesses —

CHESTER: Mmmm, not the least trace of an accent. You fooled *me*.

JOSEPH: I suppose you're wondering how I came to speak the language of this country.

CHESTER (*nodding*): Hmmm.

JOSEPH: Well, I was fairly young when I came over — twenty, perhaps twenty-five, I don't know — and I'd got this idea it might be a bloody lot easier to pick up on the language from scratch. So I got myself placed with a young couple, moved right in with them. They had a kid about a year old and I watched him real close, see? He was at the stage where he was just beginning to babble, so they put me in with him. We had the same room. Well, after a week or two, I was prattling on like a native — peepee, caca, the four elements — you know, the whole lot. See, I wanted to take my time — I had plenty of time then, I didn't know anybody and wasn't likely to until I picked up on the language — so I paced myself real slow, with the kid.

CHESTER: Ah.

JOSEPH: Yeh, I thought, why not learn to speak like a native while I've got all this time on my hands. You can see my reasoning, can't you?

CHESTER: Mmmm.

JOSEPH: So, anyhow, after a bit it became hard on the little blighter's parents, who both had to work for their keep — which is how I was able to hang about there without paying; I was really a sort of baby sitter, you know? Anyhow, the kid's mother couldn't get into the spirit of the thing — it was making her uneasy. So, to put her mind at rest, I had to sort of help the illusion along. Yeh, they put this nappy on me and I had to sit in the playpen like that with the little lad. Just to keep her sweet, I even went through the toilet training. Can you imagine a man of the age I was then, squatting on a pot in the kitchen beside the kid, the pair of us straining like bloody hell whilst the mother coaxed it out of us? I mean, you got to admit, I was really determined to speak the language of this country like a bleedin' native! I put all the lustful thoughts I had for the kid's mother out of my head — I mean, when you're being washed and nappied at the age of twenty-seven by a good-looking bird, it in't so easy to control your emotions, you know? Well, she was a bit of all right. She made a proper job of it, and I thought if that's what it takes to keep her sweet, blimey, it's no skin off *my* nose, so I went along and *got* along. It wasn't so bad, once you got accustomed to it —

CHESTER: Hmmm —

JOSEPH: You'd be surprised. And, well, look at the result!

JAKE (*to* CHESTER): Yeh, look at the result.

JOSEPH: Don't get smart. (*To* CHESTER) He can laugh. He don't know what I had to go through.

CHESTER: What about the husband?

JOSEPH: Huh —

CHESTER: The boy's father. What was he doing while all this was going on?

JOSEPH: He was there.

CHESTER: Ah —

JOSEPH: That was the worst part.

CHESTER: Mmmm. So, how long were you with them?

JOSEPH: Let me think. Four, no, five. Five years. Just long enough to put myself on my feet.

CHESTER: It's a long time.

JOSEPH: Well, how do you measure these things, really? In terms of time, money, what? I don't know, I'm asking you.

LUBA: Ready for dessert?

JOSEPH: I'll have some more wine.

> JAKE *refills* JOSEPH's *glass.*

Ah, good.

> JOSEPH *takes a long swill.*

Ah. Nothing like it, eh Chester? We haven't had a good sit-down like this in ages. How long is it, Jake?

> JAKE *shrugs.*

Anyhow, I miss the old dinners. (*To* JAKE *and* LUBA) Remember? (*To* CHESTER) Oh, they were the thing. Even when we were living like rats, we always had a good sit-down dinner; never spared the horses on *that* account.

LUBA: Are you ready for dessert?

JAKE: Let's get on with it.

> LUBA *rises, gathers up the plates.*

JOSEPH: Yeh, it wasn't easy to make ends meet in those days. (*To* JAKE) It wasn't so long ago.

> JAKE *is ogling* LUBA's *figure.*

(*To* CHESTER) Yeh. When Jakey here was a concert pianist, we used to have to rub his fingers with this special cream all the time. Got it all over the doorknobs. I couldn't take no more! I said, Jake, you got to give it up! That's what I told him.

LUBA *to the kitchen with the plates,* JAKE *ogling her.*

Finished his career on the concert stage. Couldn't play a note without the bleedin' cream! Who'd have thought it? A little thing like that! And there was no getting him back to it either. What's done is done, he said — didn't you, Jake? I didn't labour the point. No. I always said I'd rather live in my own shit than put up with cream on the doorknobs. The money never meant a thing to me. I mean, what if there was a fire? We'd never have got out! So, I kept quiet. I mean, you should never lose your sense of perspective. Isn't that so, Jake?

JAKE (*distracted*): Yeh, right.

JOSEPH: So. There it is. I did all I could for him, though, after that. I mean, I never shirked on my responsibilities. I knew I was partly to blame for Jakey's musical paralysis. So I said, We'll just have to tighten our belts for a bit, that's all, till Jake finds a new line of work. Things were pretty dodgy then. I took a job as a lavatory attendant for a bit, but I had to pack it in. The trade union forced me out.

CHESTER: Mmmm, must have been a hard life.

JOSEPH: I could take it. I took it in stride. Mind you, those lads play it rough! Anyhow, we didn't have long to wait. Jake started cranking out poems by the dozens; a regular ball of fire, he was. Always at the typewriter, you should have seen him. We peddled his works from door to door, Luba and me. Did a fair business for a while, too, depending on the neighbourhood of course. Then Jake comes out of his typing stupor and says, We're goin' about it all wrong. That's what he said, I remember it like it was yesterday. No, he says, we got to get the stuff published and sold in the shops. This is monkey nuts, he says. Well, the moment he said it I knew he was on to something; I mean, I could see the difference it would make. He'd just completed this huge epic. A classic, a real classic. (*To* JAKE) What was the title?

JAKE: *Bugger the Bride.*

JOSEPH: That's it. *Bugger the Bride,* a real classic. You know, he couldn't find a publisher to bring it out? Cor, with a title like that you'd think they'd want to snap it right up, things being what they are. We all thought it had mass appeal. Jakey used to read parts of it to Luba and me at night, when there was nothin' else to do, and we thought it had mass appeal. We thought he'd go far. (*To* JAKE) How about it, lad?

JAKE: What's keeping the dessert?

JOSEPH: Who knows what's under all that sand? (*Laughing*) Eh, Chester?

> CHESTER *grins sheepishly.*

> Here, Jake, talkin' of sand and the desert, why don't you recite a few lines from the desert scene of your epic?

JAKE: Huh? Look, I can't remember. You think I can remember everything I write, just like that, and spew it all out on a moment's notice?

JOSEPH: All right, then, something shorter. Before your sister comes back, you know how she takes on.

JAKE (*demurring*): Aw —

JOSEPH: Come on. Just a few lines. Something short. What about it, Chester? Wouldn't you like to hear the sort of thing Jake can come up with when he sets his mind to it?

CHESTER: Of course. Why not?

JOSEPH: Good! It's settled, then. Come on, Jake, before your sister comes back.

JAKE: Uh, well —

CHESTER: Yes, come on. Jolly up the evening with a little recitation.

JOSEPH (*to* JAKE): There. You see? He wants to hear you.

JAKE: Yeh, well. All right. Right. Right, I think I can recall one. It's a short one. Yeh. All right.

> *Pause.*
> *He clears his throat.*

> Right —

JOSEPH: Tell us the title.

JAKE: Oh. *The Six Percent Solution.* It's called *The Six Percent Solution.*

> *Pause.*

> Doctor Watson dreamt that he had seen
> A nude girl in a washing-machine;
> He awoke from his nap
> With a dose of the clap
> And his shirt-tails suspiciously clean.

Pause.

CHESTER: Very good.

JOSEPH (*beaming*): There. What did I tell you?

CHESTER (*to* JAKE): Got any more like that last?

JAKE: Listen.

Pause.
Then, with appropriate gestures...

> Carlene Jupiter's buttocks are grand;
> I would rather have one in each hand
> Than —

JOSEPH (*grabbing* JAKE's *arm*): Sssh!

Enter LUBA.

LUBA: The dessert will be a while yet. Any wine left?

She sits.

CHESTER (*refilling her glass*): We've missed you.

JAKE: Yeh.

JOSEPH (*to* CHESTER): So, you see what I was on about. The lad has a God-given talent there, like Machiavelli. A sense of form. All his poems are like that. You think it's easy to make rhymes? The lad's got a real sense of form, not at all like this modern trash. All that rubbish! That's why he can't get his work published. It's a crime.

The doorbell.

What's this? Luba?

LUBA (*rising*): Don't look at me. I'm not expecting anyone.

She goes to the door.

JOSEPH (*oblivious*): Well. You'd best answer it, all the same. (*To* JAKE) I wonder who it could be?

JAKE *shrugs.*
LUBA *opens the door.*
Enter JOSH *and* LYLA, *heavily peppered with snow.*

JOSH (*to* LUBA): Sorry to trouble you. Our car's broke down. We were wondering if we could use —

JOSEPH (*removing his napkin*): Hah!

JOSH (*glancing uneasily at* JOSEPH, *to* LUBA): If we could use your phone.

CHESTER *and* JAKE *gape at the intruders, who gape back at them. All, including* LUBA, *are uneasy, as though trying dimly to recall where they could have met before.* JOSEPH *is the exception.*

LUBA: Uh, well. Hmm. Yes, of . . . course —

JOSEPH (*softly*): Well, if this don't beat everything.

CHESTER (*suspiciously*): Eh?

JOSEPH: The nerve.

JAKE: What —

JOSEPH: The bloody nerve of him!

JAKE (*softly*): Here, settle down, will you?

LUBA (*to* JOSH *and* LYLA): Uh, look, you may as well get your wet things off. You can hang them in the bathroom.

LYLA: Fine. Thanks

JOSH and LYLA remove their coats, gloves, etc.

JOSH: It's, uh. It's really coming down out there.

LYLA: Mmmm, must be nearly a foot high in the drifts.

JOSEPH (*to himself*): Hah.

LUBA: Really? I haven't looked out for a while.

She goes to the window.

LYLA: Mmmm. Everything's stopped. You could hear a pin drop out there.

LUBA parts the curtains and raises the shade. The snow is falling thick and heavy.

LUBA: Mmmm. (*To the men at table*) Look.

JOSEPH: Pull that shade!

LUBA complies, and draws the curtains.
JOSH to the bathroom, with coats, etc.

LUBA: The telephone's right over here.

LYLA: Ah.

JOSEPH: I don't like it. I don't like it a bit.

JAKE: What are you on about now?

LYLA sits on the bed, lifts the receiver to her ear, and listens, pressing the cradle button rapidly several times.

LYLA (*ringing off*): Nothing. Dead. I can't think what we're to do now.

LUBA: Well, wait a bit and try again. I'll make some coffee.

LYLA (*rising*): Oh, please, don't go to any trouble.

LUBA (*to the kitchen*): It's no trouble. Only two more cups, is all.

LYLA: Let me help you.

LUBA: No, I can manage. Sit down.

Enter JOSH, *passing* LUBA *as she exits into the kitchen.*

JOSH (*to* LUBA, *calmly*): There's a hair in the sink.

JOSEPH (*livid*): You *would* mention a thing like that, in front of all these people! (*To* JAKE) There's a hair in the sink, did you hear him? You see how calmly he takes it that there's a hair in the sink, as if it were nothing at all!

JAKE: Here, come on —

JOSEPH (*to* CHESTER, *rising*): There's a hair in the sink, Chester. (*To* JOSH) There! Now are you satisfied? Chester knows about the hair in the sink. Cor, what a family!

CHESTER (*rising*): Steady on. It's nothing. A hair, that's all.

JOSEPH: I know that! You think I don't know that? (*Indicating* JOSH) He's just trying to change the subject. He thinks I was born yesterday. Eh, Josh?

LYLA (*to* JOSH): What's he —

JOSEPH: Listen, Jake. You know what I've always said, Live and let live. But there's a limit! (*Indicating* JOSH) There he is, look at him. The only times we ever see him he's with some tart!

JAKE: Here. Relax, will you —

JOSEPH (*to* JOSH): So. You've brought another one of your filthy scrubbers in here! Always sleeping with tarts. A fine example to your younger brother here. Myself, I don't mind; but what's *he* supposed to think? Do I have to remind you that we've just been eating, that we're entertaining a guest? Quit sleeping with tarts! Go home to your wife and children!

JOSH (*stammering*): Luh, listen. I — I don't have to stand here and listen to this! Come on, Lyla, we're off.

JAKE (*pushing* JOSEPH *into his chair, to* JOSH): He's not himself tonight.

JOSH: Well, who the bloody hell does he *think* he is, talkin' to me like that?

JOSEPH (*to* JAKE): He never could take constructive criticism —

JAKE: Right. Just —

JOSEPH: Even when he was a lad —

JAKE: Yeh, relax —

JOSEPH: He never listened.

CHESTER, *meanwhile, is polishing off the rest of the wine.*

I mean, you've got to draw the line somewhere. He's been bringing his tarts back here for years now, and I never said a word. A different whore each night, and I never said a thing. I was hoping it was just a phase. He'll get over it, I said, give him time. But you've got to draw the line somewhere. I mean, we've got to think of Luba. You know how naïve she is. What sort of an example is he setting for Luba? I ask you, Chester, am I wrong? Is a father wrong to want the best for his children?

CHESTER: I don't know. You know, these things are always more complicated than they seem. I mean, I'm no psychologist.

JOSH *and* LYLA, *standing near the door, become gradually more angered and less perplexed.*

JOSEPH: Perfectly reasonable. But psychology has nothing to do with it. Oh, I know, I know, there's a lot to be said for infantile sexuality. But in a case like this? I mean, where's the psychology in sleeping with tarts? You get what you pay for! No, I shouldn't have let Machiavelli stand in my way.

CHESTER: Hmmm?

JOSEPH: Yeh. I thought the best way to handle the situation would be to sit back and roll with the punches. You know, wait my chance and let the rest pass with a cynical Renaissance pragmatism.

CHESTER *pulls at his collar.*

But I see, now, that I was mistaken. Should have laid down the law right off.

In the beginning I said, Josh, whatever you do, mind the clap. I said, You've got your wife and children to think of; what are you going to look like in ten years walking round with a metal nose in the middle of your face? It in't kosher; it just in't kosher, I said. (*Indicating* JAKE) *He* knows. You don't find Jakey bringing home a different tart every night.

JOSH (*as* LYLA *restrains him*): Listen, you old bastard —

LYLA: Come on, luv —

JOSH: No! (*to* JOSEPH) I've had quite enough of this! I'll . . . (*Brandishing his fist*) Keep it up. Just keep it up, and I'll shut your bloody mouth for you with this!

JOSEPH: You see, Chester? You see how he talks to his father? If I'd spoken to my father like that he'd have strung me up with piano wire and left me to die in the ice house, I can tell you — it happened more than once. (*Indicating* JOSH) But this one, just listen to him. Listen to the mouth on him! I'm glad his mother's not here to see this, God bless her.

JOSH: Of course she's not here, you lying old sod, after what *you* did to her!

JOSEPH (*uneasily*): What's that?

JOSH: Don't come that crap with me. You know exactly what I'm talking about.

JOSEPH (*swallowing hard*): What's he saying, Jake? (*To* JOSH) What do you mean?

JOSH (*threateningly*): Old man —

JOSEPH (*rises, pacing*): Your mother, your mother. It was all so long ago, I can't even remember what she looked like, I swear it!

JOSH: Hmph —

JOSEPH: Jake, I don't think he's your brother at all. He couldn't be. I think he's playing some sort of game with us. What do you think, Jake? You think he's your brother? Luba certainly is taking her time with that coffee.

JOSH *grips* JOSEPH *by the lapels and pulls him close.*

JAKE (*trying to intervene*): Here, easy. Easy —

JOSH (*to* JOSEPH): Here, listen, you. You bag of piss.

JOSEPH (*to* JAKE, *faintly Yiddish*): Listen how he talks.

JOSH: I'll give you something to talk about.

> *He pushes* JOSEPH *away and sweeps* LYLA *into his arms, caressing her intimately. They tear at one another's clothing, mad with passion. Enter* LUBA, *bearing a bowl of fruit. She sets it on the table.*

LUBA (*cheerfully oblivious*): Coffee in a minute.

> LUBA *returns to the kitchen, completely unaffected by the antics of* JOSH *and* LYLA, *who toss her uniform, etc., off the bed and hurriedly begin to disrobe, tossing their clothes in every direction.*

JOSEPH (*very Yiddish*): Josh! (*Wringing his hands*) Oy.

CHESTER (*to* JOSH): Look here, what are you trying to prove? This doesn't prove anything. Be reasonable.

JOSH: This has nothing to do with reason.

> JAKE *looks on in amazement, takes his seat and enjoys the spectacle.* JOSEPH *lifts an apple out of the bowl as* CHESTER *drums nervously on the table with his fingers.*

JOSEPH (*still Yiddish, bewildered*): Josh. You vanna piece fruit?

> JOSH *and* LYLA *are naked. For a moment they stand motionless, facing one another,* LYLA *to the near,* JOSH *to the far, side of the bed.* JOSEPH *chucks the apple back into the bowl and continues as though they weren't there.*

(*To* CHESTER, *his Yiddish accent gone*) You see what he's like?

> JOSH *and* LYLA *climb into bed.*

You see what I've got to put up with?

> JOSH *and* LYLA *pull the covers up and lie, side by side on their backs, motionless, their heads alone visible above the bedclothes.*

I tell you, Chester, I can't take much more of his sleeping with tarts.

> JOSH *and* LYLA *close their eyes. Sleep.*

I'm a nervous man!

> *Enter* LUBA *with four cups of coffee, the cream, the sugar, on a tray.*

Sssh! (*Softly*) Act as though nothing happened. (*Awkwardly loud*) Well, here's the coffee! Here it is.

> LUBA *sets a cup and saucer down before* JOSEPH.

Thank you, luv.

LUBA: You're welcome.

> *She serves* CHESTER *and* JAKE, *then takes her seat.*

(*To* CHESTER) Sugar?

CHESTER (*nodding*): Mmmm.

LUBA: How many?

CHESTER: Two.

> *She drops two lumps of sugar into his cup, passes the sugar bowl to* JAKE, *etc.*

LUBA: Cream?

CHESTER (*shaking his head*): Uh, I never take it.

> JOSEPH *drops five lumps of sugar into his cup as* LUBA *passes the cream to* JAKE, *etc.* JAKE *takes cream.*

JOSEPH (*declining cream*): Nnnn. Got to stay awake.

> *They sip their coffee.*
> *Pause.*

The light. It hurts my eyes.

LUBA: You mean the kitchen?

JOSEPH: No. That's all right. Jake, switch it off.

LUBA (*rising*): I'll get it —

JOSEPH: No! Let Jake. He's closer. (*To* JAKE) Well, go on.

    JAKE *switches off the night-table lamp and returns to his chair.*

Ah, that's better. That's much better.

JAKE: A bit dark, don't you think?

JOSEPH (*chuckling, nervously*): Not a bit. I can still see clear enough. (*To* CHESTER) The old peepers in't what they used to be, but I get on well enough. Blimey, in the old days candlelight was all we had! Women used to sew by candlelight, it never bothered 'em. Yeh, in those days you could count on women. You could do anything you liked with 'em. Now, I'm not sayin' it was any better then. Perish the thought. I was younger, that's all. You got different ideas when you're a young man. Like Jake.

JAKE: What?

JOSEPH: Pay attention! What I've got to say is important!

JAKE: All right, all right!

JOSEPH: No, Chester. I in't the man I used to be. None of us is. Not even Jake.

JAKE: Who'd you used to be, Dad?

JOSEPH: When?

JAKE: Just now.

JOSEPH: What —

JAKE: Just now. Who did you used to be —

LUBA: Jake.

JAKE: No! I really want to know.

JOSEPH (*flustered*): What? You got eyes in your head! You can see things, even in *this* murk! You ask me a question like that and expect me to answer it right off, without thinking it over?

JAKE: By all means, think it over. (*To* CHESTER) He's stallin' for time. Always has to be the centre of attention, like Kaiser Wilhelm — you know: the corpse at every wedding, the bride at every funeral?

CHESTER: Hmmm?

JOSEPH (*to* JAKE): Ah, so you want to turn this into a political discussion. You weren't even born then! The Kaiser had his faults — I never said he didn't — just like anyone else. (*To* CHESTER) To tell the truth, I never believed half the stories they told about him. I mean, there was a war on; you've got to take that into account. Propaganda, that's all it was. I never did believe that story about the Red Cross nurses, the camel, and the vat o' vinegar. I mean, not that he wasn't a capable man — let's not take anything away from him — but, really, it was a physical impossibility! Anyone with brains in his head could've seen that right off! Ach, you know reporters. If there's no story they make one up, just to fill the empty space. I'm not criticising them, I can understand that. I can understand it. They got to eat, like anyone else. The space has got to be filled, Chester. It's *got* to be. They can't just leave it and go on about their business. I mean, there's a void. A tremendous void, when you come to think of it. It's got to be filled. A man's entitled to a few indiscretions in his life. Where would Luba and Jakey be today without my indiscretions? Live and let live is what I say. Let the Kaiser have his camel, and let him the bloody hell alone! I mean, a man's entitled, once in a while. What about it, Chester? I mean, am I daft, or what?

CHESTER: No, you make a lot of sense.

JOSEPH: Because, if you'll forgive my sayin' so, we in't heard aught from your end of the table this evening. So, what about it, then?

CHESTER: No, it's true what you said about the Kaiser. It's true.

JOSEPH (*to* JAKE): There you are. You see? Chester agrees with me. It's because he's an older man. He knows how these things are, something you'll never comprehend. Am I right, Chester? He just don't know what it's like yet. Oh, he will. He will. Give him time. That's what he wants, time. He's always on the job. Never has any time to consider the profound Machiavellian questions.

LUBA (*to* JAKE): Oh, Machiavelli again.

JAKE: He fancies Machiavelli.

JOSEPH (*rising, gesticulating*): Common sense, that's what I'm talkin' about! Common sense!

> LUBA *rises and moves to* JOSEPH*'s side, supporting him as* JAKE *and* CHESTER *finish their coffee.*

(*To* LUBA) It's nothin', luv. I'm all right. Just a bit wobbly, is all. (*To* CHESTER) Yeh, this younger generation. Take my daughter Luba here. Look at the arse on this girl. (*Appreciatively*) Disgustin', innit? I can hardly keep my *own* hands off it, and I'm her *father*, her progenital, so to speak!

> *Pause.*

Oh, I know. I know what you're thinking, Chester. You don't fool me. (*Pawing* LUBA*'s buttocks with one hand, as though by reflex*) You're just itchin' to wrap your choppers round a bit o' that, eh? I'm a very nervous man, Chester!

CHESTER: What? I —

JAKE: Like to get your hot hands on those heavenly hemispheres.

CHESTER: Listen —

JOSEPH: Cop a feel o' the mellow jello. (*To* LUBA) What you think, luv? You think Chester here wants to get his mitts on your chubby combustibles?

LUBA (*easing him into his chair*): Sit down and have a piece of fruit. A nice piece of fruit —

JOSEPH: Yes, yes. (*To* CHESTER) I know you'd like to turn her upside down, we all would. (*Pounding his fist on the table*) Damn it all, man! Try to show a bit of restraint!

> LUBA *to the kitchen, with the tray of empty cups.*

(*Picking amidst the fruit*) I don't want you to get the idea she's a tease. No, you won't catch my Luba pullin' any o' that sleight-of-heinie business on you. She's a good girl. All the same, I wouldn't want to see her a sphincter in her old age.

JAKE: Huh, look who's talkin'. Sphincter.

JOSEPH (*to* CHESTER): So, I've got to ask you. (*To* JAKE) Ask him what are his intentions.

JAKE (*to* CHESTER): What are your intentions?

CHESTER: As to what?

JOSEPH (*to* JAKE): As to your sister.

JAKE (*to* CHESTER): As to my sister.

CHESTER: Look, I don't see —

JOSEPH: Now, don't get me wrong! Don't get me wrong. You're both young. You've got plenty of time to come to a decision. I can see your side of it, Chester, don't think I can't. No need to rush into things. I know how it is. Huh, you don't have to tell *me*. Bleedin' women are like squid; once they get their testicles round you, you're done for. And mind the clap!

Pause.

Now, you take Doc Whatsup — remember him, Jake? — old Doc Whatsup. You come down with a leaky tap and he could stop the drippin' quick enough, without a fuss. You take my meaning? Yeh, I'd have been up and around long before this if old Doc Whatsup was still in the profession. Yeh, when Luba and the lads was young, I used to go to him all the time. He had a clinic over on the Northwest Side. You know, for gentlemen's diseases? Proper den of iniquity, it was too. I mean, it wasn't just a clinic. No. The Doc liked to have a few laughs while he was on the job. He was a funny sort o' bloke. Said the work depressed him no end, but he went right on with it, all the same. You should've seen some o' the punters in the waiting room. Cor, it was a sight! But what could he do? He couldn't just walk out o' there. I mean, the man weren't fit to clean shit off the streets! He had to live. You couldn't expect him to chuck six months of medical school and a stint in veterinary hospital out the window, could you? No, Chester. He was a dedicated man, Doc Whatsup. He worked some really fantastic cures, you wouldn't believe it. Hah, but I was *there*! Saw it all with my own eyes. I remember it like it was yesterday. The chancres, the pus, the mercury. One bloke come in with a faulty pisser. I can't piss, Doc, he says, I'm ready to burst! Well, the Doc knew it was all psychological, see? He says, Take down your trousers, Jake — I'm callin' him Jake on account of I can't remember the geezer's name — he says, Take down your trousers, Jake, and aim at the bucket. Then the Doc presses a button under his desk and this gorgeous bit o' crumpet comes out dressed to the nines, with a jewelled cigarette holder in her mouth — no cigarette, mind, just the holder. That's the sort o' bloke Doc was, he couldn't abide smokin'. Just didn't hold with it. Always said cigarettes and syphilis go hand in foot. Here, Jake, you wouldn't have a fag on you? (*To* CHESTER) I keep tellin' him to quit but, cor, he's got to have some vices, otherwise where the bloody hell would he be?

JOSEPH *takes a cigarette from* JAKE's *packet.* JAKE *offers one to* CHESTER. *The three men light up, together, from the centrepiece candle.*

So there's Jake with his whacker hangin' out over the bucket and this high-class bint walkin' about, swingin' her arse in every direction, bendin' over the bucket to give him a good look at her vats, sayin', Come on, luv, you can do it, nothin' to it, the strain is half the pain, and rubbish like that; you know, little rhymes and jingles the Doc taught her. Doc told me she was a registered nurse — come from one o' the best o' families, as well — a true professional. I mean, there's certain things *nobody* can teach you. You gotta be born to it. I mean, women like that don't sprout from trees; they're not thruppence a bushel —

JAKE: So, what about this Jake, then?

JOSEPH: Ah. (*Flicking ashes into the fruit bowl*) He was all right.

JAKE: That's all?

JOSEPH: Yeh. I mean, he filled the bucket, and after that he was right as rain. Must've poured off three stone at least. Yeh, and that was only one case. Old Doc Whatsup. He and I were pretty close, you know. Mind, I was a lot younger then. Whenever he had what looked to be an interesting case, he'd ring me up and scream into the phone — he was a bit hard of hearin' — Joseph, get your arse down here, I got one for the books! He thought I had a flair for diagnosis. Used to let me watch the more interesting examinations through a hole in the wall; then he'd come in back and say, Well, Joseph, what do you think it could be?

JAKE *and* CHESTER *flick their ashes into the fruit bowl and, with* JOSEPH, *will continue to do so throughout.*

He never made a move without me. I was even on the lists, for a bit, as a private consultant.

JAKE: What about the girl?

JOSEPH: Eh?

JAKE: The high-class bint.

JOSEPH: I got to know all of 'em well.

JAKE: There was more than one?

JOSEPH: Yeh. Quite a few. They came and went. I knew 'em all.

JAKE: Huh.

JOSEPH: Yeh. The Doc had a whole string o' girls workin' for him. Crumpet of all persuasions — Catholic, Protestant, Oriental — wonderful girls, all of 'em. Real ladies, not like what you see today. Yeh, the Doc did a tidy little business. Wanted me to go in with him on a full-time basis. Should've done it. Biggest mistake I ever made, not to go in with him. He'd set it up so's you could contract the clap and be cured of it all in the same place, at a discount. Cut the middle man right out.

Pause.

Yeh. I shouldn't have listened to Jake's mother. I should've gone in with him. I mean, the clinic was bought and paid for, so there was no overhead. And I'd have been doing useful work. Blimey, the money never meant a thing to me, Jake knows that. I could've made something of my life. I could've had self-respect. I . . . I know there's a good deal more I could've done for Luba and the lads. Well, I made a proper mess of things, I don't deny it. Which is why, Chester, if you want to become a member of this family, we'll have to know a little more about you. We can't afford any more mistakes. We've got to be careful from now on. You can see for yourself how naïve Luba is. It's my fault. I know I've indulged her. She's got no idea what the world is like, hasn't a clue. I can't afford to have a stranger — a stranger passing in the night — trifling with my daughter's affections. You can understand that.

CHESTER: Of course.

JOSEPH: Which is why Jake here would like to ask you a couple of questions.

JAKE: Eh?

JOSEPH (*to* CHESTER): Nothing to upset yourself about.

CHESTER: I understand.

JOSEPH: Just a few questions, so we know where we stand.

CHESTER: Press on.

Pause

JAKE: Uh. Before I ask you any questions, uh. I'd like your opinion of a dream I had last night.

JOSEPH: What are you on about? We don't have time for that —

JAKE: Now, wait. Hold on —

JOSEPH: Chester's a busy man! I mean, you can see it just to look at him. Get on with it!

JAKE: Calm down, will you —

JOSEPH: Tell him the dream afterwards, when we're more settled —

JAKE: Just keep your trousers on, this won't take long. You don't mind, do you, Chester? I mean, you got nowhere to go.

CHESTER: Not at all.

JAKE: Good. (*To* JOSEPH) See? He doesn't mind!

JOSEPH *puffs on his cigarette.*

(*To* CHESTER) Right. It isn't actually a dream.

CHESTER: Uh?

JAKE: No. I just said that, I don't know what got into me.

JOSEPH (*To* CHESTER): What's he talking about?

CHESTER *shrugs.*

JAKE: No. It's more a theory. This theory I've been developing.

CHESTER: Ah.

JAKE: Yeh. I got this theory about Faust.

CHESTER: What —

JOSEPH (*choking on his cigarette*): What?

Pause.

JAKE: You all right?

JOSEPH *waves him off, hacking and wheezing.*

You know, you really ought to cut down at your age. You'll get cancer.

JOSEPH (*coughing*): I'm all right. I'm all right. Get on with it!

JAKE: Right.

Pause.

(*To* CHESTER, *causally*) Here's what I think about Faust. During the time of his blood covenant, as all his wishes were acceded to — wealth, power, voluptuousness — Mephistopheles concealed from Faust the crowning irony of his condition. Those for whom Faust worked his so-called miracles saw him for the mass of fleshly corruption that he was, an old, half-blind mendicant worthy only of their contempt. They knew his hideous appearance, nothing more. But Faust saw a handsome image in the mirror, mistook their cowering behaviour for awe, and was deceived.

CHESTER (*nervously*): No. No, that's impossible. There must be some other explanation, I . . . I can't accept that. (*Tugging at his collar*) No. Because, in recognising him for what he appeared to be on the physical plane, he... They never realise who he is. They catch no glimpse of his true identity.

JAKE: Which is that of a tramp in rags.

CHESTER: Which is that of Doctor Faustus, a great and tragical necromancer. (*Feverishly*) Always the secret drama. One knows only that Faust is not himself. And one, not excluding Faust himself, cannot even be sure of that! (*Mopping his brow*) No. I don't understand what you're saying. (*To* JOSEPH) Do you understand what he's saying?

JAKE: Illusions.

CHESTER (*gasping*): Yes, that's it! Illusions . . . on both sides. Now I see it.

JAKE: Now we're getting somewhere.

CHESTER (*chuckling nervously*): Yes. Yes, there's something to *that*. I can see you've given it a lot of thought.

JAKE: Yeh. I mean, the two conditions of Faust — Faustus the perceived, and Faustus the perceiver — are at one and the same time mutually exclusive and mutually dependent, right?

CHESTER: You can't have the one without the other.

JAKE: You can't have the one either with *or* without the other. Which is why, now that we've agreed upon the Faustian condition, I must enquire into the present state of your health.

JOSEPH: Good. That's good, Jake. That's what I was leading up to before with that business about Doc Whatsup. But you've done it much better, more subtle. My hat's off to you.

JAKE: Thanks.

CHESTER: What was the question again?

JAKE: Never mind. I've just come up with a better one.

CHESTER: Ah.

JAKE: Yeh. There's been a lot of talk about —

JOSEPH: What? There's been a lot of talk about? Who's talking —

JAKE: Cheese it a minute, will you? (*To* CHESTER) Christ, can't even get a word in.

ACT TWO

Pause.

Chester, I'm gonna give it to you straight. I'm not at all keen on this sort of thing.

CHESTER (*sheepishly*): What sort of thing?

JAKE: Here, don't take the mickey. Look at him.

Pause.
They look at JOSEPH. JOSEPH *looks at them.*

What do you see?

CHESTER: Eh?

JAKE: Come on, just to humour me. What do you see when you look at him like this across the table?

CHESTER: Nuh, nothing. I don't remember —

JAKE: Ah.

CHESTER: What is this, a fishing expedition?

JAKE: Where do you live?

CHESTER: Huh?

JAKE: Your domicile, your digs, your almost-present whereabouts. What's the address?

CHESTER: Uh, fff — 432 Kelipawt Street.

JAKE: A house?

CHESTER: No.

JAKE: A flat.

CHESTER: Mmmm.

JAKE: Can you describe the building?

CHESTER: Large. It's a large building.

JAKE: I see, I see. And your mode of livelihood? Are you presently employed?

CHESTER: Yes.

JAKE: Your employer's name?

CHESTER: Self-employed. No employer.

JAKE: Address?

CHESTER: Not far.

JAKE: Can you describe the building?

CHESTER: Yes.

JAKE: How long have you been in business?

CHESTER: Not long.

JAKE: And your secretary?

CHESTER (*suspiciously*): What?

JAKE: Your secretary. I take it you've got a secretary.

JOSEPH: More than one?

CHESTER: She reads Chinese!

JAKE: I see, I see —

CHESTER: Chinese.

JAKE: She's an Oriental.

CHESTER: How do *I* know? That's *her* business!

JAKE: Who's the President?

CHESTER: You mean the King.

JAKE: Who's the King?

JOSEPH (*to* CHESTER): The King. Did you vote for him in the last erection?

CHESTER: No, the Queen.

JAKE: The Queen what?

CHESTER: Pay attention!

JOSEPH: Somebody killed the King?

JAKE: Pay attention!

JOSEPH: Nobody told me.

JAKE (*to* CHESTER): I'm trying to piece it together.

CHESTER: What are you trying to piece together?

JAKE: The whole thing. I'm trying to piece it all together —

JOSEPH: Piece it together —

JAKE: I'm trying!

JOSEPH: Well, try harder!

JAKE: I'm trying —

JOSEPH: Or I'll get Chester to handle the questioning.

JAKE (*to* CHESTER): What have you got against Orientals?

CHESTER: Huh —

JAKE: Take your secretary. You got all nervous when I mentioned she was an Oriental.

CHESTER (*defensively*): I gave her work!

JAKE: I mean, that rubbish about the President and the King. I mean, who can keep those things straight any more? You were trying to confuse me, to get me off the subject of your secretary.

CHESTER: You're the one who brought up the President!

JAKE: And you had the poor taste to correct me, at a time like this! It was an honest mistake! (*To* JOSEPH) I think we're on to something. Definitely something to do with the secretary. (*To* CHESTER) Hair?

CHESTER: What?

JAKE: What colour's her hair?

CHESTER: I don't know. I don't remember. Who notices a thing like that?

JAKE: Is she good-looking?

CHESTER: Not bad.

JAKE: She. You know, does she go?

> *Pause.*

Come on. You can tell us. Come on.

> CHESTER *nods.*

How fast?

CHESTER: Look, what do you want? I can't give a precise answer to —

JAKE: How many kilometres per hour —

CHESTER: One hundred forty-five.

> *Pause.*
> JOSEPH's *accent becomes gradually more Yiddish.*

JAKE: Not bad.

JOSEPH: Not bad, not bad. (*To* JAKE) Now, ask him, with that kind of speed what does he want with Luba?

JAKE: He wants to know —

CHESTER: I understood the question!

JAKE: Look, she in't half bad. I don't blame you. She's built. Just my type, too. She's got If! You lucky sod. (*To* JOSEPH) Here, why don't we have her back in? What's she doin', anyway?

JOSEPH: Ask him does he intend to support her in a manner to which she's become unaccustomed.

JAKE (*to* CHESTER): He wants to —

CHESTER: Right. Well, what can I say? Tell him I'll give her whatever she wants.

JAKE (*to* JOSEPH): He says he'll —

JOSEPH: Ask him has he got faith.

JAKE: In what?

JOSEPH: In anything! Ask him.

JAKE (*to* CHESTER): Have you got faith in anything?

CHESTER: Yes.

JOSEPH: T'ank God. I'm relieved. (*To* JAKE) Ask him where did he get that suit.

CHESTER: It's not a suit. (*Standing*) The jacket's separate.

He models the jacket.

JOSEPH: It's nice material.

CHESTER: (*sitting*) Thanks.

JAKE (*to* JOSEPH): Listen, this isn't getting us anywhere.

JOSEPH (*with resignation*): Okay, Mister Fancy Pants. You could do better?

Pause.

JAKE (*to* CHESTER): Right. Now. Just for openers, could you give me the address of this girl?

CHESTER: What girl?

JAKE: You know, the one-hundred-forty-five-kilometre one.

CHESTER: Oh. How do *I* know where she lives?

JAKE: Oh. (*Leering*) You mean you get all your business done at the office, eh?

CHESTER: That's right.

JAKE: Maybe I'll pop in at the office sometime.

CHESTER: I'm usually not in the office.

JAKE: Good. That's even better.

JOSEPH: Schmendrick! What are you talking the office? Feh.

JAKE: Just keepin' my hand in.

JOSEPH (*to himself, sarcastically bewildered*): He'll pop in at the office.

JAKE: Listen, Chester, I just can't place you. You seem familiar, but I just can't place you.

CHESTER: Hmmm.

JAKE (*indicating* JOSEPH): How about the old geezer? It bothers me, Chester. I tell you, it bothers the bleedin' hell out o' me.

CHESTER: Mmmm —

JAKE: I mean, I don't know where I stand anymore! Haven't a clue.

CHESTER: Uh-huh —

JAKE: Yeh. I'd like to know. I mean, I'd really like to know. I mean, it would make a change, wouldn't it?

CHESTER: Mmmm —

JAKE: From the old routines?

CHESTER: Uh-huh —

JAKE: From the how's-your-father?

CHESTER: Yes.

JAKE: From the penny-dreadful inconclusions?

CHESTER: It would —

JAKE: I mean, we can't just sit here all night groping round the big question.

CHESTER: Ah, right —

JAKE: The question that's on all our minds here, and that we're all afraid to ask.

CHESTER: Right.

JAKE: That's right. It can't go on like this much longer.

> *He rises, snuffs out his cigarette in the fruit bowl, beckons* CHESTER *down right, and puts his arm round him.*

(*Confidentially*) Listen, I want to help you. I really do.

> JOSEPH *snuffs out his cigarette in the fruit bowl.*

Look at him over there. He's lost. He don't want to let on, but he's lost. I'm sure of it. Look, just play along for a bit. Be a little more coöperative, eh? Feed me some information. Anything, I don't care. Just enough to keep Old Joe off me back. He's a very sick man. Right?

CHESTER: I'll do my best.

JAKE: I couldn't ask for more.

> *He gestures toward the table.* CHESTER *resumes his seat.* JAKE *flashes the 'okay' to* JOSEPH, *walks back to the table, and resumes his seat.*
>
> Ah. Now, let's see. Where did we leave off?

CHESTER: Why don't you ask me about my hopes, my dreams.

> JOSEPH *returns to his normal mode of speech.*

JOSEPH: That's good. (*To* JAKE) Ask him what are his hopes and dreams.

JAKE (*to* CHESTER): He wants to know —

CHESTER: In the beginning I had no hopes at all, absolutely none. The snow fell, and I was content.

JAKE (*softly*): That's it. Keep it up.

CHESTER: I had no dreams, and I was content. (*Rising*) I was content to have no dreams.

> *He paces the floor.*

I realise, now, that I was wrong.

JAKE (*to* JOSEPH): You see? He was wrong.

CHESTER: Yes, I was wrong. I had no idea. I just had no idea.

JAKE: So, when did you begin to dream?

CHESTER: Later. Much later. After the snow fell.

JOSEPH: The snow! Always the snow! (*To* JAKE) Change the subject!

JAKE: To what? I thought he was all right. I thought he was doin' all right —

JOSEPH (*rising*): I'd like to forget about the snow!

CHESTER: Why?

JOSEPH: It reminds me.

JAKE: Of what? It reminds you of what?

JOSEPH: I don't know!

> JOSEPH *and* CHESTER *pace the floor in a state of agitation.* JAKE *lights another cigarette from the centrepiece candle and begins to pace. The pacing is timed so that the character speaking finds himself walking out of the penumbra into the area between the centrepiece candle and the light spilling dimly in from the kitchen. The pacing appears random enough, and becomes gradually more frenzied.*

I just don't know. It makes me uneasy, that's all. There must be another way—

CHESTER: Another way. There's always another way, if you look about for it.

JOSEPH: That's it, Chester. That's what I've got to know. I can't take much more of this.

CHESTER: The doubts. The nagging doubts.

JOSEPH: Always the doubts, tucked away in the back of your mind.

JAKE: You can never be sure. You can never be too sure.

JOSEPH: And there's Luba to consider. Her naïveté.

CHESTER: Her gullibility.

JAKE: Her inexperience.

JOSEPH: Her eyes.

JAKE: Her hair.

CHESTER: The colour of her hair.

JAKE: Yeh, there's always that.

JOSEPH: I'll have to speak with her, set her to rights. Things being what they are.

CHESTER: Unavoidable, in the present situation.

JAKE: In the present Faustian situation. (*To* JOSEPH) I wouldn't want to be in your shoes.

JOSEPH: Nor would I. It's a good job I'm not in them. I can be grateful for that.

CHESTER: To who? Grateful to who?

JAKE: To whom.

JOSEPH: That's always confused me. I never know what it's supposed to be.

JAKE: Whom, as the object.

CHESTER: The object of what?

JOSEPH: Yes. That's it. What is the object?

CHESTER: The object of 'whom.'

JAKE: Of the preposition 'to.'

JOSEPH: That, too? We may have preposed.

JAKE: We may have presupposed.

JOSEPH: It's always possible that we may have presupposed. That we may have taken far too much for granted.

JAKE: That must be it. That has to be it. There can be no other explanation.

> CHESTER, *exhausted, resumes his seat. The pacing slows.*

JOSEPH: No other explanation but that we may have presupposed.

JAKE: Let's examine the facts at leisure.

JOSEPH: It's our only alternative.

> *Pause.*
> JAKE *and* JOSEPH *stand on either side of* CHESTER, *each draping an arm casually on the back of* CHESTER's *chair.* CHESTER *mops his brow.*

JAKE: Claims have been made.

JOSEPH: Where?

JAKE: Here. In this very room.

JOSEPH: Oh, yes. Claims have been made in our presence. Phantastic claims.

JAKE: Phantastic more for what they omit than for what they have emitted.

JOSEPH: Yes. The omissions are phantastic. Quite phantastic.

JAKE: It follows, therefore, that these emissions, such as they are, leave a great deal to be desired.

JOSEPH: A great deal, yes. A great deal, these emissions. These nocturnal emissions.

    CHESTER *begins to breathe heavily.*

They've not left us much to go on, Chester, you've got to admit.

CHESTER *(gasping)*: It, uh. It must have been the wine.

JOSEPH: Yeh. *(To* JAKE*)* It could have been the wine —

JAKE: Possibly —

CHESTER *(tearing at the buttons of his shirt)*: Water.

JOSEPH: You've not left us much to go on, Chester, with these emissions.

JAKE: Nocturnal emmissions —

CHESTER *(gasping)*: No.

JOSEPH: What about these nocturnal emissions, then, Chester?

CHESTER *(panting)*: Nuh, no.

JAKE: We've been given to undersand your secretary dyes her hair.

CHESTER *(closing his eyes)*: No.

> CHESTER *is weakening; his breathing becomes more and more erratic, and he begins to sink in his chair. His eyes remain closed as* JAKE *and* JOSEPH *quicken the pace of their hectoring.*

JOSEPH: No. She reads, eh?

JAKE: She reads. (*To* CHESTER) What does she read?

CHESTER: No —

JAKE: The Encyclopædia?

CHESTER: No.

JOSEPH: Ventriloquial Concatenations?

CHESTER: No.

JAKE: Chronicles of the Merovingian Period?

CHESTER: No.

JOSEPH: Malthusian Eviscerations?

CHESTER: No —

JAKE: Faust?

CHESTER: No —

JOSEPH: Faust?

CHESTER (*groaning*): No.

JOSEPH: Faust!

> CHESTER *sinks to the floor.*

Faust!

> CHESTER *lies motionless beneath the table.*

Faust!

> *The telephone rings.*

JAKE: He's dead.

JOSEPH (*shaking his head, with conviction*): No.

> *Enter* LUBA, *in an apron, as* JAKE *makes for the phone.* JOSEPH *catches* JAKE *by the arm and holds him fast. A determined look on* JOSEPH's *face.*

LUBA: What — oh, my God! (*Running to the table*) Joseph! Joseph, what have you done?

> *She kneels beside* CHESTER.
> *Second ring.*
> JOSEPH *switches on the night-table lamp.* JOSH *and* LYLA *have vanished; it is as though they were never there.* JOSEPH *sits on the edge of the bed, lifts the receiver and puts it to his ear. He listens and turns pale.*
> *Begin fade to black; a pale, narrow pool of light on* JOSEPH's *horror-stricken face.*
> *Pause.*
> JOSEPH *groans.*
> *All to black.*

ACT THREE

A second old house parlour, later that night. All the furniture of Act One, but in an entirely different arrangement. In the right wall: a door giving on the kitchen. In the left wall: a narrow vestibule conceals the door upstage; downstage, a window with curtains drawn. Up centre, the L-shaped stair of Act One. The lighting is subdued. Down centre, PEG *reclines on a couch. She is casually dressed (slacks, etc.) and reading a magazine. The phone on the desk rings twice, down left.*

PEG (*into the phone*): Hallo. (*Brief pause*) No, you've got the wrong number. (*Brief pause*) Uhm-hmm. Yes. Well, the number is right, but there's nobody here by that name. (*Brief pause*) No, it isn't. Sorry. (*Brief pause*) Good-bye.

She rings off, stretches, and goes to resume her position on the couch. A knock from beyond the kitchen, loud and insistent.
Exit PEG *to the kitchen. Sound of a door opening, off right.*

PEG (*off*): Well —

JOSEPH (*off*): I came through the back, just to be sure no one followed me.

Sound of the door closing.

PEG (*off*): What are you doing about in this weather? Here, shake the snow off —

JOSEPH (*off*): I'd —

PEG (*off*): Stand on the mat.

JOSEPH (*off*): I'd have called first, but —

PEG (*off*): That's right —

JOSEPH (*off*): But I didn't want to take the —

ACT THREE

PEG (*off*): Here, steady on. Take your time.

JOSEPH (*off*): I didn't want to call. I couldn't take the chance he might be listening.

PEG (*off*): What? Here. No, just hang it on the door.

Enter PEG, *bottle and glasses in hand.*

You look as though you could do with a drink.

She sets the glasses down on the coffee table in front of the couch, sits, and pours.
Enter JOSEPH, *sporting an elegant blazer whose stripes match those of his Act Two pyjamas. His shirt and trousers are black. He wears no tie. His collar is buttoned.*

JOSEPH (*pacing nervously*): Where's Rapitrone?

PEG: He's not here.

JOSEPH: What?

PEG: Corby took him out on a job.

JOSEPH: What, at this time of night? You know what it's like out there?

PEG: Oh, he doesn't mind. (*Handing him the drink*) Here. He goes out quite a lot with Corby. Says the night air does him the world of good. It helps him to sleep. You know how difficult it is for him —

JOSEPH: Yes, but aren't you the least bit worried? I mean, have you looked in the yard? The drifts are halfway up the dust bins. It took me more than an hour to get here, and I fell three times! (*Collapsing into a nearby chair*) Once you fall, it's the devil trying to get up again. And at my age. Huh, you can well imagine. You oughtn't to have let him go.

PEG: Corby'll look after him. He always does. Watches over him like a hawk.

JOSEPH: When do you expect him back?

PEG: He should be back any time now. What is it? What's got you out after him so late at night?

JOSEPH: You don't know?

PEG: No. How would I know?

JOSEPH: I got a call. Where'd they go?

PEG: On a job. You know. The usual sort of thing.

JOSEPH: Ah. Well, to tell you the truth, I can't understand why Corby takes him along. I mean, it can't be easy getting him into the lorry and out again at every stop, the way he is. You know. I mean, I'm not telling you anything you don't already know.

PEG: Yes, well. Corby says he's an asset.

JOSEPH: Oh?

PEG: Mmmm. You know. One look at Andy and the clients come round, without a fuss.

JOSEPH: Mmmm. I never thought of it that way; but, yes, I can see what he's about.

PEG: So, tell me; you didn't come here to discuss my husband's nocturnal escapades.

JOSEPH: No.

PEG: Well, out with it, then. What's brought you here after so long?

JOSEPH: Business. Has it been that long?

PEG: Mmmm. What sort of business?

JOSEPH: Can't say.

PEG: Come on, Joseph —

JOSEPH: I mean I'll wait for Rapitrone. It — I mean, it'll —

PEG: He's got worse, you know.

JOSEPH: No. Much worse? How bad is he?

PEG: Bad. He's very bad.

JOSEPH: Worse than before?

PEG: Much worse.

JOSEPH: Oh, it's a shame. You ought to have called me, I —

PEG: I called. You were never there.

JOSEPH: Yes. That's part of it.

PEG: What?

JOSEPH: Part of my business with Rapitrone. But if he's so much worse, I don't see—

PEG: That's another reason why you should tell me. You've got no idea what he's become. I might be able to help you myself.

Pause.

JOSEPH: Yes, I know. It's just that . . . Oh, I don't know, I'm not even sure of what the problem is myself.

PEG: What?

JOSEPH: Oh, don't get me wrong. There's a problem, and no mistake. What I mean is, it's the *nature* of the problem that's the problem right now more than anything else.

PEG: I don't follow. I mean, either there's a problem —

JOSEPH: No. Here's what I mean. The problem is there, there's no getting round it, but if it turns out not to be the problem that it *seems* to be — and that's the crucial point — then, whatever steps I'll have taken to alleviate it will have disastrous effect. Disastrous effect.

PEG: It sounds serious. But I'm still not sure what you're on about.

JOSEPH: I have to determine, beyond a shadow of a doubt, the true nature of the problem before I can take any decisive action. I mean, there are certain measures I could immediately take if the problem is merely what it appears, to the untrained eye, to be.

PEG: Ah. Well, as I said, Andy's not in a fit state to be much help to anybody.

JOSEPH: What about this Corby?

PEG: Oh, you know him —

JOSEPH: Huh —

PEG: You've met.

>JOSEPH *shakes his head.*

>Oh, I'm sure of it.

JOSEPH: The name. I'd have remembered the name.

PEG: You met him through Andy —

JOSEPH: No, Lyla. I'm certain —

PEG: Peg.

JOSEPH: Peg. I'm certain I'd have remembered the name.

PEG: Strange, I would have sworn . . . Finish your drink.

>JOSEPH *complies.*

>That's right.

>*He shudders.*

>You're cold. I'll pour you another, to settle your nerves.

JOSEPH: No. Perhaps later. I'm really beginning to feel my age. The cold never used to bother me. Now . . . All that snow. That bloody snow. I didn't think I would make it here. I mean, it's not that far; but it was —

PEG: Where were you coming from?

JOSEPH (*vaguely*): That place.

ACT THREE

PEG: What place?

JOSEPH: Over . . . Not far from here, really. Not all that far.

PEG: So, you moved.

JOSEPH: Huh?

PEG: That explains it —

JOSEPH: Yeh. What?

PEG: Changed your address. It explains why you never answered.

Pause.

JOSEPH: Uh —

PEG: The phone.

JOSEPH: Ah.

PEG: They must have kept your number.

JOSEPH: Who?

PEG: Whoever wasn't there after you moved away.

JOSEPH: After I moved —

PEG: I mean, it doesn't make sense, does it?

JOSEPH (*vaguely*): It doesn't make sense.

PEG: I mean the phone company would've taken it out.

JOSEPH: Uh.

PEG: The phone. If there was no one to move in after you. They'd have taken it out.

JOSEPH: Mmmm.

PEG: Corby was saying the other day, he was saying there's lots of them now.

JOSEPH: Lots of what?

PEG: Vacated premises.

JOSEPH: Oh, yeh. I could've told you that. The old place is vacated, all right.

PEG: You should've called.

JOSEPH (*without emphasis*): I know. I've not been well.

PEG: Oh?

JOSEPH: Yeh.

PEG: Nothing serious?

JOSEPH (*vaguely*): Well . . .

PEG: You *look* a bit peaky, now the flush's gone out of your cheeks.

> *Pause.*

So, what was it? Did you see a doctor?

JOSEPH: Nah. I came through it all right. Left me a good deal weaker, though. This is my first night out in a long while.

PEG: Mmmm, then it must be serious indeed.

JOSEPH: Huh?

PEG: This thing. This problem of yours. It must be serious.

JOSEPH: It *is* serious.

PEG: Well. You still haven't told me what it is.

JOSEPH: I'll tell you what it is, but I want you to tell me about Corby.

PEG: All right.

ACT THREE

JOSEPH: Right. I've brought something with me. It's outside.

PEG: I didn't see anything —

JOSEPH: It's at the end of the yard, buried in a drift. I couldn't take the chance of bringing it in. I didn't know who would be here.

PEG (*chuckling*): What is it, a dead body?

JOSEPH: Yes.

PEG: What?

JOSEPH: That's right. That's what it is. In a manner of speaking.

PEG (*rising*): But this is serious!

JOSEPH: Huh. You're telling me.

PEG: I mean, what if — what do you mean, in a manner of speaking?

JOSEPH: I mean that's all I hope it is, a dead body

PEG: You're having me on, aren't you? This is some sort of joke.

JOSEPH (*rising*): It's no joke.

> *She sits, pondering.*
> *Pause.*

PEG: What did you mean when you said you hoped that's all it was?

JOSEPH: That's a long story. (*Sitting next to her*) First, you promised to tell me about Corby.

> *Pause.*

PEG: There isn't all that much to tell, actually. Andy brought him home one night when he was out on one of his runs.

JOSEPH: Hmmm?

PEG: You know. Before, when he was still able to get work. He literally picked him up off the street. Corby was lying in a gutter. Some roughs had worked him over, and he was coughing blood. His nose was broken. He'd been lying there so long his hand was half embedded in a puddle of ice. As it was, they nearly had to cut it off. He lost a couple of fingers; but, to look at him, you'd never know it.

JOSEPH: He sounds a hard case.

PEG: Mmmm. But he's done a lot for Andy. I'm not complaining. We wouldn't be able to see it through, now, without him. And Andy seems happy in the work. Night work. It's what he used to do. He doesn't say much. Can't. But I know he's happy in it. It gets him out of the house for a bit each week.

JOSEPH: What sort of work is it?

PEG: Collections.

JOSEPH: Ah —

PEG: And tours of the Underground.

JOSEPH: The Underground?

PEG: The old city. You know.

JOSEPH: No. I've never heard of it.

PEG: Corby takes them down in great baskets.

JOSEPH: Who?

PEG: Why, the clients, of course.

JOSEPH: What for?

PEG: To have a look. To help them decide whether or not they want to hide out there. It's a very exclusive clientele. You know. People on the run, deserters . . .

JOSEPH: Are there many deserters?

PEG: Mainly officers.

JOSEPH: Who'd have thought it? You never hear anything about —

PEG: Oh, it's all been hushed up. I mean, what would happen if it were to get about that there are over a hundred officers hiding out in the Underground?

JOSEPH: That many?

PEG: At least. Corby says it's not so bad down there.

JOSEPH: Oh?

PEG: Mmmm, he says some of the old buildings are still intact. There's even a sort of restaurant.

JOSEPH: Huh. Sounds a bit farfetched to me. Nnnn, this Corby. He doesn't sound the dependable sort to me.

He rises and begins to pace.

What you've been telling me doesn't exactly inspire confidence.

PEG: Well. Now I've told you about Corby —

JOSEPH: There's nothing else? Nothing else you can tell me about him?

PEG: I don't actually know him all that well. He's quite aloof. Andy'd be able to tell you more, but . . . Don't worry, Corby's just the man to help you.

JOSEPH: What you said about the Underground. It mightn't be such a bad place for my travelling companion outside. But first, I've got to be sure. I've got to be absolutely sure.

PEG: I've told you, Corby's all right —

JOSEPH: I'm not talking about Corby. He'll do well enough. No, I'm thinking about the one out there. As soon as they come back, we'll bring him inside.

PEG: Just who is it, anyway? Or shouldn't I ask?

JOSEPH: Ah, that's the crux of the matter right there.

PEG: What?

JOSEPH: Who. Who it is. If I were certain of that, I could be rid of him tonight, pack him off to the Underground for good and all. We'll bring him in as soon as they get here. Lucky there's no one else in the house. I don't know what I'd have done if —

PEG: Uh, but there *is* . . . someone else.

JOSEPH: What? But you never said —

PEG: Now, it's all right. It's all right, honestly. It's only the lodger.

JOSEPH (*sitting*): What lodger? You never said anything about —

PEG: Now, it's no problem, really. Really, it —

JOSEPH: But of course it's a problem! We can't be bringing everyone into this! What're you doing taking in lodgers?

PEG: We can do with the extra money. Corby brought him to us. A disappointed client.

JOSEPH: A client.

PEG: A defector.

JOSEPH: Mmmm.

PEG: Mmmm. He didn't fancy the Underground. Didn't like the look of it. Corby took him down in the basket. Said it made him nervous. So, Corby brought him here to us.

JOSEPH: What's his name?

PEG: I don't know. He will have his privacy. Perhaps Corby knows, perhaps not. I mean, it's worked out all right. And the money . . . I've no complaints.

JOSEPH: Doesn't he get mail?

PEG: Of course not. I told you —

JOSEPH: I know. Which room does he have? Is he here now? Christ!

PEG: We've tidied the garret up for him. Yes, he's here. Now, will you stop worrying? He's all right, I promise you. He's quiet. We never hear a peep out of him. Anyhow, he's been ill.

JOSEPH: Ill?

PEG: Mmmm, so he won't be troubling us.

JOSEPH: You're sure of that?

PEG: Yes.

JOSEPH: I mean, you're sure of that; because it's positively essential what I'm doing here tonight doesn't get out.

PEG: Look, I told you. He's a defector. Even if he *were* to find out something, what good would it do him? Who could he possibly tell without involving himself in it and giving his own game away?

JOSEPH: You're forgetting one thing.

PEG: What?

JOSEPH: The phone. All he's got to do is pick up the phone and make an anonymous call. Why else do you think I'm here?

PEG: What?

JOSEPH: That's the reason I'm here. I got a call.

He walks to the L-shaped stair.

It was him.

PEG: No, it couldn't —

She joins him at the foot of the stair.

JOSEPH: It *must* have been him —

PEG: It couldn't have been. There's no phone up there.

JOSEPH: Maybe he slipped down here to make the call.

PEG: Impossible. I've been in all day.

JOSEPH: In here? In the parlour?

PEG: In the kitchen. In the parlour.

JOSEPH: You didn't go to the lav?

PEG: Well. Yes, I went after supper.

JOSEPH: How long did you take?

PEG: Here, listen —

JOSEPH: What time did you finish eating?

PEG: About two hours ago.

JOSEPH (*to himself*): Two hours. (*To* PEG) All right. After that.

PEG: After that, I was in here the whole time. How long ago was the call?

JOSEPH: I don't know, an hour. An hour and a half.

PEG: Well, there it is. It couldn't have come from here. I was here the whole time.

JOSEPH: Nnnn, I still don't like it.

PEG: You don't believe me —

JOSEPH: Ach. No, it isn't that.

He sits on the second step

The voice said, Find Rapitrone.

PEG: Ah.

She sits down beside him.

Anything else?

JOSEPH: I'd rather not say.

PEG: Why not? You can trust me.

Pause.

You won't tell me, then?

JOSEPH: It's too... personal. Something that only I... Perhaps later. When I'm sure.

PEG: Hmmm, sounds awfully intriguing. (*Rising*) I'm not at all sure I'll be able to stand the suspense.

She leans, buttocks against the desk, and folds her arms.
Pause.

JOSEPH: Could your husband have anything to do with this?

PEG: What do you mean? How could Andy have —

JOSEPH: Rapitrone, he said. Find Rapitrone.

PEG: Yes, but —

JOSEPH: Perhaps they know one another.

PEG: Or perhaps someone gave the caller my husband's name.

JOSEPH: Mmmm —

PEG: And how do you know the caller wasn't doing the work of someone else?

JOSEPH: I know. (*Shaking his head*) That voice.

Pause.

What's the typewriter for? You writing a novel?

PEG (*smoothing some papers*): Just some work I'm doing for Corby.

JOSEPH: Something to do with the Underground.

PEG: No.

JOSEPH: The collections, then.

PEG: No, it's something completely different.

JOSEPH: This Corby sounds a very busy man. How old is he?

PEG: It's difficult to say. Perhaps a few years older than me, I can't tell.

 She sits on the couch, slumping back.

 I wonder what's keeping them. They should've been back by now.

JOSEPH: It's the snow. I don't know how they can see to drive in it. Perhaps they got stuck in a drift.

 He collapses into a nearby chair.

PEG: You look tired.

JOSEPH: I *am* tired. Tired of the whole bloody mess.

PEG: The body. You carried it all this way?

JOSEPH (*shaking his head*): Dragged it. I dragged it. And quite a load, too.

PEG: Huh, I'll bet it was.

 He sighs.

JOSEPH: Well. I don't know, I've got to collect my wits. Got to sort it all out, before it's too late.

PEG: Well, you've come to the right place, I can say that. Corby can easily dispose of the body.

JOSEPH: That's not the main problem.

PEG: Well, what is, then? Look, you still haven't explained —

The doorbell. They rise.

JOSEPH: Later.

PEG opens the door within the vestibule, off left.

PEG: (*off*): Well, at last. I thought you'd got lost.

Enter CORBY *and* RAPITRONE, *heavily peppered with snow, followed by* PEG. CORBY *pushes* RAPITRONE *in in a wheelchair.* RAPITRONE*'s face is wan and lifeless; he sits with his head slumped forward, steel-rimmed spectacles masking his eyes (the lenses black), hands folded under the afghan that blankets his legs — he is completely paralyzed.* CORBY *has no fingers missing, no broken nose.*

CORBY: We nearly did. Whew! It's coming down worse than ever. I had to leave the lorry at the corner. Couldn't get past the drifts.

He doffs overcoat, cap, gloves, boots, etc., in the vestibule.

Couldn't see a bleedin' thing, coming up the street with him. Had to lift the chair up in the deepest places. (*Rubbing his arms*) Oooo! I'm not used to this.

PEG cups her hand under RAPITRONE*'s chin, lifts it, then lets it drop again.*

PEG: He seems none the worse for it.

CORBY: Oh, he's all right. (*Producing a flask*) I had him take a good stiff belt of this before we got out of the lorry.

He drinks from the flask.

PEG: I'm glad you thought of that.

CORBY: Ah. (*Handing her the flask*) Here. Put it over on the desk, that way I'll remember it.

She complies.

So, you've got company.

PEG: This is Joseph.

CORBY (*shaking hands, to* JOSEPH): 'Evenin', squire.

JOSEPH: Hallo. (*To* RAPITRONE, *with forced cheerfulness*) Well! (*Chuckling nervously*) There he is! There's your husband, Peg, home from the wars! (*Shouting into* RAPITRONE*'s ear, rapidly and with an almost mocking cheerfulness*) Rapitrone, Rapitrone, Rapitrone!

CORBY (*to* PEG, *softly*): Don't I know him?

PEG: That's what *I* thought, but he says no.

CORBY: Hmmm. Face is familiar. (*To* JOSEPH) We've met before, haven't we?

JOSEPH (*confused*): Huh? No.

CORBY: Let me think.

> *Pause.*

Hmmm, no. No, I can't quite place you. What brings you out on a night like this? (*To* PEG, *indicating* RAPITRONE) I'll get his coat off.

PEG: No, I'll do it. You sit down. Joseph's here on business. He came to speak with Andy.

CORBY (*to* JOSEPH): Well, then. You'd best speak with *me*.

JOSEPH: Yes, I can see that.

> PEG *proceeds with the awkward and rather laborious task of removing* RAPITRONE*'s cap, overcoat, boots, etc., as* CORBY *steers* JOSEPH *to the couch.*

CORBY: So, you've got business with Rapitrone.

JOSEPH: Uh, yeh. (*To* PEG) I'd best not say any —

PEG: No. No, don't worry. (*Struggling with* RAPITRONE*'s coat*) He's, ach! He's all right. He'll help you. (*To* RAPITRONE, *softly*) Easy. Now, easy —

> *As* CORBY *and* JOSEPH *sit* . . .

CORBY (*to* JOSEPH): Yeh, you've got nothing to worry about. I take it your business needs require a modicum of . . . discretion?

JOSEPH: That's right —

PEG (*to* CORBY): He's got a stiff in the yard.

CORBY (*to* JOSEPH): You don't say! (*Pouting appreciatively*) Your wife's lover?

JOSEPH: No, nothing like that.

CORBY: Worse luck.

PEG: Why worse luck?

CORBY: Well, I mean, that would *really've* been something, wouldn't it? A bloke his age. (*To* JOSEPH) How old are you, squire?

JOSEPH: Eighty.

CORBY (*to* PEG): Eighty.

PEG: Eighty? Are you that old, Joseph?

JOSEPH (*vaguely dissembling*): I'm eighty, that's right. Eighty.

CORBY: You look older.

PEG: Huh, a proper diplomat, you are.

CORBY (*to* JOSEPH): Well, anyway. Get on with it.

JOSEPH: It's like this. I got this call to come over here —

CORBY: Here, hold on a minute. Hold on a minute. Who's the stiff?

JOSEPH: Why have you got to know that?

CORBY: No reason. You're right. It's better I don't know. (*To* PEG) I must be dead whacked. (*To* JOSEPH) Right, go on.

JOSEPH: I got this call, see?

CORBY: When?

JOSEPH: Earlier.

CORBY: What, this evening?

JOSEPH (*nodding*): Yeh —

CORBY: Right.

JOSEPH: Yeh. Well, this voice — I recognised the voice, you see — this voice tells me to find Rapitrone.

CORBY: Yeh, anything else? A man's voice, was it —

JOSEPH: Yeh —

CORBY: Well, what else did he say?

JOSEPH (*uneasily*): Nothing.

PEG: Ah, Joseph. That isn't what you told *me*. (*To* CORBY) There was more, but he wouldn't tell me.

CORBY: Ah, well —

JOSEPH: It was personal. I can't tell you. I mean, I need time to sort it out, first. Time to test out my theory.

CORBY: Ah, you've got a theory, then.

JOSEPH: Yeh —

CORBY: I see —

JOSEPH: Yeh, I. I mean, why don't we bring it in?

CORBY: You've got it in the yard.

JOSEPH: Buried in the high drift.

CORBY: Well, let's leave it for a bit. It'll come to no harm. I mean he — it *is* a he, in't it?

JOSEPH: Mmmm.

CORBY: Well, he's not feelin' a thing out there. Here, nobody saw you bury him, did they?

JOSEPH: No, I don't think so. No. I'm sure —

CORBY: That's all right, then. Let him rest. (*To* PEG) Best keep the dead on ice, eh?

JOSEPH: But that's just it!

CORBY: What —

JOSEPH: What I was trying to tell her before. (*To* PEG) You remember what I said before?

PEG: You mean that it might be —

JOSEPH: I'm not at all sure that he's dead.

CORBY: What do you mean, you're not sure he's dead? He *must* be dead. Out there, in —

JOSEPH: It all depends.

CORBY: It all depends? On what?

JOSEPH: It all depends on whether or not he's who I think he might or might not be.

CORBY: I thought you said you knew him. (*To* PEG) That's what he said. Didn't you hear him say that —

PEG: Hear him out.

CORBY: Right. (*To* JOSEPH) Go on.

JOSEPH: Right. (*Brief pause*) Disposing of the body is the least of my worries.

CORBY: Yeh. That's not a problem.

JOSEPH (*pacing the floor*): It's like this. For a long time, I didn't understand. Now I'm beginning to understand.

CORBY: Mmmm —

JOSEPH: Or, at least, I think I am. That's where the trouble is. I can't be certain.

CORBY: I don't follow.

JOSEPH: I can't be certain whether it's him doing it all along or it's only me imagining that he's there, and that nothing has actually happened. That wouldn't bother me so if I hadn't this blasted trouble remembering. You see, I'm working at a disadvantage. I'm working at a tremendous disadvantage here. There's no way I can —

CORBY: Here, hold on a minute. I can't make any sense of what you're talkin' about.

Pause.

JOSEPH: Right. It's like this. We've got to bring him in here. Certain tests have got to be made. If he's dead, there's an end of it, we get rid of him. Right?

CORBY *flashes a questioning look at* PEG.

CORBY (*dubiusly*): Right. Yeh, right. (*Rising*) I'll fetch him in.

JOSEPH: I'll help you.

CORBY: No, sit down. I can manage it. (*To* PEG, *conspiratorially*) Why don't you give him a drink or something, he's making me nervous.

PEG *nods. Having disencumbered* RAPITRONE, *she has draped the afghan over his legs again and wheeled him up beside the couch.* CORBY *throws his coat on and steps back into his boots.*

(*To* JOSEPH) Where is he exactly?

JOSEPH: At the far end of the yard. Down by the dust bins, a bit to the left.

JOSEPH *collapses on to the couch.*

You're sure you don't want me to come?

CORBY: No. I'll find him all right.

PEG: Want me to help?

CORBY: No, I can manage. Only, open the door when I knock.

PEG: Right —

CORBY: And get the lad here a drink.

PEG: Yeh.

CORBY: I'll be wantin' one myself, when I come in.

> *He lumbers to the desk in his unbuckled snow boots, and slips the flask into his coat pocket.*

(*To* JOSEPH) Thirsty work.

> *Exit* CORBY *to the kitchen.* PEG *pours another drink for* JOSEPH, *and one for herself. Sound of the back door opening, closing.*

PEG (*handing* JOSEPH *his drink*): Here. Now, for God's sake, try to relax.

> JOSEPH *drinks.* PEG *sits down beside him.*

JOSEPH: I should be able to relax. I'm tired enough. (*Indicating* RAPITRONE) How is he? I mean, it was a terrible shock to see —

PEG: Ssssh!

JOSEPH: He can hear, then.

PEG: Yes, he can hear well enough.

JOSEPH: Ah. Tell him I'll try to come round more often.

PEG: You tell him.

JOSEPH (*leaning over the arm of the couch, to* RAPITRONE): Rap . . . Rapitrone?

PEG: You needn't shout. He can hear you.

JOSEPH (*softer*): 'Ere, Rapitrone. I'll not wait so long the next time. I'll come round more often, eh? Yeh. (*To* PEG) Mmmm. (*In vague confusion*) I'll come round. Yeh. I'll pop round and see him.

Pause.

PEG: So, you've been —

JOSEPH: Are you sure he's all right?

PEG: Yes, you don't —

JOSEPH: I mean Corby.

PEG: You don't have to worry. I mean, you've been behaving very secretively about all this. You're even making Corby a bit nervous.

JOSEPH: I've been trying to explain. Just you wait. When Corby brings him in, you'll see. So, he's nervous too, eh?

PEG: A bit.

JOSEPH: Huh, if he only knew.

PEG: What?

JOSEPH: If he only knew the half of it.

PEG: Eh? What are you talking about?

JOSEPH: The whole business. It's so bloody daft. I just can't seem to get a hold on it. It's like having to feel your way through the dark with thick woolen gloves. You take the gloves off and there's another pair beneath. You take off that pair and there's another. You keep going, on and on, one pair after another, without ever reaching the last, as though there were nothing but the layers of wool; one after another, without ever coming to the skin, till you forget about the skin altogether, because you no longer remember what it's supposed to feel like. And because you no longer remember — because you *can't* remember — you finally come to the skin, and it's just another glove. You come to the muscle, another glove. To the bone. Then, nothing. You're in the dark.

ACT THREE

Pause.

That's it. That's the game. (*Brief pause*) That's the game I've been playing with the thing I buried out there. The whole idea of the thing is not to be aware that you've been playing at all. And I'm still not certain. He may know or he may not know, himself. Perhaps I'm only guessing. I hope I'm wrong. I hope I'm deluding myself, because I'm tired and I don't want it to go on any longer. I've been ill. (*Shuddering*) I, uh! I've not been well, Lyla.

PEG: You're trembling.

She touches his forehead with the back of her hand.

Well, you're not feverish.

JOSEPH: I'm not feverish! I'm not feverish, I'm getting close now. Closer than I've ever been, you understand? I was trying to tell you, and I nearly had it. I nearly had it, Peg! I nearly had it.

PEG: It's difficult, Joseph. You know, it's quite difficult —

JOSEPH: I know. I know, you don't understand. (*Brief pause*) You will, you might, when Corby brings him in. If he's not dead. If he's dead, then there's an end of it. (*Leaning over the armrest*) Rapitrone, you hear what I'm saying. (*To* PEG) Can he speak at all?

She shakes her head.

(*To* RAPITRONE) Think about it, old friend. Turn it over in your mind. (*To* PEG) If he could speak. If he were the way he used to be . . .

PEG (*wistfully*): Ah —

JOSEPH: Mmmm. What a terrible thing. I mean, I had no idea he'd . . . I never thought I'd find him like *this*. I mean, he's still a young man. (*Softly*) What was it, an accident?

PEG: No.

JOSEPH: Was it sudden, then? I mean, it *must've* been. There was nothing wrong with him. Nothing at all, only a —

PEG: It was no accident, Joseph.

JOSEPH: What are you saying? (*Brief pause*) Sometimes, I get the feeling you're not quite the —

A loud knocking at the back door.

PEG (*rising*): Oh, here he is.

JOSEPH rises as PEG hurries into the kitchen. Sound of the back door opening, muffled noises. JOSEPH opens the kitchen door a crack, and peers in.

(*Off*) What!

CORBY (*off*): Look for yourself.

He mutters something unintelligible.

PEG (*off*): But, I don't understand! It can't be. Joseph!

Enter PEG in a rush, flustered, JOSEPH backing away as she advances on him.

Joseph, what does this mean?

JOSEPH: What're you talking about? I —

PEG: You deliberately kept it from me! Why —

JOSEPH: What? I —

PEG: Why didn't you tell me? You knew I'd find out soon enough! Why did you keep it from me?

Enter CORBY, dragging SHEM's lifeless body by the heels.

JOSEPH: I don't understand. What are you talking about?

PEG (*indicating* SHEM): Him, of course! The lodger!

JOSEPH (*swallows hard*): What?

CORBY: Yeh. It's Shem all right —

ACT THREE

JOSEPH (*to himself*): Shem —

CORBY: And no mistake. (*to* PEG) Where you want him?

PEG: Put him on the couch.

    CORBY *drags* SHEM *toward the couch.*

CORBY: I don't get it. He was always so careful with himself. Not that I'm blamin' you, squire. (*To* PEG) No, Shem was nobody's fool. He knew whatever he was getting into. Not the sort of bloke you'd want to mess about with. There must be a lot more to the old man here than I thought.

JOSEPH: But, I don't —

CORBY: You don't have to say a thing, guv. Mum's the word, as far as it goes with me. The less I know, the better. Oh, I could tell you a thing or two about Old Shem here. (*To* PEG) Here, gimme a hand, will you? Get his legs.

    She complies.

    Right?

PEG: Mmmm.

    They lift SHEM *on to the couch.*

CORBY: I'll get his coat off.

PEG: What for? He's dead.

CORBY: Oh. Yeh. Well, he was one hell of a bloke when he was alive, Shem was. Last of his kind. Now he's pegged out it don't matter, I can tell you everything. I mean, the burden's off now. It's completely off. I can breathe a sigh of relief.

    CORBY *sighs with relief.* JOSEPH *ponders, more perplexed than ever.*

PEG: Well, I wish you'd clue me in on what's going on. (*To* JOSEPH) The pair of you.

CORBY: Yeh, well. I wouldn't pressure the old man — right, squire? — he's probably got a lot on his mind right now.

JOSEPH (*to* PEG): You say this is the lodger?

PEG: It *was* the lodger.

JOSEPH: What do you mean, was?

CORBY: Here, what do *you* mean? He's *your* stiff. (*To* PEG) And *what* a stiff. Christ!

PEG: What do you mean, Corby? Listen, if this means we've got to have the police, I'm not —

CORBY: Hold on! No police. No police, that's for bleedin' sure —

JOSEPH: Peg, look in his mouth.

PEG: Huh —

JOSEPH: Don't be afraid. It's perfectly normal. Just have a look.

> *Reluctantly, she kneels beside* SHEM *and peers into his open mouth.*

Well? Anything?

> *Pause.*

PEG: I can't see anything. Lots of fillings.

CORBY: Gold?

PEG: No.

CORBY: Oh.

JOSEPH (*to* PEG): Put your finger under the tongue.

PEG: What?

JOSEPH: It's all right. Just stick it in and tell me if there's anything.

> *Even more reluctantly, she slips her finger into* SHEM*'s mouth.*

(*Staring straight ahead*) Well? Have you got it in?

PEG (*squeamishly*): Yes.

JOSEPH: Under the tongue?

PEG: Wait.

> *Pause.*

JOSEPH: Don't worry. There's nothing to be ashamed of —

PEG: Yes.

JOSEPH: Feel anything?

PEG: Only the tongue.

JOSEPH: Ah.

PEG: It's cold, like an icicle.

JOSEPH: Nothing else. You're sure?

PEG: Nothing.

> *She takes her finger out and hurries into the kitchen.*

JOSEPH: Where are you going?

PEG (*off*): To wash my hands.

JOSEPH: Ah.

> *Pause.*

CORBY: What's up —

JOSEPH (*pondering*): Hold on a minute.

> *Pause.*

Hmph. (*To* CORBY) You say he's the lodger?

CORBY: Mmmm. I can't get him out tonight. Maybe after the snow stops I can level a few of the drifts and dig out a path for the lorry. We shouldn't have too much trouble. It'll mean a bit of a wait, though.

JOSEPH (*still preoccupied*): It doesn't matter.

CORBY: What?

JOSEPH: It doesn't matter about the waiting. I can do with the time, in any case.

CORBY: Huh?

> JOSEPH, *who has been standing behind the couch, leans forward over* SHEM's *upturned face.*

JOSEPH: Shem! (*Brief pause, then louder*) Shem! (*Brief pause, still louder*) Shem!

> SHEM *opens his eyes, but remains motionless, as* PEG *enters.*

PEG: What's this —

JOSEPH (*extending his arm, his gaze riveted on* SHEM's *eyes*): Ssssh!

> *She joins* JOSEPH *and* CORBY *behind the couch.*
> *Long pause.*

(*To* SHEM, *in a beckoning whisper*) Shem.

> *Pause.*
> SHEM's *eyelids flutter. He remains otherwise motionless.*

(*In conversational tone*) Shem.

> *Pause.*
> SHEM's *fingers twitch.*

(*Falsetto*) Shem?

> *Pause.*

(*In his normal tone*) Ah, Shem. I knew you were still with us. I knew.

ACT THREE

>SHEM's *stomach heaves upwards. He begins to wheeze and creak with life, like an old pneumatic effigy.*

>(*To* PEG) Listen to him.

CORBY: Jesus Christ.

PEG: It's impossible. I don't believe it.

JOSEPH: Yet there he is.

PEG: What about his tongue? Why did I have to put my finger under his tongue?

JOSEPH: Just a precaution.

CORBY: A precaution against what?

JOSEPH: I don't know, it's always done.

>*Pause.*

PEG: Strange. Very strange. Look at him. He doesn't seem alive —

CORBY: Mmmm —

PEG: I mean, he doesn't actually seem in control. His breathing's forced.

JOSEPH: Maybe now he can die. (*In admonition*) Hope that he dies.

PEG: What? What are you saying? After all this?

JOSEPH: It would be better for everyone if he dies now.

>*Pause.*
>*He leans down close to* SHEM's *face.*

>Give it up, Shem. Give up the ghost. Let it go.

>SHEM's *breathing becomes gradually more regular. His eyes close. He appears to sleep.*

PEG: Look, he closed his eyes.

JOSEPH (*resigned*): He'll live. I can't answer for him now. I *won't* answer for him.

SHEM (*with sepulchural intonation*): Joooseph. (*Brief pause*) Joooseph Golem —

JOSEPH (*unnerved*): Eh? What's that?

> *Pause.*
> CORBY *and* PEG *lean over the couch, straining to hear* SHEM*'s words, as* JOSEPH *takes a few steps backwards.*

SHEM (*less hollow*): Joooseph. (*Brief pause*) Joooseph.

> *Pause.*

Where are you, Joseph?

JOSEPH (*tensely, holding his ground*): Here. I'm here.

SHEM: Where were you?

JOSEPH: Huh?

SHEM: Where were you *then?*

JOSEPH: What?

> SHEM *heaves a long sigh.*

(*To* PEG) He's out of his mind. I knew it'd be like this.

PEG: He's bound to be a bit confused, isn't he? I mean, after all he's been through...

CORBY: Yeh, we got to allow for that. You'd never know it was the same bloke, though.

PEG: How's that?

CORBY: You know. He seems more relaxed than when I knew him.

PEG: Oh, yeh.

Pause.

JOSEPH: I don't think —

SHEM: Joseph.

JOSEPH: Yes?

Pause.

SHEM: Cold. So cold.

He sighs.

Soft, it falls. Cold, white.

Pause.

What have you done, Joseph? What have you done?

He opens his eyes.

Closer. Come, closer.

JOSEPH *leans over the couch.*
Pause.

Yes . . . Joseph.

JOSEPH: Yes?

SHEM: Where were you?

JOSEPH: Huh? I was here. Here, I was —

SHEM: In '43.

JOSEPH: Eh?

SHEM *grips* JOSEPH *by the lapel.*

What are you —

SHEM: You were needed. They really had need of you, Joseph. Where *were* you?

JOSEPH (*nervously*): Uh, in '43? I was younger then —

SHEM: Never younger —

JOSEPH: I was —

SHEM: Then and before. They had need of you, Joseph —

JOSEPH: No —

SHEM: And you betrayed them. '43 and before —

JOSEPH: No —

SHEM: You betrayed them —

JOSEPH: No —

SHEM: Betrayed them. Left them all to die like rats.

JOSEPH (*tugging at* SHEM's *clenched fist*): What are you saying?

> *He extricates himself from* SHEM's *grip and staggers backwards as* SHEM *plants his feet on the rug, rises to a sitting position, and stares straight ahead throughout.*

No! You can't say that. You can't say a thing like that to *me*. You're imagining things. You made it up. You only *think* you remember —

SHEM: A thousand betrayals, Joseph.

JOSEPH: No, it's impossible. You can't expect me to —

SHEM: A hundred thousand betrayals —

JOSEPH (*laughing*): Hah! You think I was born yesterday?

SHEM: And more. So many —

> JOSEPH (*angered*): Listen, Rabbi, you can't hang that phoney rap on *me*. That

has nothing to do with either one of us. It never happened. You know it never happened. It *couldn't* happen, a thing like that.

He approaches SHEM.

Or you *don't* know. You only *think* you know. You can't be sure. There's an image there. Even though we're always meeting again for the first time, there's an image.

SHEM: What?

JOSEPH: Yes. (*Screaming*) Shem! Shem! Shem!

SHEM *looks at* JOSEPH *for the first time. Pause.*

SHEM: I'm cold.

CORBY (*to* PEG): Get him a drink.

SHEM *snatches the bottle from her, puts it to his lips, and drinks.*

SHEM (*wiping his lips with the back of his gloved hand*): Ah. Much better.

PEG: Can I take your coat?

SHEM: No, thanks. I'll keep it on.

CORBY: Here, Shem, I didn't say nothing.

CORBY *takes a drink from his flask.*

SHEM: Eh?

CORBY: You know, about why you're here.

SHEM: You know? How do you know?

CORBY: Mum's the word.

SHEM (*dubiously*): Of course.

CORBY *hurries into the vestibule and removes his coat, etc.*

(*To* JOSEPH) Who is he?

JOSEPH: Hah!

PEG (*to* SHEM): You ought to relax. Perhaps you should lie down again. Why don't you let Corby help you to your room?

SHEM: Corby?

CORBY (*off*): Yeh. There's a few things we might want to talk over, private like.

SHEM (*to* PEG): I'm all right. I'll stay here.

JOSEPH (*sarcastically*): Now do you know who he is?

SHEM: Perhaps, perhaps not. What about you, Joseph?

JOSEPH: The same.

SHEM (*rising*): Well. Now we've got *that* settled . . .

His gaze falls on RAPITRONE.

(*To* JOSEPH) What have you done to him?

JOSEPH: You don't know that! Ask Peg. He was like that when he got here!

PEG (*to* SHEM): My husband. You know, my —

SHEM *passes his hand before* RAPITRONE*'s face.*

SHEM (*to* JOSEPH): He reminds me of someone.

JOSEPH: He reminds me of you.

SHEM (*to* PEG, *indicating* JOSEPH): He doesn't take to me. Must be something I've said —

PEG: Oh, he's been acting strangely all night.

ACT THREE

SHEM: He wants a sedative, something to send him to sleep. (*To* JOSEPH) You want a sedative. You've been up too long.

JOSEPH: That's right.

SHEM (*at the desk*): What's all this, then?

PEG: Corby's theory.

CORBY (*to* SHEM): You know, my theory.

SHEM: Huh —

CORBY: Faust.

Pause.

SHEM: Faust.

JOSEPH: Faust.

CORBY: Yeh. I mean, I can't take *all* the credit. Rapitrone and I sort of worked it up together.

PEG: You never told me that.

CORBY: Yeh, in the beginning at least.

PEG: Oh?

CORBY: Yeh. He was quite a lot of help to me. Set me straight on a lot of things.

PEG: He never mentioned it.

CORBY: No. Well, he wouldn't, would he? I asked him not to.

PEG: Ah.

SHEM (*leafing through the pages*): Looks as though you've put a lot of thought into it.

PEG: Huh, I'll say. It's his great obsession.

SHEM: Fancy that, Joseph. The man's obsessed.

JOSEPH: One look at him'll tell you that. I spotted it right off.

CORBY (*to* SHEM): Yeh. I never discussed it with you because you always seemed so aloof, so preoccupied.

JOSEPH (*to* PEG, *aside*): He doesn't know. He really doesn't remember *anything*. He's feeling his way, just like me.

PEG: What are you on about?

JOSEPH (*to* CORBY): This Faust theory. I mean, what's it all about?

CORBY (*flustered*): Uh, no. No, I don't want to bore you.

JOSEPH: What's the matter, can't you remember?

CORBY (*stammering*): Uh, of course. Of c-course. I remember —

JOSEPH: Well —

CORBY: But, uh. But I'm no good at, at verbal elucidation — that's it, I always get it wrong when I try to explain it! The theory, I mean. I'd have to make notes first. Extensive notes.

SHEM: Then, why don't you just read it out?

CORBY: Huh?

JOSEPH: Yeh. Read us something of what you've got there. Something concise, to the point. Something we can all understand.

CORBY (*shaking his head*): Uh. (*Chuckling nervously*) Hah, I can't read. I mean, I'm a terrible reader! Let Peg read it. Why don't you read it, Peg? You know about as much about it as I do, eh?

PEG (*shuffling the pages*): The Third Corollary?

CORBY (*nervously, sitting*): The Third Corollary, yeh. The Third Corollary. Fine. Yeh, that's fine.

ACT THREE

Pause.

From right to left, JOSEPH, SHEM *and* CORBY *on the couch.* RAPITRONE *remains in position to the right of* JOSEPH. PEG *sits on top of the desk.*

JOSEPH (*to* RAPITRONE): This ought to be good.

PEG *switches on the desk lamp.*

PEG: Let's see, now. Here we are. (*Reading*) It therefore follows that the Faustian identity or condition remains extremely tenuous —

JOSEPH: Follows from what? (*To* CORBY) Follows from what?

CORBY: From the first two corollaries.

JOSEPH: Ah. Yes, of course. From the first two corollaries. It would.

PEG: Can I get on with it?

JOSEPH: Any questions, gentlemen?

Pause.

No questions. (*To* PEG) Go on.

PEG: Right. (*Reading*) It therefore follows that the Faustian identity or condition remains extremely tenuous in all its supposed manifestations. That the said manifestations are in fact supposed, as opposed to concretely substantive, subsumes them — with all relative hypotheses as to their origins, pro and con — under one or more of the generally accepted mystagogic criteria which, for the sake of clarity, we may designate as dualistic, whereas the victim, qua Faust, takes upon himself the task of performing — with or perhaps without the aid of necromancy, chiromancy, cartomancy, and ventriloquial concatenations — all the miracles attributed to his name, in the first instance, or, in the second instance, inadvertently plays the dupe of some irrevocably absconded imp, demon, or suchlike. The Faustian equation, in this sense, partakes of an exegetical guise, whereby the victim, qua Faust, exhibits all the signs of a quite justifiable confusion as to the ultimate nature of his condition, which lies beyond all powers of prognostication, mystagogic or otherwise, for to be the victim, qua Faust, in this third instance, is to have passed from deception, through delusion, into limbo — totus, teres, atque rotundus — from which there can be no escape but one.

Pause.

PEG *switches off the desk lamp, goes to the window, and thrusts her head behind the curtains.*

JOSEPH (*still staring straight ahead*): What do you see?

PEG: It's getting deeper. Drifts up to the sill. I can't make out the street for the falling snow.

JOSEPH: Any wind?

PEG: No. It's falling straight, unless the wind's coming from our direction or towards us.

JOSEPH (*to* SHEM): Well, what do you think?

SHEM (*preoccupied*): Hmmm?

JOSEPH: What do you think of Corby's theory?

SHEM (*dissembling*): Oh. Yes, concise. (*To* CORBY) Quite concise, I'll grant you that.

JOSEPH: I think there's a lot more of Rapitrone in that theory than Corby would care to admit.

CORBY (*rising*): Here, what are you trying to say, that I nicked his ideas?

JOSEPH: Why so jumpy, then? Admit it.

CORBY: What?

JOSEPH (*rising*): Admit you drained him.

CORBY: What —

JOSEPH: Sucked him bone dry, eh?

CORBY: Listen, you're —

JOSEPH: And left him an empty shell of a man —

CORBY: No!

JOSEPH: Sans eyes.

CORBY: You're bleedin' daft —

JOSEPH: Sans tongue —

CORBY (*to* PEG): Look, will you tell him —

JOSEPH: Bereft of wit and limb —

PEG: Joseph!

RAPITRONE (*weakly*): Uuuuuuhhh . . .

> PEG *rushes to* RAPITRONE*'s side.*

CORBY (*with emotion*): Rapitrone —

PEG: What is it, Andy? What is it? What's the matter?

> *She cups her hand under his chin, lifts it, then lets it drop. Pause.*

SHEM: Perhaps he's ill.

JOSEPH (*sarcastically*): What's your prognosis?

SHEM: He's come over sick, that's all. Maybe he's gone down with something.

CORBY (*to* PEG): It's possible. It's possible. He might've caught a chill.

PEG: Hmmm, this isn't like him —

CORBY: I mean, he didn't make a sound in the lorry. Not a sound the whole time.

JOSEPH: And what about before? What about that, eh? What sort of sound did he make before?

CORBY: Before what?

JOSEPH: Before. When you were working it up. You know, kicking it about, so to speak. (*To* SHEM) He must have had the answer. (*Indicating* RAPITRONE) Look at him! Look what it's done to him! (*Pacing*) We keep forgetting — I'm not the *only* one. So, maybe I'm imagining the whole thing. Maybe someone else is. Eh, Rapitrone? (*To* SHEM) It's you, isn't it? Perhaps it's been you all along. It's . . . Or perhaps it isn't. I may be deluding myself. (*Tearfully*) All I know is, I'm tired. I want to sleep and can't shut my eyes or open them wide enough, I don't know which it is. But I'll tell you this . . .

> *He pulls* SHEM *up by the lapels.*
> *The* VOICE *of* SHEM *or* CHESTER *or* SPAHDA, *from beyond the top of the stair, resonating as from an empty room* . . .

VOICE: Luuuuuuba . . .

JOSEPH: Hah! (*To* PEG) Your lodger's restless tonight.

PEG (*to* SHEM): Who is it —

JOSEPH: Who's in the garret, Shem?

RAPITRONE: Uuuuuuuh . . .

JOSEPH: Eh, Rapitrone? Who've you got living up there?

CORBY: This is insane. It's insane.

JOSEPH: Who is it, Corby? What have you done to the lodger that he calls down to us like a dying man?

SHEM (*nervously*): He's where you left him. It's him I brought you to see.

JOSEPH (*tightening his grip on* SHEM): You, old man. You can't toy with me any longer, I'm ready to *die!* But if I die, then who'll die *with* me? (*Pointedly*) Eh, Shem?

VOICE (*more resonant*): Luuuuba . . .

JOSEPH (*mockingly to the stairs*): Luuuuba!

> *He throws* SHEM *back against the couch, then pulls the window curtains wide on thick-falling snow and a high drift banked halfway up the panes. He whispers into* PEG's *ear. She gazes, horrified, at* SHEM.

SHEM (*weakly from the couch, to* PEG): Don't listen to him. He's a liar —

VOICE (*more insistent*): Luuuba —

SHEM (*to* PEG): He doesn't know, himself! I'm sure of it!

> PEG *begins to undress, staring daggers at* SHEM.

(*To himself*) No. (*To* PEG) No!

JOSEPH (*to* PEG): He knows. You see? He already knows. He's been anticipating. Perhaps he's the one. (*To the dumbfounded* CORBY) Perhaps it's been him all along. (*To* PEG) Perhaps he's the one who's imagined it all. Are you, Shem? Is it you?

SHEM: Nuh, no! It's Rapitrone! Can't you see? It's Rapitrone —

RAPITRONE: Uuuuuuh —

VOICE: Luuuba —

JOSEPH (*to* SHEM): If you're the one, you can stop it. (*Through his tears*) Stop it! Try to stop it, the way I'm trying. There's always a chance, eh? I'm tired sick of it! Old Corby's got a bit of life in him yet, for all his theories, and Peg. But Rapitrone — look at him, Shem — he's already long past it. We're done in, Shem, you and I —

VOICE: Luuuba —

JOSEPH: And even now, like me, you're not certain. You think it might be one of the others. Well, who is it, then? Which one of us? What do you think, Shem? What's going through that subtle brain of yours, old man, eh? Tell me, I'd like to know.

VOICE: Luuuba —

JOSEPH (*with a sweeping gesture, toward the stair*): Perhaps it's him, eh? Perhaps it's the one upstairs who'll play Faust tonight!

> PEG *stands naked.*

Have a good look at her, Shem. Feast your eyes, you miserable, wretched old ghost! You and I will never see the like of *her* again. (*To* CORBY) Corby, the lights.

    CORBY *switches off the lamps, one by one, until the room is in darkness.* SHEM, *still in his overcoat, stands in a shaft of moonlight emanating from the window. A second shaft of moonlight falls across the L-shaped stair from an oval window on the landing.*
    Pause.

VOICE (*longingly, or like a dying man*): Luba.

    Silently, the nude woman begins to mount the stair. JOSEPH *catches her by the arm and, with a fierce sadness in his face, removes her blond wig. She turns and faces* SHEM *across the darkness.*
    It is LUBA.
    Pause.
    Silently, LUBA *mounts the stair into the upper shadows.*

(*Mechanically reverberating*) Luba . . . .

    SHEM *collapses at the sound of the* VOICE. *He lies motionless. Quick fade to black.*

January 1980

II.
Joseph in the Underground

Or vedi la pena molesta
Tu che, spirando, vai veggendo i morti:
Vedi se alcuna è grande come questa;
— INFERNO, XXVIII

DRAMATIS PERSONÆ

JOSEPH, *a man of seventy-five*

SHEM / CANAMINE } *a man in his forties*

GUS / RANTZ } *a stocky man in his fifties*

SILVO / STILLER } *a man of sixty*

BOCH / BLOCKER } *a man in his forties*

FLINT / FINCH } *a man in his forties*

COATES / HODGE } *a man in his forties*

GUTHRIE / DOOLEY / PATIENT } *a dilapidated man of sixty-five*

CORBY / GAD } *a man in his late twenties*

RAPITRONE / ASHER / JOSH } *a man in his middle thirties*

PEG / MEG / MAGGIE / MAGDA / MADGE } *a blonde in her twenties*

LUBA / RUTH } *a brunette in her twenties*

MAN, *a pianist*

YOUNG JOSEPH
GUARD } *in his twenties*

ACT ONE

Scene 1

Down centre: slow descent of JOSEPH *and* SHEM *from the flies in a small wicker gondola. Darkness surrounds them.* JOSEPH *cranes his neck upwards, around, downwards, squinting for some feature in the immense subterranean blackness.* SHEM *lies inert, silent, at* JOSEPH*'s feet.* SHEM*'s legs — the only visible part of him — dangle over the front of the gondola. From time to time, an ascending shadow.*

Cavernous, pre-recorded voices are heard. JOSEPH, *in coat, muffler and gloves, oblivious throughout.*

VOICE OF JOSEPH: The whole business. It's so bloody daft. I just can't seem to get a hold on it. It's like having to feel your way through the dark with thick woolen gloves. You take the gloves off and there's another pair beneath. You take off that pair and there's another. You keep going, on and on, one pair after another, without ever reaching the last, as though there were nothing but the layers of wool; one after another, without ever coming to the skin, till you forget about the skin altogether, because you no longer remember what it's supposed to feel like. And because you no longer remember — because you *can't* remember — you finally come to the skin, and it's just another glove. You come to the muscle, another glove. To the bone. Then, nothing. You're in the dark.

   Pause.

   What do you see?

VOICE OF PEG: It's getting deeper. Drifts up to the sill. I can't make out the street for the falling snow.

VOICE OF JOSEPH: Any wind?

VOICE OF PEG: No. It's falling straight, unless the wind's coming from our direction or towards us.

Pause.

VOICE OF CORBY: Jesus Christ.

VOICE OF PEG: It's impossible. I don't believe it.

VOICE OF JOSEPH: Yet there he is.

VOICE OF PEG: What about his tongue? Why did I have to put my finger under his tongue?

VOICE OF JOSEPH: Just a precaution.

VOICE OF CORBY: A precaution against what?

VOICE OF JOSEPH: I don't know, it's always done.

Pause.

VOICE OF PEG: Strange. Very strange. Look at him. He doesn't seem alive —

VOICE OF CORBY: Mmmm —

VOICE OF PEG: I mean, he doesn't actually seem in control. His breathing's forced.

VOICE OF JOSEPH: Maybe now he can die. (*In admonition*) Hope that he dies.

Pause.

(*With forced cheerfulness*) Well! (*Chuckling nervously*) There he is! There's your husband, Peg, home from the wars! (*Shouting, rapidly and with an almost mocking cheerfulness*) Rapitrone, Rapitrone, Rapitrone!

Pause.

Well, what do you think?

VOICE OF SHEM (*preoccupied*): Hmmm?

VOICE OF JOSEPH: What do you think of Corby's theory?

VOICE OF SHEM (*dissembling*): Oh. Yes, concise. Quite concise, I'll grant you that.

VOICE OF JOSEPH: I think there's a lot more of Rapitrone in that theory than Corby would care to admit.

VOICE OF CORBY: Here, what are you trying to say, that I nicked his ideas?

VOICE OF JOSEPH: Why so jumpy, then? Admit it.

VOICE OF CORBY: What?

VOICE OF JOSEPH: Admit you drained him.

VOICE OF CORBY: What —

VOICE OF JOSEPH: Sucked him bone dry, eh?

VOICE OF CORBY: Listen, you're —

VOICE OF JOSEPH: And left him an empty shell of a man —

VOICE OF CORBY: No!

VOICE OF JOSEPH: Sans eyes.

VOICE OF CORBY: You're bleedin' daft —

VOICE OF JOSEPH: Sans tongue —

VOICE OF CORBY: Look, will you tell him —

VOICE OF JOSEPH: Bereft of wit and limb —

VOICE OF PEG (*cavernous reverberations*): Joseph!

VOICE OF JOSEPH (*shouting, rapidly and with an almost mocking cheerfulness; cavernous reverberations*): Rapitrone, Rapitrone, Rapitrone!

VOICE OF SHEM: A thousand betrayals, Joseph.

VOICE OF JOSEPH: No, it's impossible. You can't expect me to —

VOICE OF SHEM: A hundred thousand betrayals —

VOICE OF JOSEPH (*laughing*): Hah! You think I was born yesterday?

VOICE OF SHEM: And more. So many —

VOICE OF JOSEPH (*angered*): Listen, Rabbi, you can't hang that phoney rap on *me*. That has nothing to do with either one of us. It never happened. You know it never happened. It *couldn't* happen, a thing like that. Or you *don't* know. You only *think* you know. You can't be sure. There's an image there. Even though we're always meeting again for the first time, there's an image.

VOICE OF SHEM: What?

VOICE OF JOSEPH: Yes. (*Shouting, with cavernous reverberations as recording ends*) Shem! Shem!

JOSEPH (*Immediately, thunderously*): Shem!

> *Pause.*
> *He chuckles sardonically, kicks* SHEM *once, twice.*

(*To* SHEM) Dead, eh? Dead at last. I thought it would never end.

> *He prods* SHEM *with his foot, to no effect.*

(*Contemptuously*) Hmph. (*Hand to ear*) Huh? Can't hear you. What's that?

> *Pause.*
> *He gazes down at* SHEM.

Shem. (*Brief pause*) I'll be rid of you soon enough. It won't be much longer now, I'll be rid of you for good and all. (*Looking about*) It's dark. (*Shivering*) Uuuuh, cold. I can't see anything. (*Peering over the edge of the gondola*) We should be touching bottom soon; can't be much longer, what do you think?

> *Pause.*

No answer. Good. That's what I like to hear, silence. You hear it, Shem? The pin's dropping. Listen. (*Brief pause*) Yes. It's dropping.

> *Pause.*

(*Looking about*) So, this is what it means to bury yourself alive. Who'd have thought it, Shem? Who could have imagined one of us would still be round to tell the tale after that frightful business at Rapitrone's, eh? I'd thought we'd go together, you and I, into the ground. Hmph. Corby would've had to shovel us under, side by side in the yard. That's how I thought it would be. I hadn't counted on surviving. I didn't want it. You forced my hand. Those last moments, those seconds when I felt it all falling together. You forced me to act. And we lost Peg. We lost her, Shem. Up the spout. Corby and I looked all over for her. It happened so quickly. (*Brief pause*) Corby had switched off the lights. I could see you . . . standing like stone by the window. You knew the game was up. We both knew. Only, you couldn't see *me* there. (*Brief pause*) And I *felt* something . . . the cool flesh of Peg standing beside me. I felt her breath on my ear as the other woman started up the stair. And I knew then what had happened. The woman the lodger was calling to in his sickness: Luba . . . I recalled the name. (*Brief pause*) And when it was all over and the lights were on again, you were lying on the floor. I was still standing, still breathing. Corby, he was in shock. Rapitrone was slumped in his wheelchair; the afghan had slipped from his legs and his head was twitching, it was horrible. I told Peg to go to him. I thought she was standing behind me. I still had the scent of her. (*Brief pause*) She was gone.

Pause.

I went up into the garret after Luba and the lodger, and found a little hole of a room that smelled of stale breath and medicine. Old clothes lying about everywhere. A camp bed had been dragged under the dormer. The snow was falling through the open window on to the sheets. They must've gone out on the roof, crawled to the south side of the house and shinnied down the spout into the drifts. The wind would've covered their tracks. Peg said he was a defector. I found his uniform under one of the piles. He was a fool to have kept it. That was careless.

The gondola touches down. JOSEPH *opens its wicket, turns his back to* SHEM, *lifts* SHEM's *legs on to his shoulders, and hauls him slowly into the shadows.*
Fade to black.

Scene 2

A seedy public house in the Underground, dimly lit. Right wall: the bar, no stools; downstage, an upright piano, a microphone. Left wall: downstage, a doorway with a sign above the lintel that reads PRIVATE. Chairs, tables. The floor strewn with sawdust. Rear wall, right to left: a wide, grimy window giving on the outer

blackness; *a door that jingles when opened. On a scarred wooden bench beneath the window: torches, weatherproof lanterns, one to account for each of the pub's occupants.*
  GUS *is tending bar.*
  FLINT *and* COATES *sit at a downstage table,* JOSEPH *at a table hard by. At separate tables:* SILVO, GUTHRIE, BOCH. *All, save* GUS, *are unshaven and tattily dressed, slumped over their tables in an advanced state of unconsciousness. Their overcoats hang from the backs of their chairs.* JOSEPH's *striped blazer, black shirt and trousers are wrinkled, soiled, worn thin at the elbows and knees.*
  Bottles — most drained to the dregs, some overturned, beside a filthy glass — at each occupied table.
  Sounds of stupor: smothered murmurs, occasional grunts.
  GUTHRIE *lets out an agonised moan.*
  Pause.

GUS (*banging a mallet on the bar top*): Right! Showtime!

> *Wails and protests from the groggy men.* JOSEPH *still unconscious.* GUS *speaks a broad East End cockney.*

Come on! What're you sods bloody waitin' for, Eugene bleedin' O'Neill? (*Brief pause*) Look sharp! Time to freshen-up the empty glasses!

> GUTHRIE *tries to stand, reeling.*

'Ere, Guthrie! Sit down before you bleedin' *fall* down!

SILVO: Sit down, Guthrie.

> GUTHRIE *falls.*

Bleedin' great pillock.

GUS: Pick him up. I don't want no drunks on my floor.

> SILVO *rises, staggers toward* GUTHRIE *and falls, knocking one of* GUTHRIE's *bottles to the floor.*

(*Exasperated*) Jesus Christ —

SILVO (*spitting*): Ptugh! Sawdust, ptugh! What're you put that fuckin' sawdust all over the floor for?

GUS: To keep your breath from burnin' the place down.

FLINT *and* COATES *chuckle.*

Huh, don't laugh.

SILVO: Somebody get me up.

BOCH: What about Guthrie?

SILVO: He can fend for himself. Come on, Boch!

BOCH *staggers to* SILVO *and helps him into a chair at* GUTHRIE's *table.*

Where's my bottle?

BOCH: What *is* this, the two o'clock feeding? There's another man here lying in the dust!

SILVO: Bleedin' sawdust.

BOCH *helps* GUTHRIE *to his feet and lowers him into a chair beside* SILVO.

BOCH (*to* FLINT *and* COATES): Pah! You lot are a great help.

FLINT: What're you on about, Boch? You can do with the exercise.

BOCH: You hear that, Silvo? I can do with the exercise.

SILVO *and* GUTHRIE *have passed out.*

(*Exasperated*) Jesus.

BOCH *sits down with* FLINT *and* COATES. GUS *sets new bottles on their table and takes the empties away, shambling from table to table as the dialogue proceeds, placing a full bottle beside each of the three unconscious men, vainly trying to wake them with a nudge, a tickle, a slap.*
BOCH *drinks from the bottle,* FLINT *and* COATES *from a glass.*

(*To* FLINT) Here, is it my imagination or are the nights getting longer?

COATES: It's your imagination.

BOCH: How would *you* know, Coates?

GUS: It's your imagination, Boch. You're imagining things.

FLINT: How much do we owe you for, Gus?

GUS: You in't paid me for the last two nights, but it's been taken care of. (*Indicating* GUTHRIE) 'Ere, look at this geezer. (*Shaking* GUTHRIE) Looks like he's made out o' rubber.

COATES: What do you mean it's been taken care of? Who took care of it?

GUS: The gent upstairs.

COATES: What, Canamine? Since when?

GUS: Since he told me he was takin' care of it. What you askin' so many questions for?

FLINT: Canamine, eh? (*To* COATES) It don't figure.

BOCH: What don't figure?

FLINT: You know. Why should a bloke like Canamine — a regular spiv, *you* know—

BOCH: Regular? There in't no regular spivs down here.

COATES: Yeh. If he was a *regular* spiv, he wouldn't be down here.

BOCH: Yeh.

FLINT: Yeh. I guess you're right. What do you think, Coates?

COATES: I think maybe he's —

GUS: What you goin' on about —

COATES (*to* FLINT): I think maybe he wants something out of us.

BOCH: Pah! Don't make me laugh.

FLINT (*to* COATES): Yeh. What would a geezer like him want with us?

COATES: What time is it?

ACT ONE 163

FLINT *shrugs.*

Here, Gus. What time is it?

GUS *takes a whack at* JOSEPH*'s head.* JOSEPH *still unconscious.*

FLINT: Here! Don't hit the old man —

BOCH (*to* GUS): What'd you want to do that for? He's not bothering anybody.

COATES (*to* GUS): Yeh. Leave him be.

GUS: 'Ere, get off my back, will ya? I know my own business. Don't tell me I don't know my own business! This geezer come in here last night, looked like he in't shut his eyes in a week.

BOCH (*to* FLINT *and* COATES): *I* don't remember him.

FLINT *and* COATES *shake their heads in agreement.*

GUS: That's because you was all dead blind by then. Guthrie here was the only one awake. He had his eyes open. He seen him come in. I was upstairs with Mister Canamine and the birds.

Lewd chuckles.

'Ere, what you laughin' at, eh? I brought up a tray, is all. Mister Canamine was entertainin' a couple o' clients. Had 'em up there all night.

He goes behind the bar, tosses the empties away, busies himself.

FLINT: Must've been quite a party. Anybody we know?

GUS: No. Nobody you know.

FLINT: Ah.

GUS: Anyhow, Guthrie crawls to the foot of the stair and yells. An old geezer just come in, he says, Looks like he's ready to peg out! So I rush down, stumble over Guthrie who's still crawlin' about, and there's the old man — right where he's sittin' now — tryin' to get his coat off. He was —

BOCH (*his mind wandering*): When the hell are you gonna get some coat racks in here?

COATES: Put a sock on it! Can't you see we got men here tryin' to wake up? You wanna bruise their sensibilities?

GUS (*to* BOCH): There in't no coat racks because I can't find one big enough for you to shove up your arse!

FLINT: Lads, lads!

GUS (*indicating* BOCH, *exasperated*): Bleedin' piss-artist.

COATES: So, what about the old man, then, Gus?

GUS: He was talkin' to himself.

COATES: Huh?

GUS: Yeh. He was talkin' to himself sort o' funny-like. It didn't make no sense.

FLINT: Was he on the piss?

GUS: What, you mean when he come in?

FLINT: Yeh.

GUS: Sober as a judge.

COATES: Must've polished off a bottle or two since then, by the look of him.

GUS: He didn't have much. One, maybe two glasses.

COATES: Mmmm?

GUS: Just enough to steady himself. He was a bit shaky — *you* know, he had trouble holdin' the bottle. I had to pour for him. Could hardly keep his eyes open.

FLINT: What'd he say his name was?

GUS: He didn't say.

BOCH: Wake up, Guthrie.

GUS: Aw, he don't know nothin'.

COATES (*to* BOCH): What difference would it make if he told him his name? Have you forgotten where the hell you are?

FLINT: He's right, Boch. If that's your name.

BOCH: Right, right. I get the point. (*Brief pause*) Sometimes I forget. You know, I was up north with the army when —

COATES: We know. We know, you were up north —

FLINT (*to* BOCH): You gonna start up with that again?

GUS: Let him be.

BOCH (*to* COATES, *indicating* GUS): See? He *knows*. He was *up* there. He told me —

FLINT: I didn't know that, Gus. You never said you were in the service.

GUS: I wasn't. I was up there on business a few years back.

COATES: What sort of business?

GUS (*smiling*): Never you mind.

    They chuckle.

FLINT: You mean you actually got into the camp without having —

GUS: I wasn't in the camp. Never said I was.

BOCH (*to* FLINT): He wasn't in the camp —

GUS: I was in the town.

FLINT (*to* BOCH): You never said anything about a town up there.

BOCH: I was never in the town. They never let us in the town. They were afraid of . . . What's the word?

GUS: Contagion. He's right, that's all they ever talked about up there. Electrified fences, barbed wire all over the place. I had to strip off before they let me in. Gave me a proper search, I can tell you that.

COATES (*lewdly*): They find anything, Gus?

GUS (*grinning*): Only what I was preservin' for the ladies.

FLINT (*smiling*): Oh, yeh? The ladies, eh?

GUS: Yeh.

> GUTHRIE *cries out in his stupor. They ignore him.*
>
> It was quite a town, I'll tell you that. I never seen anythin' like it. The women? Cor cripes, you'd burn your bleedin' hands off if you was to hold 'em too far out in the streets.
>
> *Appreciative grunts.*
>
> I remember, there was this one place everybody used to go to, on account o' the speciality. That's what they called it, the speciality. Cor, it weren't half exotic.
>
> *He comes out from behind the bar.*
>
> You went in and there was this ... It was like a cave, dark, with soft-coloured lights reflectin' off the rocks, and fountians cascadin' down into a pool. You had to take off your shoes and socks and roll up your trouser legs to reach the other side. The pool was all lit from underneath, green like an emerald, and full o' mermaids—only, the sort o' mermaids what don't have no fins. (*Winks*) Know wha' I mean?

COATES: They were starkers from the waist down.

GUS: 'Ere, they was starkers from the *head* down!

> *Appreciative grunts, etc.*
>
> There was these two rubber tracks under the water so's you could walk across without slidin', 'cause the floor o' the pool was smooth as ice, you see. Only, the tracks was so narrow, you couldn't walk normal. You had to walk with your feet apart, one on each track, like this ...
>
> *He demonstrates, to appreciative laughter.*
>
> And them mermaids would swim 'twixt your legs. And sometimes one of 'em

would slip her hand up your trousers and grope your pockets for loose change.

FLINT (*laughing*): Leave off.

GUS: 'Strewth, it is. You don't believe it? Well, listen to *this*.

COATES: Here, what was the name of this place?

GUS: It didn't have no name.

COATES: What? You mean it didn't advertise?

GUS: What'd they want to advertise for? Nobody would —

BOCH: Then, how'd *you* find out about it?

GUS: Through the grapevine. I was taken there.

BOCH: Who took you?

GUS: Some lads I was doin' business with over there.

BOCH: Oh —

GUS: Yeh. They knew where everything was over there.

BOCH: Ah. You mean they were a —

FLINT: For Christ's sake, let him finish the story! Go on, Gus.

GUS: Well —

> GUTHRIE *cries out in his stupor. They ignore him.*

I get to the other end of the pool and all me change is gone. Me pockets are empty. And there's this grotto — you know, pissin' statues and the like. The blokes I was with said it was blended whiskey, but I didn't want to take the chance. (*Brief pause*) We put our shoes and socks back on. Next thing I know, the floor's movin' under me — turnin' about, you know, on a pivot? — and risin' toward the ceilin' o' the cave. And I'm thinkin', Blimey, this is the end, we'll all be crushed, and me but a young man o' fifty and not yet past me prime.

They chuckle.

Then, at the last moment, just when everythin' is beginnin' to go black, a hole opens in the rocks above our heads, and we come to find ourselves standin' in the middle o' this room, and the floor still turnin' about under us. And we're surrounded . . . by wild animals! Cor, fifteen, perhaps twenty o' them, all round us. It took a bit before it came to me the animals was stuffed. Mind, I'm not talkin' about toys. I mean the real thing, the genuine article — the sort you shoot in a safari — lions, tigers, elephants, rhinoceroses.

BOCH: Was there a zebra?

GUS: Yeh, there was a zebra —

BOCH: Mmmm, I'm partial to zebras.

GUS: Yeh, there was a zebra.

FLINT: So, what happened then?

GUS: Well, I bleedin' near empty me bowels over these great animals. The blokes with me, they had a good laugh over it. As soon as we stepped off the revolvin' disc, the floor closes over it. And one o' the lads hoists himself up on a rhinoceros and says to the rest of us, Choose an animal and climb on. So, I decide on the camel, on account of he's sittin' close to the floor with his legs folded under him. Cor, what a mistake! Blimey, soon as I get on I hear this bleedin' spring go off inside the camel, and the camel stands up! Before I can catch me breath, we're all of us glidin' toward this door at the other end o' the room, on a sort o' runway. And I'm hangin' on to the camel with me eyes half closed, on account o' me fear o' heights. (*Brief pause*) There's this bloke in front o' me. (*To* BOCH) On a zebra.

BOCH: Ah.

GUS: Yeh. And I can hear the rest o' the lot cheerin' me on from behind. Only, I don't turn round, see, 'cause I'm scared o' fallin' off, even though it's a tolerable smooth ride.

COATES: Yeh?

GUS: Then, the door opens. The first bloke goes in on the zebra. He was maybe ten, fifteen feet in front o' me on the runway. The door closes, and that's the last I see of him.

ACT ONE 169

FLINT: Uh-huh?

GUS: Then, just as the camel and me are about to crash into the door, it opens again. (*Lowering his voice*) And I see these legs.

BOCH (*expectantly*): Yeh?

GUS: Female legs, in stockings and heels; stickin' down out o' the ceilin', they were. The genuine article. Hundreds of 'em.

> *Pause.*
> *He swallows hard.*

Well, there it was, and me the most astonished man that ever rode camel. Cages, all round the place, in a blood-red light. And the floor was crowded with people drinkin', dancin', gamblin' at the tables. The cages were high up, all along the walls. There were naked women in the cages, but not like the mermaids in the pool. No. These women were wild and filthy, crouchin' like apes, snatchin' at scraps o' meat tossed up to them by people on the floor. I never seen the like. They called 'em Zombie Women. It's the truth. They were brought there from the camp. Don't ask me how I found out about that. They were halfway between the sickness and full recovery. Only, later, none of 'em would remember they'd ever been in the cages.

> *The door jingles.* SILVO *comes to.*
> *Enter* CORBY *and* RAPITRONE. CORBY *pushes* RAPITRONE *in in a wheelchair.* RAPITRONE'*s face is wan and lifeless; he sits with his head erect, steel-rimmed spectacles masking his eyes (the lenses black), hands folded beneath the afghan that blankets his legs — he appears to be blind and paralysed. A weatherproof lantern hangs from* RAPITRONE'*s neck.* CORBY *wears a small lantern strapped to his head, is unshaven and somewhat dishevelled.*
> GUS *goes behind the bar, leaving* BOCH, FLINT *and* COATES *to drink and murmur amongst themselves and to cast side glances at the newcomers from time to time, as* CORBY *switches off the lanterns, sets them on the bench, and wheels* RAPITRONE, *absentmindedly, to* JOSEPH'*s table.*

What can I do for you lads?

CORBY (*unbuttoning his overcoat*): Pint o' bourbon, two glasses.

GUS: Comin' up.

> *He puts the bottle and two shot-glasses on the bar as* CORBY *doffs his overcoat and hangs it over the back of a chair.* SILVO *carries his bottle to* JOSEPH's *table and sits, facing* RAPITRONE, *as* CORBY *counts off six notes from a thick wad and hands them to* GUS, *who hands one note back.*

It's too much.

CORBY: Keep it.

GUS: Thanks.

> *He pockets the money, all six notes.*
> CORBY *carries bottle and glasses to* JOSEPH's *table, pours two shots, downs one, and holds the second glass as* RAPITRONE *drinks from it.*

SILVO (*to* CORBY): Is he all right?

CORBY: He's all right. Nothing that a dram o' piss won't mend. (*To* RAPITRONE) Eh, mate?

> *He wipes* RAPITRONE's *chin with the afghan, and proceeds with the awkward task of removing* RAPITRONE's *gloves, muffler and overcoat.* JOSEPH *still unconscious.*

SILVO: I was the greatest bloody magician in the country. Nobody could come near me for pulling strange objects out of the most unlikely places. I was a fucking genius! I once pulled a bouquet of African violets out of a woman's arse. (*Brief pause*) Before a national audience of well-wishers and conventioneers, I depantsed several now-infamous politicians without using my hands, causing flocks of orange, yellow, and green canaries to flutter to the rafters from beneath their private organs. You may have seen it. (*Brief pause*) As an apprentice, I startled my mentors with the suavity of my legerdemain. The force of gravity was at my beck and call. (*Gesturing*) The merest flick of the hand sufficed to transform a twenty-one-stone dowager into a gypsy moth. (*Brief pause*) Strong men wilted beneath my hypnotic gaze. Women swooned. There was no theatre, no lecture hall, no supper club whose walls did not but tremble at my prestidigitations. It was nothing for me to be swaddled in a mummy's winding sheet and locked into a tinder-box chained to the bed of a lake. Often, I remained submerged for days. Then, when the box was hauled to the surface and blasted open with a charge of dynamite, all they would find was an ocarina or a plasterer's trowel. (*Brief pause*) I'd allow myself to be frozen in a cake of ice and make my escape before thousands of people in a matter of seconds!

He reaches across the table and extracts a ludicrous feather duster from beneath RAPITRONE's *jacket.*

CORBY (*indifferently*): Very impressive.

> SILVO *lays the feather duster on the table, in front of* JOSEPH. CORBY *hangs* RAPITRONE's *overcoat on the back of a chair, and sits between* RAPITRONE *and* JOSEPH *as* SILVO *drinks from his bottle, lost in thought.*
> JOSEPH *slowly raises his head for the first time, and stares blankly at the feather duster.* CORBY *suddenly recognises him.*

Good Lord, it's . . .

> JOSEPH *grips* CORBY *by the arm to silence him, and turns to* SILVO.

JOSEPH (*to* SILVO): What time is it? Is it night or day?

RAPITRONE (*suddenly agitated*): It's you, it's —

> CORBY *clamps his hand to* RAPITRONE's *mouth.* JOSEPH *gapes at* RAPITRONE *in surprise.* RAPITRONE *silenced.*

SILVO: Here, Gus. What time is it?

GUS: Gettin' on for nine.

> CORBY *pours out a shot.*

JOSEPH (*to* SILVO): Day or night?

SILVO (*turning to the window*): It's black as pitch out there.

> CORBY *holds the glass as* RAPITRONE *drinks from it.*

JOSEPH (*without looking back*): Oh. Nine in the morning. (*To* CORBY) This blasted place. I've been down here too long. (*Now turning to the window*) Look out there. Does that look like nine in the morning to you?

CORBY (*to* RAPITRONE): That's right. (*To* JOSEPH, *wiping* RAPITRONE's *chin with the afghan*) You should be used to it by now.

> CORBY *pours himself a dram, drinks.*

SILVO: So, you gentlemen are aquainted.

CORBY: You know how it is down here.

SILVO: Hah, I could write a book.

JOSEPH (*wearily*): Yeh. My son used to write. Never got anywhere with it, though. *I* thought he had talent. The rejections came in hand-over-fist. We could've papered the walls with 'em.

SILVO: Ah.

JOSEPH: In the end, he couldn't even flog the stuff door to door.

SILVO: Mmmm.

JOSEPH: No. He never cracked it as a writer. He was too sensitive.

SILVO (*nodding*): Mmmm. The literary world is no place for a man of sensitivity.

Brief pause.

JOSEPH: Neither is this.

SILVO: What's your name, squire?

JOSEPH *and* CORBY *exchange glances.*

JOSEPH (*to* SILVO): Loew.

SILVO: What's that, L-O-W? As in Low?

JOSEPH: No. L-O-E-W, as in Loew.

SILVO: That's not your real name, is it?

JOSEPH: It's as good as any other. What about yours?

SILVO: What?

CORBY: Your name. What's your name?

SILVO: Silvo.

JOSEPH: Ah.

SILVO: That's not my *real* name. (*To* CORBY) And what do *you* call yourself?

CORBY: I call myself Nash.

SILVO: Mmmm.

CORBY: That's not my *real* name.

SILVO (*indicating* RAPITRONE): And what about him?

CORBY: He calls himself Coates.

SILVO: We've already got a Coates down here.

He points to COATES, *who waves back drunkenly.*

Coates is a good name. It's got some stuff to it. Keeps the wind out.

CORBY (*indicating* RAPITRONE): His real name is Wally Floone.

SILVO: Eh?

Pause.

JOSEPH: Cor, what a morning *this* is!

SILVO: You can't always be sure.

JOSEPH: What?

SILVO: That it's morning. You can't always be sure, if you've been sleeping it off.

JOSEPH: What do you mean? (*To* CORBY) What's he talking about —

SILVO: Sometimes they switch the power off in the streets in the middle of the night. (*To* GUS) Right, Gus?

GUS: What?

SILVO: I said they turn the power off sometimes.

GUS: What, you mean outside?

JOSEPH (*to* CORBY): Who turns the power off?

SILVO (*to* GUS): Yeh.

GUS: Yeh. They switch it off sometimes.

JOSEPH (*to* SILVO): Who switches the power off? What are you talking about?

SILVO: Canamine would be able to answer that.

JOSEPH: Who's Canamine?

SILVO (*pointing upwards*): The man upstairs —

JOSEPH (*to* CORBY): Who's Canamine?

SILVO: He hasn't been down here long, but —

CORBY (*to* JOSEPH): He doesn't know anything.

>   *Pause.*

SILVO (*musing*): Morning, morning... What's the use of having it at all if you can't have it?

JOSEPH (*nods, then*): What?

CORBY (*to* SILVO): Here, piss off!

>   SILVO *staggers, bottle and feather duster in hand, to his original table, where he passes out.*
>   JOSEPH *looks about to make sure no one else is listening.*

JOSEPH (*to* CORBY, *indicating* RAPITRONE): My God, he can *talk*.

RAPITRONE: Joseph —

JOSEPH (*to* CORBY, *an urgent whisper*): Corby!

CORBY *clamps his hand to* RAPITRONE*'s mouth.*

CORBY (*to* RAPITRONE): Here, not so loud. You gotta watch what you say here.

RAPITRONE *nods.* CORBY *removes his hand.*

JOSEPH: Mmmm. How long has he *been* like this, able to talk?

CORBY: Since that night.

RAPITRONE: That ... That night.

JOSEPH (*his hand on* RAPITRONE*'s arm*): Ah, Rapitrone.

RAPITRONE *recoils.* CORBY *removes* JOSEPH*'s hand.*

(*To* CORBY) What is it? What's wrong, Corby?

CORBY: He blames you, Joseph. He blames you for —

RAPITRONE (*stammering*): Puh, Peg —

CORBY (*to* JOSEPH): He blames you for what happened. For Peg.

JOSEPH (*shakes his head, sadly*): Uh, he's got every right to blame me. It was my fault. I should never've taken it as far as I did without the absolute certainty that ...

CORBY: What?

Pause.

JOSEPH: No. I can't say. It's over now, really over. That's the important thing. Shem is dead and buried.

CORBY: Ah, you found time to bury him before you came down here.

JOSEPH: No. I brought him down with me in the basket.

CORBY: That's dangerous. You mean you buried him down here? That's not a —

JOSEPH: It wasn't easy, I can tell you, finding a place, dragging about that load of flesh on my back through the dark. You didn't tell me I would need a lantern.

CORBY: I didn't think of it. At the time, I was —

JOSEPH: I know, I know. I'm not blaming you.

Pause.

(*Indicating* RAPITRONE) So, you've stayed with him.

CORBY: Mmmm.

JOSEPH: Good.

CORBY: There was little else I *could* do, with Peg gone.

JOSEPH: Quite. And the lodger. What about the lodger? Did he and the other woman ever return to the house?

CORBY: He's down here.

JOSEPH (*excited*): You've seen him?

CORBY: No. And even if I did, he wouldn't acknowledge me. You know how it is down here.

JOSEPH: How do you know he's down here, then?

CORBY (*indicating* SILVO): Him. *He* told us, just now.

JOSEPH: You mean the —

CORBY: Canamine.

JOSEPH: Ah.

CORBY: He didn't even bother to change his name. He must be barmy.

JOSEPH: Or cunning. Sounds as though he might have connexions down here you don't know about.

CORBY (*pensive*): Hmmm . . .

ACT ONE 177

JOSEPH: That business about switching the power off.

CORBY (*indicating* SILVO): That's what *he* says. What does *he* know?

JOSEPH: You're probably right.

Pause.

CORBY: Still, the very last thing he wanted was to come down here. He was a sick man. Didn't at all fancy the idea of coming down. I brought him down once on a trial run, and he didn't take to it. Said it made him nervous.

JOSEPH (*to himself*): Nervous. Why?

CORBY: He didn't say.

JOSEPH: Maybe he was lying, to cover himself.

CORBY: It's a possibility. I wouldn't rule out anything where a defector's concerned.

JOSEPH: I don't even know what he looks like. An officer?

CORBY: Hmmm.

JOSEPH: Mmmm. Peg told me there were more than a hundred of 'em down here.

CORBY: Huh, more than that. (*Brief pause*) Look around you.

JOSEPH: You know these men? (*Indicating* SILVO) You know *him?*

CORBY: The magician? I've heard of him. I don't know him.

Pause.

JOSEPH: So, what do you think we should —

RAPITRONE: Tricks. Cheap doctor's tricks.

CORBY *pours out another dram.*

Peg!

CORBY: Here.

He holds the glass as RAPITRONE *drinks from it.*

(*To* JOSEPH) I had to bring him down with me. Some unfinished business. I couldn't leave him up there all alone. (*Brief pause*) I was hoping I'd run into you, Joseph.

JOSEPH (*pained at* RAPITRONE'*s condition, to* CORBY): The Underground's a very large place. Larger than I'd imagined. A man could easily get lost in it.

CORBY: That's the whole idea.

He wipes RAPITRONE'*s chin with the afghan.*

JOSEPH: How long has it been? How long have I been down here, Corby?

CORBY: You mean you don't know?

JOSEPH: A week, a fortnight. Perhaps a month, I don't know.

CORBY: Try three days.

JOSEPH (*helpless chuckle*): Three days. (*Pensive*) Seems like so much longer. I'd never've said three days.

CORBY: It's only three days. Three days since . . .

JOSEPH (*shaking his head*): Hmmm.

    Pause.

What about the woman?

RAPITRONE (*to himself*): Peg.

JOSEPH (*to* CORBY): I mean the other woman. Luba. The one this . . .

CORBY: Canamine.

JOSEPH: Canamine. The one Canamine was calling for at the end —

RAPITRONE (*to himself*): That man.

ACT ONE   179

Pause.

JOSEPH: What is it, lad?

Pause.

RAPITRONE: The lodger.

CORBY: Here, easy. Easy. You know you shouldn't wear yourself —

JOSEPH: No. Let him talk (*To* RAPITRONE) Go on, Rapitrone. Go on, lad.

As RAPITRONE *tells his tale,* CORBY *tries to conceal his own growing uneasiness.*

RAPITRONE: Joseph.

Pause.

Do you know what it means to be blind?

CORBY *pours himself a dram, gulps it down.*

You hear things, things a normal person wouldn't hear. You smell things, things you shouldn't or wouldn't want to smell, if it were left to you. You can measure the distance of a wall or the closeness of a locked door by the sound of your own breathing. And when it rains, when the rain falls, all the raindrops puddling in the mud, in the streets and on the pavements, the murmurs in the grass, the flooded downspouts and the gutters droning on, that rustle of starched curtains across the roof tiles when the wind shifts — you hear it all, unmixed, as though each element of the storm was untouched by any other, and the drops themselves were falling all alone. (*Brief pause*) I've grown used to it now. It's not so much a question of remembering where things are; it's learning, with your ears and nose, and through the pores of your skin. Learning to sense where the empty spaces end.

Pause.

Canamine lived for a long time in our house, but it wasn't till that last night that I heard him speak.

CORBY *pours out another dram.*

He was a sick man and needed constant looking after —

CORBY *holds the glass to* RAPITRONE'*s lips.*

CORBY: Here, don't upset yourself. There's no point in —

RAPITRONE (*turning his head away*): No.

CORBY *downs the dram in one gulp.*
Pause.

Canamine was a sick man. In the daytime, he seldom left his bed. Peg was always having to go up to him, up to that room in the garret. She told me about that room and the things in it, as if it needed telling. I could smell it on him whenever he came down to supper, which wasn't often. That smell of dead moths, medicines, and musty sheets. (*Brief pause*) He never spoke.

Pause.

I wasn't in the chair then, not at the beginning. I couldn't see, and my speech was going — I was down to a few words, my last few syllables, before the silence set in — but I was still able to hobble about a little on my own. (*Brief pause*) For a long time I used to go to bed early. Peg would tuck me up on the nights Corby didn't call for me. We made the collections together, Corby and I. But on those other nights, Peg would put me to bed early, and I would sleep for a few hours. My sight came back to me, in dreams. (*Brief pause*) It happened one of those nights, in the small hours. I heard her tiptoeing barefoot on the carpet, and felt her creep into bed beside me. She reached across me to switch the nightlight off, and thought I was still asleep. She was naked. The must of the garret room was on her. I could smell it in her skin. The dead moths. The medicine. The stinking bedsheets. What could I do?

Pause.

You killed the wrong man, Joseph, when you did Shem in. You dragged the wrong ghost with you into the grave.

JOSEPH: I never killed anyone. He died. He *had* to die. You were there —

RAPITRONE: And Peg? Did she have to die, too?

JOSEPH: Look, you don't understand. That's nothing to do with me. Nothing. I wouldn't have harmed a hair of her head. I don't *know* what happened. It was Shem, *he* was the —

RAPITRONE: Shem, or the other one? The one upstairs. He'd grown tired of her. Wanted an excuse to slip off quietly, without a fuss.

JOSEPH: No. You're ignoring the most important —

RAPITRONE: *He's* the one you should've murdered. *He's* the dangerous one.

> *Pause.*
> CORBY *sits with his head in his hands.*
> RAPITRONE *still physically impassive as* JOSEPH *ponders his words.*

JOSEPH: I went up there. Up to his room in the garret. The window was open. They were gone, the pair of 'em, Canamine and the woman. I looked out. No tracks, nothing. As though they were never there. (*Brief pause*) And Peg, I searched everywhere. Believe me. Corby and I looked everywhere.

> *Pause.*

Shem was lying in the parlour, where I'd left him. His eyes were shut. (*Brief pause*) When I came down from the garret, I opened his left eye and could see, by the way it had flattened in the socket, that he was dead. The iris was eclipsed. It appeared to have blotted up so much of the darkness that the white of the eye had gone grey and was already drying up.

> *Pause.*

(*To* CORBY) I couldn't get him into the lorry. By then, most of the drifts were above my head. When I reached the corner with him, half an hour after leaving the house... When we'd got as far as the corner, I found the lorry and the street lamp buried so deep they seemed to fuse under the snow. The street, all the hedges, the trees, the roofs of the houses in the high drifts, were drooping and looked as though they might collapse. And I remember thinking, the sheer tonnage of snow — the snow that was still coming down — should be more than enough to rupture the crust of earth and send us all tumbling into the Underground.

> *Pause.*

I don't know how long it was. It must've taken long, a long time, to pull him so far. Half the night at least. It seemed so far, but it couldn't have been. If I'd gone to sleep, I would've died. I was moving so slow with him, and the blizzard fell so thick, so heavy, that the trench we left in our wake was soon covered over. From time to time, I'd stop to kick the snow off him. It filled his nostrils, When it froze, the snow stitched his eyelids shut and sealed the grimace on his lips.

Pause.

His lips were black. There was no moon. No star beneath the clouds. But there was moonlight, a soft polar light, where the snow irradiated the sky. And all in silence as I dragged Shem behind me. (*Brief pause*) His face was shadowless.

Pause.

I dug for the hole to the Underground with my hands. How I came to it, I'll never know. But it was there, a lid cut into the brown grass and the weeds, beside a wall. Then, I hesitated. (*Brief pause*) It seemed to me that Shem should not be buried in the Underground, where I was taking him, but six feet under the sod in daylight with the sky grey, the earth white, as it was, and dead trees thin in the distance. But there was only the wall, and the lone tree just beyond it. An old locust tree. So, I had to bring him down. (*Brief pause*) Before I leaned into the hole and pulled the rope for the basket, I took a pocket-knife, chipped the ice from Shem's lips, and pried them apart. Then I scooped up a handful of snow, packed it hard into a ball, and stuffed it in his mouth, shutting the lips again.

CORBY: Why?

Pause.
JOSEPH *looks at* CORBY.

JOSEPH: I don't know.

Pause.

I buried him not far from here. Tore the cobbles out of a narrow alleyway and put him under. (*Touching* RAPITRONE) We're rid of him at last.

Sounds of laughter, off, growing louder.
Enter CANAMINE *from left, a big cigar in his mouth, with* LUBA *and* MEG *on each arm, a nondescript* MAN *following hard at their heels, all laughing uproariously.*
CANAMINE, *clad in an expensive three-piece suit, carries a walking stick, and sports a large campaign button, reading:* I Quit. *He is darkly bearded, well groomed, and wears black-rimmed glasses.*

LUBA *(who carries* CANAMINE*'s briefcase) and* MEG *wear provocative evening gowns.*
The MAN *may seem, at first, to be a well-dressed hoodlum.*

GUS *(grinning)*: 'Mornin', Mister Canamine!

CANAMINE: Gus.

FLINT, COATES *and* BOCH *drunkenly salute* CANAMINE.

(Returning their salute) As you were, lads. As you were.

CANAMINE *mumbles something to the women, who giggle suggestively as* JOSEPH *stares at him in shocked disbelief.* RAPITRONE *turns his head in* CANAMINE*'s direction.*

GUS: What'll it be, Mister Canamine?

CANAMINE: Nothing, Gus. Not a bloody drop. A bit early in the day for us. Right, girls? *(To* GUS*)* Guthrie still out?

GUS *(pointing to* GUTHRIE*)*: Over there. Silvo, too —

CANAMINE: Ah.

He catches sight of JOSEPH, *who has mastered himself and stares back defiantly.* CANAMINE *meets* JOSEPH*'s stare with an ironic smile as he takes the cigar from his mouth for the first time.*
Pause.
From now until the end of the play, JOSEPH*'s behaviour vis-à-vis* CANAMINE *is that of one who, for reasons of his own, plays along with the latter's games and strategies, sometimes with ironic detachment, at other times so completely immersed in his various 'rôles' that it becomes difficult, even impossible, to determine whether he is play-acting or in earnest.*

(Bowing ceremoniously) Good morrow, Master Doctor.

He chukles sardonically.
JOSEPH *is not amused.*
MEG *saunters past* RAPITRONE, *who suddenly reaches out and grabs her by the hips.*

MEG (*struggling*): Here —

RAPITRONE: That scent —

MEG: Here! Watch it —

RAPITRONE (*pawing her hips, waist, buttocks*): It can't be —

MEG: Watch your hands —

RAPITRONE (*to* CORBY): That voice —

MEG (*struggling*): Come on —

RAPITRONE (*to* CORBY, *still pawing*): It's Peg —

MEG: Ease off, will you?

CORBY (*tugging at* RAPITRONE's *arms*): Here, let go. Come on. It's all right. She's not goin' anywhere.

> CORBY *forces* RAPITRONE *to release his grip.* MEG *stumbles backwards, smooths her dress, etc.*

CANAMINE (*to* MEG): Any damage?

MEG: I've had worse.

CANAMINE: I meant the dress.

> MEG *turns, arms akimbo, as he inspects the dress.*

All right.

JOSEPH (*sarcastically*): For a man who's been down here only a short time, you've done well for yourself.

CANAMINE: I'm a simple business man, that's all.

JOSEPH: Pretty successful, I'd say.

CANAMINE *chomps his cigar and snaps his fingers.* LUBA *opens his briefcase at* JOSEPH's *table, extracts a roll of toilet tissue, and hands it to* CANAMINE.

GUTHRIE *cries out in his stupor. They ignore him.*

CANAMINE (*proffering the toilet roll to* JOSEPH): Look at this. Imported. Here, smell it.

JOSEPH *is not amused.*

It's a precious commodity down here. Very hard to come by. You ought to know that. (*To* GUS) Here. On the house.

He tosses the toilet roll to GUS.

GUS: Here, thanks, Mister Canamine. I can really do with this.

CANAMINE: Don't mention it, Gus. (*To* FLINT, COATES *and* BOCH) Anything I can do for you lads? Are you comfortable?

They laugh, cynically.

JOSEPH: You've found a niche for yourself.

CANAMINE (*indicating the women*): More than one.

JOSEPH: Really made yourself at home down here.

CANAMINE: I get by.

RAPITRONE: Joseph, Corby, you can see her. It *is* Peg, isn't it? It's my wife.

MEG: Here, what's your name, luv?

RAPITRONE: It's me. It's Andrew.

MEG: Andrew, eh? Well, listen, Andrew. My name's Meg. Meg, got it? And I'm nobody's wife. At least, not any more, I'm not. (*To all and sundry, with a wry smile*) A tragic case, my husband. He fell asleep in the car-wash with the windows open and was sudsed, rinsed, buffed and squeegeed to death.

Cynical laughter of all but JOSEPH, CORBY, RAPITRONE.

RAPITRONE (*his head bobbing uncontrollably*): No. No! (*Brief pause*) No.

CORBY *steadies him.*

CANAMINE (*to* JOSEPH): If he wants to see her privately, it'll cost him.

He wraps his arm round LUBA*'s hips and lays his hand on* RAPITRONE*'s shoulder.*

(*To* CORBY, *confidentially*) I'd like to help you lads out, I really would. Stick around. I might have a little job for you, eh? (*Loudly*) Meg! How about a song for the lads here?

FLINT, COATES *and* BOCH *noise their approval.*
The MAN *sits down at the piano and begins to play.*
Blue spotlight follows MEG.
CANAMINE *sits down beside* JOSEPH, LUBA *on his lap.*
MEG *sings "Neon Blue" with style.*

MEG (*singing*):   Keys to dark hotels,
Rooms with no view;
All the mean streets are
Laid out under signs, neon blue.
O neon-blue names,
They fade away;
When daylight comes
They're dead letters in grey:
Old neon-blue names.

She makes a turn of the drunkards' table, then sits on BOCH*'s lap.*

Midnight clocks that chime
Ring the night through;
And the images climb
Out of my eyes, neon blue.

She postures, sitting on the drunkards' table.

O neon-blue dreams
Bloom and decay;
Bright coals to ashes,
They flicker away:
Old neon-blue dreams.

ACT ONE

She rises; approaching RAPITRONE, *she sings to him.*

> I used to be someone who lived for
> No one but you, and then
> You were gone from me;
> Now there's nothing I wouldn't do
> To feel your lips on mine again.

She crouches, face to face with RAPITRONE.

> Dark clouds swell with rain,
> Hearts break in two;
> Though I can't stand the pain,
> There's not a thing I can do.

She caresses RAPITRONE*'s face.*

> O neon-blue skies,
> They're here to stay,
> So dark I can't tell
> The night from the day.

She slowly removes RAPITRONE*'s glasses.*

> Old neon blue,

She rises, puts on RAPITRONE*'s black spectacles. He stares up at her, his mouth gaping, as in a trance.*

> Neon blue.

With the last chords, fade to black

ACT TWO

A room above the public house, night. Rear wall, right to left: a wide, rectangular mirror above a battered chest of drawers; a door giving on the outer hall; a bare, grimy window. Beneath the window, a creaky brass bed, its dilapidated headboard flush with the left wall; a night table and lamp beside the bed, down left. Right wall: a closet door; the bathroom door, ajar, upstage. Downstage, right to centre: crates, boxes, rolls of toilet tissue, stacked pell-mell round a desk; outdated parlour furniture, a floor lamp, a motheaten couch, all hideously mismatched. The room is wide and deep, with dingy, wood-coloured walls and the vague suggestion of a warehouse about it.

Darkness, save for the dim, bluish light that filters in through the window from the silent street below.

Pause.

Sounds of a woman waking, yawning. MEG *stretches, tosses the covers aside and sits naked on the edge of the bed. With a drowsy sigh, she fumbles at the night table, lights up a cigarette and shakes out the match, tossing it into an ashtray.*

Pause.

She switches on the night-table lamp, shivers, squints at the alarm clock, coughs, scratches her hip, then rises, slipping into the flannel dressing gown draped across a nearby chair on a pile of men's clothing.

MEG *leans over the bed and shakes a sleeping figure, who remains completely hidden under the tousled covers.*

MEG: Here, wake up.

> *She shakes the sleeper again.*

Come on, it's late. Up you get.

> *She shakes the sleeper harder.*

Here, wake up. Come on. Wake up, Guthrie!

> *No response.*

Christ.

She goes to the desk, rummages amid its litter of notes and papers, picks up a receipt, reads it, appears momentarily impressed, glances at the toilet rolls, gives the receipt a last look, then tosses it back on to the cluttered blotter.
Exit MEG *to the bathroom, shutting the door.*
Pause.
A knock.
Pause.
Enter CORBY *and* RAPITRONE *from the outer hall.* RAPITRONE, *still in his wheelchair, but without spectacles and no longer blind, is able to propel himself, having regained the use of his arms.*
They speak in hushed voices.

RAPITRONE: You said she'd be here.

CORBY: The light's on. Look.

They approach the bed from the window side. CORBY *lifts the edge of the covers, the sleeper still unseen by the audience.*

RAPITRONE: What's *he* doing here?

CORBY: We must be in the wrong room. I *told* you it was —

RAPITRONE: No. No, this isn't the wrong room. He said the door at the top of the stair, didn't he?

CORBY: Yeh, but —

RAPITRONE: Well?

A toilet flushing, off right. CORBY *lets the covers fall as they were.*

There, you see?

CORBY: What?

RAPITRONE: It's past midnight, isn't it?

CORBY: Yeh, well?

RAPITRONE: Well, she used to get up a lot in the middle of the night to go to the loo.

CORBY: That doesn't prove a thing. Look, I told you, it can't be —

RAPITRONE: I know. I know what you told me. But *you* saw her. And Joseph, as well.

CORBY: You know what Joseph said.

RAPITRONE (*wheeling toward the desk*): I know, I know. He's not sure.

CORBY (*following*): Well, it's just that he —

RAPITRONE: He's an old man, out of his depth. He's not sure of anything. It's *his* fault, his more than anyone else's, and now he isn't sure. Don't make me laugh.

Pause.

Look at all this. It's disgusting. When I think of her living down here, like this.

CORBY *inspects the crates and boxes.*

(*Brief pause*) How much did you give him?

CORBY: Canamine?

RAPITRONE: Yeh.

CORBY: Nothing. Nothing at all.

RAPITRONE: Don't lie to me, Corby —

CORBY: I'm not lying —

RAPITRONE: You *know* he said it would cost me.

Pause.

CORBY (*peering into one of the boxes*): We managed to work something out. You know, I did a lot for him up there —

RAPITRONE: Yeh, and look where it's got you.

CORBY: He owes me plenty. He owes the pair of us, and he knows it. That business downstairs, all that talk, that's just for Gus and the horns. Things are different down here, you know that. You know how it is down here. Canamine owes us, so we get a free ride. But he's got to keep up a front for the others. Nobody here can afford to let on too much about himself. (*Rummaging in one of the boxes*) It's best to forget the old life, all the old lies and deceptions, and let the past be buried.

RAPITRONE: By burying yourself down here?

CORBY: You got a better suggestion? Are you forgetting what it was like up there? Are you forgetting the collections?

RAPITRONE: No, I'm not forgetting.

> CORBY *extracts a dusty, feathered toque from the box, and puts it on his head.*

CORBY: Well?

RAPITRONE (*sourly*): Charming.

CORBY: Here, come on, jolly up. Everything's gonna come out right in the end.

RAPITRONE: That's not what Joseph says.

CORBY: Joseph has his own business to take care of down here.

RAPITRONE: With Canamine.

CORBY (*nodding*): Mmmm.

> *Enter* MEG, *still in the flannel dressing gown.*

MEG: Oh, it's you lot. I thought it was somebody else. (*Snatching the toque from* CORBY*'s head*) Here, gimme that.

CORBY: I didn't know it was yours. What, are you goin' to a costume ball?

MEG: It's not mine, silly.

> *She puts on the toque.*
> *Pause.*
>
> You're a quiet pair, I *must* say. (*To* CORBY, *indicating the sleeper*) Here, how'd you like to lend me a hand with that lot over there? I gotta get him out of here. There's going to be a party up here in half an hour.

CORBY: A party, at this time of night?

MEG: I mean a client (*Brief pause*) Mister Canamine send you?

CORBY: Not exactly.

MEG: What does *that* mean?

CORBY: He owes us one.

MEG: There's a switch. Well, wait'll we get Guthrie out of here.

CORBY: I don't think he'll give us any trouble.

MEG: What are you gonna do, roll him under the bed?

CORBY: Forget Guthrie, *that's* not what we're here for.

MEG: Oh, I thought —

CORBY: Yeh, I know. It's all right.

> RAPITRONE *stares.*
> *Pause.*

MEG (*to* RAPITRONE): What's the matter, cat got your tongue? (*To* CORBY) What's the matter with *him?* He was feeling chipper enough downstairs. Nearly tore my dress off.

CORBY: He's all right. He's tired.

She goes to the closet.

MEG: Look, one of you lads'll have to turn round while I slip into something warmer. I'm freezing.

    CORBY *turns and rummages in another of the boxes as* MEG *opens the closet door, doffs her dressing gown, and hangs it up. The closet is full of expensive dresses, coats, shoes, boots, etc.*

RAPITRONE (*gazing at* MEG*'s nudity, to* CORBY, *hushed*): It's her! It's her, I tell you! The face is one thing, but the body —

CORBY: Ssssh —

RAPITRONE: Those buttocks. I'd know them anywhere —

CORBY: Here, steady on.

    MEG *puts on a fur coat and high heels as* CORBY *extracts a View-Master from the box, slips in a reel of 3-D transparencies and peers into it.*

We haven't broken the ice yet.

    He switches on the floor lamp and puts the viewer to his eyes again.

MEG: Here, you didn't tell me he could *see!*

CORBY: You didn't ask.

MEG: Well, how was *I* to know? What is this, the Court of Miracles?

RAPITRONE (*to* CORBY): Victor Hugo. It's a dead giveaway. She reads Victor Hugo—

CORBY (*clicking the viewer to another transparency*): Easy, easy —

MEG (*to* RAPITRONE): So, who down here *hasn't* read Victor Hugo? (*To* CORBY) What's *he* on about?

    CORBY*'s eyes are glued to the viewer throughout.*
    RAPITRONE *wheels himself after* MEG *as she gathers the pile of men's clothing from the chair and pushes it under the bed with her feet.*

RAPITRONE: You went to the loo.

MEG: I was thirsty.

RAPITRONE: *We* heard the toilet.

MEG: I flushed my cigarette down the jakes.

CORBY: Smoking? You'll ruin your voice.

MEG: A lot *I* care.

RAPITRONE: That face. That voice (*Brief pause*) Peg!

Pause.

MEG: Are you talkin' to *me?*

RAPITRONE: For God's sake, Peg!

MEG: Look, I told you before, my name's Meg! (*To* CORBY) Who's this Peg, anyway?

CORBY: His wife.

He clicks the viewer to another transparency.

MEG: His wife?

CORBY: You might be his wife.

MEG (*to* RAPITRONE): Listen, don't come that Underground con with *me* — you might be this, you might be that — I been with Mister Canamine long enough to be on to *that* game.

RAPITRONE (*to* CORBY): You hear? You hear what she's saying?

MEG: I'm not your wife!

RAPITRONE: Then, what're you doing with my wife's bum?

Pause.

CORBY *clicks to another transparency and peers into the viewer more intently.*

CORBY (*to* MEG): Here! This you on here?

He turns the viewer upside down and peers into it.

MEG: What if it is?

RAPITRONE: Impossible, impossible! She's only been down here three days!

MEG: Three days, huh? That's a good one.

RAPITRONE: How long has Canamine been down here, then?

MEG: I can't tell you that. (*To* CORBY) I can't tell you that.

CORBY (*still peering into the viewer*): What?

MEG: Here, put that thing away, will you? You're making me nervous.

CORBY: This is evidence.

She snatches the viewer out of his hands and tosses it into the box.

MEG: So much for the evidence.

She lies on the couch, her legs draped over the arm.

Now, you wankers gonna tell me what you're really here for? I told you, I haven't got all night.

CORBY (*to* RAPITRONE): I think we've broken the ice.

MEG *brings an emery board from her pocket and begins to manicure her nails.*
RAPITRONE *wheels himself back and forth throughout.*

(*To* MEG) I've got some unfinished business of my own down here, so we'll try not to take up much more of your time.

MEG: Good.

CORBY: Mister Rapitrone — Andrew — and myself would like to call your attention, if we may, to the possibilities, the plausible possibilities, of his case.

MEG: Hoo, *very* nice, too! I'm listening.

CORBY: The first thing we'd like to sort out is, how did Canamine get you to pose for those 3-D pictures?

MEG: Who said Mister Canamine got me to do *anything?* Your friend said himself, three days wasn't time enough for me to have —

CORBY: Then, when *did* you pose for those pictures? How long ago *was* it? Was it before you met the plaintiff?

MEG: Who?

CORBY: Rapitrone.

MEG: I never said I posed for those pictures. How do you know his *wife* didn't pose for those pictures?

CORBY: When?

MEG: *I* don't know.

CORBY: Have a guess.

MEG: I don't know, before she met him. Maybe she needed the money.

CORBY: Mmmm, the oldest profession.

RAPITRONE: Let's leave religion out of this, shall we? The woman who posed for those pictures is obviously a tart!

MEG: You haven't even seen 'em!

CORBY (*to* RAPITRONE): You wanna see 'em? The lighting's not half bad —

RAPITRONE: I don't wanna see 'em!

CORBY: Usually, they get the lighting wrong. (*To* MEG) Don't you often find that to be the case?

ACT TWO

MEG: It depends on what you consider good lighting.

CORBY: When I say good lighting, I mean artistic lighting.

Pause.

MEG: I see. (*Brief pause*) What was the question?

CORBY: You say it isn't you in the pictures.

MEG: Can you prove it *is?*

CORBY: It looks like you, you've got to admit.

MEG: I don't know. There are lots of reels in there. How do *I* know?

CORBY: The ones on the Persian rug, with the hookah.

MEG: Hookah?

CORBY: The waterpipe.

MEG: Oh. And you think that's me, eh?

CORBY: Would you mind tilting your head back a bit?

She complies. He scrutinises her from the other end of the couch.

RAPITRONE: All this is getting us nowhere.

CORBY (*to himself*): It's uncanny. (*To* MEG) Now, take off the hat. Close your eyes halfway, and open your mouth.

She complies, tossing the toque over the back of the couch; RAPITRONE *catches it, examines it, and puts it on.*

No, that's too wide. Not so wide.

She raises her eyebrows.

Yeh, that's better. Much better.

MEG (*features rigid*): Uh?

CORBY: Right, relax. (*To* RAPITRONE) An uncanny resemblance. If only there were some special feature, a pimple or a mole. That would make the whole thing a hell of a lot easier. (*To* MEG) I won't ask you to disrobe.

MEG: Thanks.

CORBY: Don't mention it.

RAPITRONE: I don't think this picture business is getting us anywhere. (*Pointing to the bed*) Ask her about *him!*

CORBY: What, about him? Over there?

MEG: What, Guthrie?

CORBY: Right.

MEG (*to* RAPITRONE): What *about* him? It's just Guthrie. When you've said that, you've said it all.

    CORBY *nods.*

RAPITRONE: He looks dead, to me.

MEG: He always looks that way.

CORBY: You known him long?

MEG: I know him. Not to *speak* to.

CORBY: What does *that* mean?

MEG: Well, *you've* seen him.

CORBY: Oh, yeh. But he's in your bed!

MEG: Guess again.

CORBY: What, that's not your bed? (*To* RAPITRONE) That's Guthrie's bed. (*To* MEG) You sleep in Guthrie's bed?

MEG: It's not Guthrie's bed.

CORBY: Then, whose is it?

RAPITRONE: Who do you think?

MEG: It's nobody's bed. We all use it. (*To* CORBY) You know how it is down here.

CORBY: Yeh, I know how it is.

> *Pause.*

(*Gesturing at the crates and boxes*) So, what about all this, then?

MEG: It's business.

CORBY: Mmmm. (*Brief pause*) There's a gum-ball machine in one of those boxes. You got any kids down here?

MEG: Other uses could be found for it. Take the dome, for instance — the glass bowl.

CORBY: Yeh?

MEG: Luba told me there was a geezer in here the other night, paid her to strip and put the bowl over her head.

CORBY: You don't say?

MEG: Yeh. Only, when she put it on, she started to sneeze from all the dust. Then the bowl fogged up with her breath, and she started to suffocate. That's when it came to her what the old sod was after all along, 'cause once she started choking, she said he came over all excited. That degenerate!

RAPITRONE: What's this, moral judgements? (*Contemptuously*) Oh, *very* nice.

MEG: You know, you're gonna wear out your arms with all that wheeling about. Take it easy, will you? You're giving me the chills.

CORBY (*to* RAPITRONE): Yeh, take it easy. Let me handle this. You'll have your say, just be patient.

> RAPITRONE *slows the pace of his wheeling, whips off the toque in disgust, and tosses it on to the bed.*

(*To* MEG) He'll be all right. He's had a hell of a time, you know? (*Brief pause*) So, what about this other girl, then? You were saying . . .

MEG: Luba.

CORBY: Yeh —

RAPITRONE: Luba. Don't forget!

CORBY: Yeh, don't worry. (*To* MEG) So, what happened?

MEG: She had trouble getting it off.

CORBY: The gum-ball dome.

MEG: Yeh. They're easy to get on, but not all that easy to get off.

CORBY: Must be the suction.

MEG: Hmmm? Oh, yeh.

CORBY: That night in the house, three nights ago, we heard Canamine calling for her. Sounded as though he were dying. Luba, Luba, he said. Joseph made me —

MEG: The old man —

CORBY: Yeh. Joseph made me turn off the lights. Is any of it coming back to you?

MEG: Why should it?

> *Pause.*

CORBY: Canamine was a sick man.

MEG: He looks well enough to me.

CORBY: He was off his food. I used to look in on him at the house. It was me that got him the room there when he needed it.

> *He pulls up a chair and sits, facing her.*
> *Pause.*

Oh, yeh, I used to look in on him all the time. Took him down here once to give him the feel of the place, it was all part of the service. But he didn't fancy the Underground then. He could've come down to stay long before this, but he didn't. That time when he was in the basket with me, coming down, I thought he was gonna pass out. (*Brief pause*) I held the lantern up to his face. He'd gone all pale. And he moaned, Get me back, get me back to the room before I die; I don't want to die down here. And he fell against me, gasping for breath.

Pause.

MEG: And you expect me to believe that.

RAPITRONE *comes to a halt beside the couch, facing* CORBY.

CORBY: It's the truth.

MEG *puts away the emery board, her hands jammed into her pockets.*

MEG (*indicating* RAPITRONE): And what about him?

CORBY: What do you mean?

MEG: How much of this can he corroborate?

RAPITRONE: Canamine was a sick man.

Pause.

He lived a long time in our house. He scarcely ever left his bed. Once in a while, he would come down to supper, but he never ate much. And I never heard him speak, until that last night. If it weren't for the sound of his footsteps on the ceiling and the stair, and that smell of the garret room about him, you'd have thought him a ghost.

Pause.

I was sick then, too. Worse than Canamine. The sickness crept into my eyes. Then, the numbness — no, the absence — the absence that was in my eyes streamed down my shoulders and arms into my legs. (*Nodding*) A slow process.

Pause.

When I could no longer hold down a respectable job, Corby took me on. (*Brief pause*) The night I met him, he was lying in a gutter, coughing blood. Some young hoodlums had worked him over. Broke his nose. It was the middle of winter, round three in the morning. He'd been lying there so long, his fingers were embedded in the ice. I cracked them loose with a screw-driver I had, and got him to hospital. (*Brief pause*) They had to cut off two of his fingers; but, to look at him, you'd never know it.

> MEG *glances at* CORBY's *hands. No missing fingers. She tilts her head back, sighs, and shuts her eyes.*
> *Pause.*

Corby here took me with him on the rounds, two or three nights a week. The collections, rendezvous with defectors, the odd tour of the Underground — oh, we've been down more than once together. (*Brief pause*) I wasn't with him the night he brought Canamine down in the basket. No. (*Brief pause*) I was home . . . with you.

> MEG's *expression slowly turns to one of sadness.*
> *Pause.*

All those nights — the nights Corby went off on his rounds alone — you put me to bed early. You stayed by me, pretending to read, watching my eyelids droop, thinking I'd gone to sleep, never realising that for me there was no real difference between the one darkness and the other. (*Brief pause*) I slept. But the sounds of the house never left me. The creak on the stair came in a murmur, and your soft footsteps across the ceiling; and in the walls, the puttering of the mice at midnight, into the still hours when my eyes would open and I'd lie in the second paralysis of waking, trying to lift the bedclothes and rise, but sinking instead, deeper and deeper, into the backward flow of my dream.

> MEG *is quietly weeping.*
> *Pause.*
> CORBY *rises and goes to the desk, where he stands leaning on the blotter, his back to* MEG *and* RAPITRONE. *The pained expression in his eyes turns gradually to one of guilt and sadness.*

MEG (*somberly*): You don't know . . . You can never know what it's been like, what it's like now, not to remember. (*Brief pause*) I was in a small room somewhere. Somewhere above the Underground. (*Brief pause*) My clothes had been taken away. They had taken away my clothes and thrown them in a heap with the other clothes. I say *they*, but I was alone there. (*Brief pause*) The smell was . . . suffocating. It was the sort of room that people go to die in. A narrow bed, a table. And, on the table, an empty, coated glass with a spoon in it.

She rises to a sitting position at the corner of the couch farthest from RAPITRONE. *Her hands remain in her pockets throughout.*

I thought someone would come to me there and take me away. Don't ask me why. I don't know why — I don't know now, I must've dreamed it. I can't even say for certain how long ago it was.

Pause.

I slept there alone, waiting. (*Brief pause*) For days and days I lay on that bed. I don't remember eating. I must've eaten. (*Brief pause*) I don't remember anything but lying there with the window shut and the blinds drawn. (*Brief pause*) I lay on that bed, staring at the hole the black smoke from an old lantern had etched in the ceiling.

Long pause.

RAPITRONE (*in hushed despair*): Who are you?

Long pause.

CORBY (*standing at the desk*): Canamine was a sick man. She used to slip up to his room — quite often, she told me — just to see if he was still breathing. She brought him his meals, but he never ate much. For him, a cup of chicken broth was something you drank to wash down the medicine. Myself, I thought he was going to die in that room. But he held on. Oh, when I'd first brought him, when I'd got you to take him in, I thought, He's faking, he's a hypochondriac. I thought he was neurotic. (*Brief pause*) But then, after a while, I began to realise how sick he really was, and that he actually seemed to be dying. She told me that . . . he'd lie there unconscious, as though he were in a coma, and nothing would wake him. So you see, he was too weak. It wasn't how you thought it was. (*Brief pause*) It wasn't really how you'd imagined it at all.

Pause.
Growing awareness in RAPITRONE*'s expression.*

The nights when you thought I'd gone off on the rounds alone, she left the back door unlocked. Other nights, when I brought you home, I never left. She'd put you to bed. I'd sit in the parlour, sometimes at the foot of the stair, waiting.

Tears stream down his cheeks. He swallows hard.

That first time, she grabbed me by the hand and led me up to Canamine's room. There was a strange, pained look in her eyes I didn't understand. I thought she was going to tell me he'd died. I thought perhaps she wanted me to carry him down to the lorry while you were asleep. (*Brief pause*) She didn't say anything. And Canamine seemed dead enough. His eyes were shut, and they were dark and hollow. His lips were blue under the light. (*Brief pause*) Then she began to sob.

> *Pause.*

You see, I . . . I really thought he was dead. I thought she was crying like that because she was afraid to have a dead man in the house. Afraid of what you might do when you found out the man upstairs had died in the room that used to be yours.

> *Pause.*
> RAPITRONE *stunned, dazed.* CORBY *turns toward him for the first time, and approaches.* RAPITRONE *shakes his head, sighing in disbelief.*
> CORBY *kneels beside the wheelchair.* RAPITRONE *turns his head away, the tears streaming down his cheeks.*

It would be wrong to blame her.

> CORBY *shuts his eyes; his head falls.* RAPITRONE*'s hands slide hesitantly up* CORBY*'s arms, as if to comfort him, then close round his neck. The two men struggle as* MEG *looks on in horror. Sounds of* CORBY *choking.*
> CORBY *goes limp, slumps forward, dead.*
> RAPITRONE *draws a revolver from inside* CORBY*'s jacket, shoves him to the floor and takes aim, with both hands, at* CORBY*'s head.*
> MEG *screams.*
> RAPITRONE *looks at her, a blank expression in his eyes, turns the gun on himself, and fires. He slumps forward, clutching at his chest, the blood gushing over his fingers, and falls to the floor on top of* CORBY *as running footsteps are heard in the outer hall.*
> MEG *drops to her knees beside the two dead men, stunned, a blank expression in her eyes.*
> GUS, *pistol in hand, bursts into the room, followed by* JOSEPH, *both dressed as before.*

GUS: 'Ere, what the bloody hell's goin' on up here?

> *He takes in the situation.*

(*Hushed*) Jesus Christ.

He stares at the two dead men, whistles, and shakes his head.

(*To* MEG) You'd best clear off out of it.

Pause.

'Ere, Meg. You shouldn't be in here, girl. (*Gently*) Come on. Up you get.

He lifts MEG *to her feet.*

Now, remember. You don't know nothin'. You in't seen nothin'. Got it? You never even been here tonight.

JOSEPH: Get her out of here. You have a key to the room?

GUS: Yeh.

JOSEPH: Right, then lock the door behind you, and don't let anyone else come up.

GUS: But Mister Canamine, I —

JOSEPH: Never mind him, I'll take care of it. (*Pointing to* RAPITRONE) Get his gun.

GUS: Right.

> GUS *picks up the revolver.*
> *Exit* MEG *and* GUS. *The door closes.*
> *Sound of a key turning in the lock.*
> JOSEPH *kneels by the bodies of* CORBY *and* RAPITRONE. *Quietly, solemnly, he studies them.*
> *Pause.*
> *The bedclothes are flung aside.* CANAMINE *emerges, dressed as before, the 'I Quit' button still pinned to his lapel, a big cigar in his mouth. He wears* RAPITRONE*'s black spectacles.*
> CANAMINE *sits on the edge of the bed and calmly lights his cigar with an expensive lighter.*
> *Pause.*
> JOSEPH *watches him without emotion.*

CANAMINE (*facing the audience*): Joseph, is that you? I can't see a bloody thing with these glasses.

> *He rises, walks haltingly from the bed to the wheelchair, groping the air with his hands, like a blind man, as they converse.*

Hell of a lot of action round here, lately.

JOSEPH: Who are you?

CANAMINE: I'm a sick man.

> *He chuckles, coughs.*

Bloody cigars, they'll be the death of me.

> *Pause.*

Well, how do you like the Underground? Are you settling in all right?

JOSEPH (*rising*): I'm beginning to get the feel of it.

CANAMINE: Good, good. If you want anything, just let me know. Money, women, the piss, it's no problem.

JOSEPH: I'll bear it in mind.

CANAMINE: Good. (*Brief pause*) By the way, you did the proper thing.

JOSEPH: Hmmm?

CANAMINE: Telling Gus to lock the door.

JOSEPH: Mmmm —

CANAMINE: He's a good man with the bottle and siphon, is Gus — dependable. But he annihilates the mother tongue. He can't be depended upon to handle — shall we say, more delicate concerns? — with the finesse I've come to expect from you, Joseph.

JOSEPH (*ironically*): You're too kind.

CANAMINE: It's the simple truth.

> *He bumps against the wheelchair, kicks* RAPITRONE's *body clear of it, and sits.*

(*Blindly wheeling himself about*) I could do with a man like you down here, to help with my mopping-up operations.

JOSEPH: Careful —

CANAMINE (*still wheeling*): Ah, you're right. You're right. Got to watch how I put things, eh? How I use the mother tongue? You're absolutely right. You never can tell who might be listening behind a wall. Even now, as we pass the time so amicably in frivolous conversation, there may be someone lurking under the bed or in one of the crates, stenographic pad and pencil at the ready, lying in ambush for the passive voice or the unfortunate participial phrase. True, we must maintain our vigilance at all times. But you needn't concern yourself. We're quite secure here, I promise you.

He ends up behind the desk, removes the black spectacles and tosses them into a drawer, opens another drawer and extracts his regular pair of glasses, which he puts on. He switches on the desk lamp and sets his cigar in an ashtray.

(*Rubber-stamping orders and receipts*) My God, the paperwork! You wouldn't believe it. Just to move a few crates and boxes out of here! I spoke to Corby about it — oh, we had quite a chin-wag over it — but he was as much in the dark as I was. He didn't know a thing. I've got no idea where they're supposed to've been sent. It wasn't *here*, that's for certain. Pull up a chair, this won't take long.

JOSEPH *complies as* CANAMINE *rounds off his paperwork with a flurry of signatures.*

Ah, that's done. (*More relaxed*) Well, what can I do for you, old chap?

He takes up his cigar and begins puffing away again.
Pause.

JOSEPH: You mentioned Corby.

CANAMINE: Yes. A fine young man, someone upon whom you could depend to take on any assignment, however dubious or unsavoury. It's Corby's sort that made this country what it is today.

JOSEPH: You're much better, aren't you? You're getting better.

CANAMINE (*coughs*): I'm a sick man. (*Puffing away, in conversational tone*) You've no idea the pain I've had to bear, the long nights of immobility, nights on which I was often called upon to witness acts of unspeakable depravity.

JOSEPH (*archly*): I see.

CANAMINE: I'm a reasonable man, Joseph. I think you know me to be a reasonable man.

JOSEPH: None more reasonable.

CANAMINE: Thank you. I appreciate that, I really do. (*Wheeling himself to the crates and boxes*) That's why I hope you won't take it amiss if I ask you to lend me a hand with these, seeing as we're locked in together. We might as well make the most of the situation. I'm not sleepy, are you?

JOSEPH (*rising*): No.

CANAMINE: Excellent! Now, let's begin. (*Pointing to a box*) Open it and we'll examine the contents.

A dozen toilet rolls are stacked on top of the box.

JOSEPH (*removing them*): What're you gonna do, wipe your arse with all this toilet tissue?

CANAMINE: It's for my mother.

JOSEPH: You mean your mother's down here?

CANAMINE: Mmmm, but keep it to yourself. (*Brief pause*) Sometimes one of the birds pops round to her and drops off a roll or two.

JOSEPH: The birds.

CANAMINE: They can keep a secret.

JOSEPH: Where is she, then?

CANAMINE: My mother?

JOSEPH: Mmmm.

CANAMINE: Who can remember a thing like that?

JOSEPH: Ah.

CANAMINE (*rubbing his hands in glee*): Anyhow, we've got more interesting fish to fry, eh?

> JOSEPH *peers into the box.*

Can you see anything?

JOSEPH: Yes, wonderful things.

CANAMINE (*chortling with delight*): Ah!

> JOSEPH *pulls a nurse's cap out of the box.*

(*Crestfallen*) What's that?

> JOSEPH *holds it up.*

(*Irritated*) Oh, *those* people.

> JOSEPH *places the nurse's cap on* CANAMINE*'s head.*

(*Dryly*) Are there any more wonderful things in there?

> JOSEPH *pulls a bath towel out of the box and holds it up for* CANAMINE *to read.*

What's that? Chubby Combustibles? (*Brief pause*) That reminds me of something. (*Vexed*) What do they send this stuff down here for? Are they daft? What *can* they be thinking of? What use could we possibly have for...for Chubby Combustibles?

> JOSEPH *spreads the towel over* CANAMINE*'s legs, letters forward. The towel's cartoon illustration: between the words 'Chubby Combustibles', a voluptuous nude woman with enormous projecting buttocks smiles and winks over her shoulder.*
> CANAMINE*'s legs assume the slackness of paralysis.*

What else is in there? Perhaps we ought to try another box.

JOSEPH *pulls a bouquet of roses out of the box.*

Ah roses.

JOSEPH *hands the bouquet to* CANAMINE.

(*Sniffing the roses*) Mmmm, *that* takes me back. (*Brief pause*) I couldn't have been much more than twenty. I met her in another country.

JOSEPH: Where? When?

CANAMINE: She was dark, beautiful. (*Brief pause*) No, she was fair. I'll never forget her.

JOSEPH: Her name.

CANAMINE: I saw her for the first time in the reading room of the library, under the great, clouded dome. There, even on the sunniest of days, the shelves and the long mahogany tables were plunged in gloom.

JOSEPH: A country in a southern latitude.

CANAMINE: A cold, northern country. (*Brief pause*) A large book lay open before her, under the green shade of the lamp.

JOSEPH: She was beautiful.

CANAMINE: Incomparable.

JOSEPH: A literate woman.

CANAMINE: In the extreme.

JOSEPH: Face like a rose.

CANAMINE: I was lonely, a sick man. Even then. I'd bring her flowers and court her under the linden trees when the leaves turned and the season of mists began.

JOSEPH: When the armies were in the north.

CANAMINE: It was a long time ago. Ah, the tricks time plays on the memory. It's a treacherous thing — dangerous, even. You go along for years thinking you've mastered it, then suddenly the trap-door springs open beneath your bed. You could be breathing your last or shagging away at the landlord's wife when it happens. Suddenly the floor gives way and you find yourself in a wheelchair, clutching a bouquet of roses.

He tosses the bouquet on to the bodies of CORBY *and* RAPITRONE.
Pause.

JOSEPH: In the north, is that where you lost your memory?

CANAMINE (*wheeling to a new position*): Don't speak to me of the north! Open another box.

JOSEPH opens another box and peers into it.

What do you see?

JOSEPH: Nothing.

CANAMINE (*apprehensively*): What?

JOSEPH: Nothing. It's empty.

CANAMINE: No —

JOSEPH: The box is empty.

CANAMINE swallows hard.

CANAMINE: Are you certain? I mean, who would take the trouble to send an empty box? Who would bother?

JOSEPH turns to box upside down, shakes it.
Pause.

JOSEPH: It must be a mistake.

CANAMINE (*with mad conviction*): Yes, that's it! Of course. It's a mistake! There's been a mistake —

JOSEPH: The man who sent it —

CANAMINE: Or the woman! The man or the woman who sent it —

JOSEPH: Whoever it was —

CANAMINE: They — they forgot to pack what they wanted to send!

JOSEPH: Or forgot what it was they wanted to send.

CANAMINE (*to himself*): No —

JOSEPH: That makes more sense —

CANAMINE (*to himself*): No —

JOSEPH: And sent . . .

CANAMINE: What?

> *Pause.*

JOSEPH: Emptiness.

CANAMINE (*shaking his head*): No.

JOSEPH: Emptiness.

CANAMINE (*pleading*): No?

JOSEPH (*bearing down on him*): Emptiness.

CANAMINE (*whining*): No?

JOSEPH: Emptiness! Nothing!

> *The two are eye to eye.* CANAMINE *stares up at* JOSEPH *in horror. Pause.*

(*Calmly*) Who are you?

> CANAMINE *wheels himself backwards. The wheelchair bumps against the bodies of* CORBY *and* RAPITRONE. CANAMINE *turns his head and looks down at them, removing his nurse's cap. He looks back at* JOSEPH, *stunned.*

CANAMINE: Who do you *think* I am?

> *He stubs his cigar out on the arm of the wheelcair and flings it away, gasping.*
> *Pause.*
>
> (*Distantly*) I am a man . . . who has seen emperors and popes lying under the mud, their faces caked in blood and the excrement of worms. (*Brief pause*) I've seen women sell their sons and daughters into bondage for a crust of bread and a cup of water.
>
> *Pause.*
>
> (*Pointedly, to* JOSEPH) I am a man . . . who has seen how a man can die.
>
> *Pause.*
> JOSEPH *takes an involuntary step backwards, but is still quietly defiant.*
>
> (*Indicating* CORBY *and* RAPITRONE) Look at them, Joseph. Time is a treacherous thing. (*Brief pause*) These two young men would still be with us now, talking, disputing, raging with lust and jealousy, if it weren't for your murderous obsession.

JOSEPH (*shaking his head, unconvinced*): No.

CANAMINE: Mmmm?

> *Brief pause.*
> *He beckons* JOSEPH *with his finger, turns, and wheels himself to the window.*

Put out the lights.

> JOSEPH *follows, switching off the lights.*
> JOSEPH *and* CANAMINE *at the window, two silhouettes against the dim, bluish haze . . .*

It'll be dawn in a few hours. Look down there, Master Doctor. In a few hours, it'll be dark as pitch. All the streetlamps will have flickered out, and the avenues of the Underground will be an abyss of wandering lanterns again.

> *Fade to black.*

ACT THREE

Scene 1

Darkness, and the distant sound of a howling wind. Two lanterns, one above the other, glide from far upstage into the dim, hazy light downstage centre. It is JOSEPH, *pushing* CANAMINE *along in the wheelchair. They seem still to be advancing as the howling wind increases,* JOSEPH *in his overcoat, a small lantern strapped to his head,* CANAMINE *in a nurse's cap and cape, the 'Chubby Combustibles' towel over his legs, holding an old lantern out before him. White nylon stockings cover their faces.*

CANAMINE (*frantic, above the wind*): Faster, Joseph! We're not going fast enough!

    JOSEPH *quickens his 'pace' to a trot.*

  At this rate, we'll never make it!

JOSEPH: What do you see?

CANAMINE: Nothing! (*Brief pause*) Faster! Go faster! (*Poining right*) There! There!

    They turn right and exit, full-speed, into the wind and darkness.

Scene 2

Darkness. As the howling of the wind dies, a low mist rolls in, gliding over the ground from right to left.
  Pause.

ACT THREE   215

Fade up slowly MEG *and* LUBA *standing up centre, side by side against the darkness, wearing nurses' caps and black full-length capes.*
Pause.
Enter CANAMINE *and* JOSEPH *from the left, as before, but without their nylon masks;* CANAMINE, *without his glasses, asleep in the wheelchair, the old lantern hanging from his neck. They stop.*
The women go to them. MEG *crouches to examine* CANAMINE — *cupping her hand under his chin, lifting it, letting it drop* — *as* LUBA *removes the lamp strapped to* JOSEPH's *head.*

JOSEPH: Where are we? What place is this?

> LUBA *sets* JOSEPH's *lantern on* CANAMINE's *lap.*
> MEG *wheels* CANAMINE *away.*

(*Calling after* MEG) Mind how you go, he's a sick man.

LUBA (*taking* JOSEPH's *arm*): She'll look after him.

> *Exit* MEG *and* CANAMINE *into the shadows right, as* JOSEPH *and* LUBA *walk to centre stage.*

JOSEPH: It's cold here.

LUBA: It's always cold here, Joseph.

> *Pause.*

JOSEPH: Luba.

LUBA: Yes.

> *Pause.*
> *Ten unidentified men emerge from the shadows right. Wearing drab overcoats and fedoras, their collars turned up to conceal their faces, they file past* LUBA *and* JOSEPH *with their hands in their pockets, followed by* YOUNG JOSEPH, *who wears an overcoat, gloves, a bowler hat, and sports a thin handlebar moustache.*

JOSEPH: Who are they? Where are they going?

LUBA: Can't you see their faces?

JOSEPH: No.

> *Exit the ten into the shadows left, as* LUBA *catches* YOUNG JOSEPH *by the arm. He appears dazed.*

LUBA (*to* YOUNG JOSEPH, *pointing right*): Look over there, Joseph. What do you see?

> *The mist subsides.*
> *Fade up on* MAGGIE *right, a girl of eighteen, standing before a low stone wall, dressed in winter gear circa 1919. Snow is falling.*

YOUNG JOSEPH (*to himself*): Maggie.

> *He goes to* MAGGIE, *joins hands with her.*

LUBA (*to* JOSEPH): It was all so long ago. Do you remember her?

JOSEPH (*ironically*): She was fair. No, she was dark. I'll never forget her.

> LUBA *smiles, bringing a bouquet of roses from under her cape.*
> JOSEPH *takes the bouquet and goes to* MAGGIE *as* YOUNG JOSEPH *steps backwards into the darkness right.*

MAGGIE: Joseph! Right on time.

JOSEPH: I set off early so I wouldn't be late. (*Handing her the bouquet*) For you.

MAGGIE: Ooo, they're beautiful!

> *She sniffs the roses.*

Wherever did you find them?

> JOSEPH *snatches the bouquet out of* MAGGIE's *hands and chucks it over the wall. He takes her in his arms, kisses her violently, passionately, groping at her long skirt.*
> *Blackout* MAGGIE *and* JOSEPH.

LUBA (*shaking her head*): Tch-tch-tch-tch-tch.

JOSEPH (*emerging from the shadows right*): The face was familiar. Bring her back, I've something to say to her.

LUBA: You should've thought of that before. What got into you? I thought you loved her.

JOSEPH (*ironically*): I'd have cut off my head for her. It's a long time since I thought of Maggie. But, seeing her again like that, standing in the snow, it all came back to me, the time I'd wasted when we could've been —

LUBA: Don't make me laugh.

Fade up on an old floor lamp, up left. MAGDA, *dressed as a flapper, is wheeled into the light, lying provocatively on a settee, vintage 1925, a long cigarette holder between her fingers.*

MAGDA (*gliding in, suggestively*): Joooseph. (*Brief pause*) Got a match?

Fade up on a sideboard, down left. YOUNG JOSEPH, *clad in a smoking jacket of many colours, stands holding a cocktail shaker, his hair slicked back à la Valentino, without his moustache.*

He sets the shaker down, strikes a match and holds it to the tip of MAGDA'*s cigarette, his cupped hands trembling. She steadies his hands for the light, then guides the match toward her lips and blows it out.*

YOUNG JOSEPH *returns to the sideboard, pours out two martinis, hands one to* MAGDA, *then leans back against the sideboard, sipping his drink.*

(*Sipping her drink*) Mmmm, I thought I'd never get the baby to bed. I really should stop calling him that, he'll be three in November. Mmmm, think of that. Already three years since little Herbert popped out of my oven. But, you've got to admit, I'm none the worse for it. (*Posturing*) I mean, look at me. Do I look like a mother of three years?

Pause.

YOUNG JOSEPH *sips his drink.*

(*Alternately smoking and sipping*) Mmmm, you and Herbert have come a long way in the past two years. I remember when you first came to us. You couldn't speak a word of the language. Now, look at you. With a bit of coaxing from Herbert and me along the way, you've learned to speak the language of this country like a native. (*Brief pause*) Oh, and with a bit of help from Voss, too, I suppose. You know, it's not been easy, Joseph. I mean for Voss and me. It's not been easy with Voss away half the time and me having to work three nights a week when he *is* here. (*Brief pause*) I get lonely.

She sits up.

Remember when we had you in nappies, you and Herbert? (*Laughing*) You were both so cute, and I had to wash and powder you both? I was glad we did it, really. It put me more at ease and helped the illusion, so I could get used to your learning the language from scratch, from the cradle up.

> *She pats the couch, beckoning* YOUNG JOSEPH, *who remains aloof, sipping his drink.*
> *Pause.*

(*Intimately*) I know you like me, Joseph. (*Rising*) I remember what happened every time I used to change your nappy.

> *She puts her arms round his neck.*

(*Pressing herself against him*) Mmmm, let's go to the bedroom. Come with Magda. (*Kissing him*) Mmmm. Lie with me, Joseph. (*Pulling him toward the shadows left*) Lie with me.

> *Blackout* MAGDA *and* YOUNG JOSEPH.
> *Pause.*

JOSEPH: I never had that much hair, even as a young man. My hair was thin.

> *Pause.*

LUBA: I've got to leave you now, Joseph.

JOSEPH: Stay. The woman was very good. Who was she?

VOICE OF CANAMINE (*in the darkness*): My wife.

> *Exit* LUBA *backwards into the shadows.*
> *Sounds of a woman weeping.*
> *Fade up slowly on* MAGDA, YOUNG JOSEPH *and* CANAMINE, *stage right.* CANAMINE *lies in a brass bed, his head visible above the covers.* MAGDA, *in a Chinese housecoat, and* YOUNG JOSEPH, *in shirtsleeves, stand together by the bed. On the near side, a night table cluttered with medicine bottles, a coated glass with a spoon in it.*
> MAGDA *is weeping.*

CANAMINE (*like a dying man*): More light, more light.

Pause.

(*To* YOUNG JOSEPH) There's no use denying it.

He brings the smoking jacket of many colours from beneath the covers.

This is proof enough.

MAGDA *throws herself across his chest, sobbing hysterically.*

(*Glancing about, gently*) Where's little Herbert? My little boy. I want to see my son once more before I die.

MAGDA (*through bitter tears*): No, no. You're not going to die. Oh, Voss! Voss!

YOUNG JOSEPH *breaks down and throws himself across* CANAMINE *'s legs, weeping hysterically.*

CANAMINE (*to* JOSEPH): He was a young man. He gave you everything. He took you in when you came from overseas, provided for your every need, gave you his money and a home, a place to eat and lie in, so you could learn the language of this country. He didn't *have* to do it! His wife looked after you, rubbed you up with baby oil, powdered your arse for you. And this is how you repaid him. (*Brief pause*) He gave you everything and you gave him ashes, and a pair of horns. (*Getting out of bed*) He handed the carving knife to you on a silver platter, and you stabbed him in the back.

Fade to black YOUNG JOSEPH *and* MAGDA. *Their weeping subsides.* CANAMINE *approaches* JOSEPH; *he is wearing striped pyjamas, the 'I Quit' button pinned above his breast pocket.*

It killed him, Joseph. He died of grief. He was a young man. He should've had more sense.

Pause.

JOSEPH (*slyly*): But I paid, didn't I? I always manage to pay in the end.

Spotlight on LUBA *and* MAGDA *up left.* MAGDA, *wearing her flapper outfit with cigarette holder, in the witness box;* LUBA, *in judge's gown, on the bench, knitting an afghan.*

MAGDA: He ... He tore the roses out of my hands and threw himself on top of me!

Male voices in the darkness: mutters and cries of outraged decency.

He was like a wild animal! (*Producing the smoking jacket of many colours*) Look, here's his smoking jacket!

The clamour increases. LUBA *bangs the gavel repeatedly.*
Blackout LUBA *and* MAGDA. *Silence.*

CANAMINE: Yes, hell hath no fury . . . You treated her badly in the end.

JOSEPH: We all pay for our mistakes. I paid.

CANAMINE (*removing* JOSEPH's *overcoat*): Yes, Magda saw to that. You paid, under lock and key!

Exit CANAMINE *backwards into the shadows,* JOSEPH's *coat in his hands, as lights come up on a long wooden table and bench down right.*
JOSEPH *is wearing pyjamas identical to* CANAMINE's. *Three large numerals above his breast pocket: 432. He stands alone at centre stage, eyeing the prisoners who sit at the table, each wearing identical pyjamas, each with a tin bowl and spoon before him, as though awaiting a meal; all with various numbers above their breast pockets.*
Unintelligible mutterings.
Upstage scrim, light up slowly: high, barred windows in dark stone.
The prisoners, facing front, from right to left: FINCH, HODGE, BLOCKER, DOOLEY, STILLER, RANTZ.

BLOCKER: Jesus —

HODGE: Aw, come off it, Dooley —

RANTZ (*to* STILLER): Shit, here we go again —

DOOLEY (*to* HODGE): What, are you sayin' I'm round the twist or somethin' —

FINCH (*disgusted*): Jesus Christ —

DOOLEY (*to* HODGE): Is that what you're sayin'?

HODGE (*to* FINCH, *shaking his head*): Shit —

DOOLEY (*to* STILLER): Is that what he's sayin' —

ACT THREE

RANTZ: 'Ere, Dooley, come on, will ya? Shut up. You fuckin' imbecile —

STILLER: 'Ere, ease off. You want the fuckin' screws to put us on another one o' them starvation diets? Let the bloke talk. (*To* HODGE) Let him talk.

HODGE (*to* DOOLEY): So, go on, talk. (*To* FINCH) It'll just be the same old story, the one he tells over and over again. I'm not listenin'.

DOOLEY: So, don't listen, then! In't nobody asked you to listen! So, don't listen —

HODGE: I won't —

DOOLEY: Fuckin' arsehole.

> *Pause.*

> Like I said, I'm sure she must've been a beautiful girl, standin' like that, half naked in the bedroom window. For all I know, she was *completely* naked, unless she was wearin' one o' them flimsy see-thru numbers and the heat o' the night made it stick to her skin. Fair or dark, I couldn't tell you. The light was behind her. She stood in the window, arrangin' a bouquet of roses in a glass vase. (*Brief pause*) She switched off the light. I waited. Then I climbed up the vine trellis, and in through the window. (*Brief pause*) I looked for her, but she was gone. Searched the house from top to bottom — nothin'. (*Brief pause*) They nicked me for breakin' an' enterin', at my age! She testified against me at the trial, and she weren't even there! She had on this turban hat with a veil down over her face. And her hair, just when I might've found out what colour it *really* was . . . (*Gesture of futility*) Fair or dark, I couldn't tell you. It was all under the hat, every strand of it. Every bleedin' strand. The eyebrows were dark — I could see 'em through the veil — but, just how dark, I couldn't tell you. I'll never forget 'em.

> *Fade to deep blue the prisoners, frozen, silent.*

CANAMINE (*strolling out of the shadows with a* GUARD): By the way, did you happen to see the part in my hair anywhere about? I seem to have misplaced it.

> *The* GUARD *shrugs.*

> Search the grounds. Leave no stone or brick unturned.

> *The* GUARD *hurries off into the shadows.*

CANAMINE *as before, save that the 'I Quit' button has moved from his left to his right side. Above his breast pocket, the number 8.*

(*To* JOSEPH) What's your name, young man? I've had my eye on you. You're the one who's in for chucking the roses away. It was in all the papers. (*With his arm round* JOSEPH, *shaking him in earnest commiseration*) A grave miscarriage of justice, my boy, a grave miscarriage of justice. You should never've left your jacket behind.

  JOSEPH *shoots him a sly look.*
  Pause.

Allow me to introduce myself. (*Proffering a cigar*) You smoke? No? (*Lighting the cigar, puffing*) Doc Whatsup's the name. Round here everybody calls me Whatsup Doc —

JOSEPH (*chiming in*): Whatsup Doc.

  Pause.
  Silence.

CANAMINE: Listen to that wind.

  Pause.

JOSEPH: What wind?

CANAMINE: I suppose you know, they've made me the prison psychiatrist.

  The prisoners at table fade to black.
  Light up psychiatrist's couch and chair down left.

Oh, I'm not saying it's the job I *wanted*, spending the whole day listening to other people's dreams — you can *have* it. You should hear the dreams some of these fools come up with. Make your hair stand on end, I'm not lyin'. Know what I think? I think they make 'em up, just to see what I'll say, that's what *I* think. Myself, I *never* dream. (*Lying on the couch*) No, I'm a man of action. Marital aids, that's my *real* line. At least it *was*, before they nicked me for running a string of whoopee parlours above the downtown surgery.

  JOSEPH *sits in the chair.*

I tried to explain that the girls were clean, every last one of 'em a registered nurse, that the beds were for patients only; but it didn't wash. We had a large and varied clientele, blokes coming in at all hours of the day and night to take our treatments. Nothing fancy. It was all fairly basic, the same treatment for everyone, with variations to suit the personal needs of the patient — that's where we made the *real* money. (*Brief pause*) Anyhow, the birds were run out of town by the coppers so they wouldn't be able to testify at the trial. Blimey, half our patients were on the municipal bench! They couldn't afford the risk. I hear from the girls, now and then. I get postcards and letters from all over the country. Most of them have gone into evangelical work. They're crackin' it fine. That's where the *big* money is. But, then, they had the proper sort of training for it. Could've been a preacher myself, one of the Lord's own, but I'd rather work with the diseased. (*Brief pause*) I'm planning to open a men's clinic when I get out. Going to go first class all the way, this time. I could do with a lad like you. You know how to listen, how to keep your mouth shut, unlike the rest of the marbleheads round here. I'd show you the ropes — you know, turn you into a proper doctor. It wouldn't take you long to catch on. We'd have a couple o' birds to help us out — only, this time it's legit, everything on the up and up — they're therapists, see? We get them diplomas to hang on the wall, from the University of Basel or someplace. You can do whatever you want as long as you got the old sheepskin, that's what my dad used to say. So, what about it, lad? Are you in?

Pause.

We can do a scarper any time we want. Escaping is the least of our worries, now they've made you a trustee.

JOSEPH: What do you mean?

CANAMINE *sits up, look about.*
Pause.

CANAMINE (*with a sweeping gesture*): Do you see any screws about?

JOSEPH (*nodding, with a smile*): Ah.

Scrim: fade to black. Sounds of a woman giggling in the dark. JOSEPH *and* CANAMINE *rise, turning toward the giggle.*
Blackout JOSEPH *and* CANAMINE */fade up on* MADGE *and* PATIENT *up right; a bed with satin sheets, an ottoman before a folding hospital screen.* MADGE *wears a short lab coat, stethoscope, high heels, black mesh stockings with red suspenders, gaudy make-up circa 1930, and nothing else. The cadaverous* PATIENT *is clad in a hospital gown and squats on the ottoman.*

MADGE *pulls at the bow of a large square box that sits on the bed, tears away the gift-wrapping, lifts off the lid and peers in, brushing the packing-tissue aside.*

MADGE (*giggling*): Ooooo —

PATIENT: What do you see?

She reaches into the box and pulls out the glass dome of a gum-ball machine, holds it aloft, and flashes the PATIENT *a questioning smile.*
Pause.
Sound of a door opening behind the hospital screen: riotous female laughter, noises of tumbling furniture, scurrying feet. The door closes: silence.
Enter CANAMINE *from behind the hospital screen, clad in pyjama bottoms and slippers, shirtless beneath his lab coat, and smoking his cigar.*

CANAMINE (*to* PATIENT): I've got the new Medical Inspector in there. Joseph and Kimberley are pullin' out all the stops to keep him entertained, but he's a hard man to please.

He brings a large roll of notes from his lab-coat pocket.

(*Counting off eight notes*) Here, do us a favour. (*Stuffing the notes into the* PATIENT*'s hand*) Pop round the corner and fetch us a couple of bottles of champagne, the cheapest you can find.

MADGE *slips the* PATIENT *into an overcoat.*

PATIENT: How many you want?

CANAMINE: Two. No, make it three. You can join us. Only, keep it under your hat.

CANAMINE *caresses* MADGE.

PATIENT: Château Merde?

CANAMINE (*distracted*): What? Yeh, fine, fine.

Exit PATIENT *as* CANAMINE *and* MADGE *collapse on to the brass bed.*
Blackout.
Fade up slowly on JOSEPH *and* RUTH *down left. They sit in wing chairs, a*

table and lamp between them, JOSEPH *reading the paper,* RUTH *knitting an afghan.* JOSEPH *and* RUTH *clad circa 1930. Their eyes never meet.*
   Long pause.

RUTH: Someone by the name of Kimberley rang up today.

   Pause.

JOSEPH *(from behind the paper)*: I don't know any Kimberley.

RUTH: She was calling for Doc What's-his-face.

JOSEPH: You know his name.

   Pause.

RUTH: This Kimberley knows *you* . . . quite well, by the sound of her.

   He lowers the paper.

JOSEPH: Oh. You mean the new girl.

RUTH: Mmmm.

   Pause.

JOSEPH: University girl. Doc Whatsup just took her on. Smart as a whip. Not my type, though. Too broad.

RUTH: You *like* broad women. *(Brief pause)* I'm broad.

JOSEPH: That's different.

   He turns the page.
   Pause.

   Did Luba take her medicine?

RUTH: I finally got her to take it.

JOSEPH: Good. Then, she'll sleep tonight.

RUTH: Mmmm.

Pause.

Do you have to spend so much of your time with that . . . veterinarian?

JOSEPH: He's a brilliant man. He's taught me a lot. The least I can do is go when he calls me.

RUTH (*contemptuously*): The Mayo Brothers. You help that quack mend a few leaky faucets and, right away, he's a brilliant diagnostician.

JOSEPH: You know we can do with the extra money.

RUTH: Why do we need the extra money, so you can —

JOSEPH: Look, Ruth, we've been over this a hundred times. Without the money I make helping the Doc with his special cases, without that extra money, I won't be able to bring my brothers over from America.

RUTH: You told me you *hated* your brothers, and you expect me to believe all this is for them?

JOSEPH: I want them here. (*Brief pause*) It'll be my revenge.

RUTH: Revenge. For what?

Pause.

JOSEPH: You'll go blind if you keep that up. That knitting. (*Brief pause*) You'll be needing glasses.

Pause.

VOICE OF CANAMINE (*in the darkness*): Sad.

Fade up on CANAMINE *centre stage, as before, wearing a stethoscope,* MADGE's *red suspenders sticking out of his lab-coat pocket, no cigar.* RUTH *and* JOSEPH *begin slow fade to black.*

You loved her, once. There was a time when you'd have eaten the hair in the sink, if she'd asked you to.

Pause.

I didn't want to put a wall between you, I really didn't. That wasn't my idea at all.

RUTH *and* JOSEPH *in darkness.*
Pause.

Joseph, the first night Ruth came to you, do you remember? You were asleep.

Through scrim, far upstage: a vast night sky, glimmering stars.
CANAMINE *in a deep-blue light.*

You were sleeping, alone in the night, under the stars, lost in an unending dream. From the hills and the lilies, Ruth came. Ruth came to Joseph, treading the waters of a hundred ponds where the wind shimmered and eclipsed the moon. Ruth came, waist-high in a barley field, into Joseph's long, unending dream.

The night sky fades to black.
JOSEPH *steps out of the shadows.*
Fade up slowly from deep blue JOSEPH *and* CANAMINE. *They stare at one another, dazed.*
Fade up on GAD *and* ASHER *down right.*
Pause.

Your brothers, Joseph, from America.

JOSEPH (*contemptuously*): Gad and Asher, my brothers.

GAD *and* ASHER *sit side by side on a couch, noisily sipping tea. A floor lamp beside the couch, a coffee table before it.*
Pause.
Fade up on RUTH *sitting in an armchair, facing the brothers at an angle far right, sipping tea. She is wearing glasses.*

(*To* CANAMINE) No!

CANAMINE (*finger to lips*): Ssssh!

RUTH *rises, sets her cup and saucer on the table, and stands before the brothers with her legs wide apart. The brothers stare up at her over their teacups.*
Pause.
Slowly, RUTH *lifts the hem of her pleated skirt, higher, higher. The brothers' eyes follow over their teacups.*

JOSEPH: No! No!

> *Quick fade to black* RUTH *and the brothers as* JOSEPH *rushes toward the scene and is engulfed in its darkness.*
> *Pause.*
> JOSEPH *emerges from the shadows.*

Did you have to show me *that?*

CANAMINE: They were your brothers. Was that the revenge you'd planned for them?

JOSEPH (*urgently*): Bring them back. I'll kill them. I should've done it long ago.

CANAMINE: They're dead.

> *Pause.*

JOSEPH (*remembering his age*): Yes.

CANAMINE: No one lives for ever, Joseph.

> *Pause.*

Ruth is dead now, as well. She died young.

> *Fade up on* RUTH. *She lies, blind, on her deathbed upstage left, beckoning* JOSEPH. *On the night table beside the brass bed, a clutter of medicine bottles, a coated glass with a spoon in it.*

RUTH (*weakly*): Joseph? (*Brief pause*) Joseph?

JOSEPH (*rushing to her bedside*): Ruth! (*His voice breaking*) Oh, my God! Ruth!

> *Quick fade* CANAMINE *to black.*

RUTH (*touching his face*): Ah, Joseph.

> *Pause.*

Do you remember our first night together?

JOSEPH: Yes —

RUTH: The night I came to you in a field of stars when you were dreaming?

JOSEPH: I remember.

RUTH: Never forget it, Joseph. Forget everything else, but never forget that night.

JOSEPH: I won't. I won't forget.

Pause.

RUTH (*gaspng*): Joseph?

JOSEPH: I'm here. I'm right here —

RUTH: Joseph, promise me. The children . . . Luba and the boys. Promise me —

JOSEPH: Yes.

Pause.

RUTH: Promise me you'll look after them. I . . .

She dies.
CANAMINE steps out of the shadows, as before, but now his lab-coat pocket is empty.
Pause.

JOSEPH: Ruth? (*Brief pause*) Oh, God! Ruth!

He throws himself across her chest, sobbing.

CANAMINE (*closing the dead woman's eyes*): I tried to save her, but there was nothing I could do. (*Sadly, with quiet sincerity*) You should have called in a *real* doctor.

Fade to deep blue.
Sound of a distant wind.
Through scrim, the grave site far upstage: fade up slowly the rise of a hill buried under the snow, a grey sky, the tops of a few dead trees looming thin in the distance; along the summit, to the right, a withered tree beside an open grave. Pall-bearers are moving toward the grave from the left, carrying a wooden coffin with large brass fittings on their shoulders, followed by a

small procession of mourners, YOUNG JOSEPH *at its head; nine men in all, one woman, all in black overcoats and hats, their faces obscured, save for* YOUNG JOSEPH, *who is bare-headed. There is no priest, no minister, no rabbi.*

Your brothers came to the funeral. They rode with you in the undertaker's car. You never said a word. You never even looked at them.

JOSEPH (*bitterly*): I looked at them.

CANAMINE: They were your brothers.

JOSEPH: I worked my fingers to the bone to bring them over.

CANAMINE: Mmmm, to take your revenge.

JOSEPH: Yes.

CANAMINE: Revenge. And for what?

JOSEPH: They broke my father's heart. All but one of them.

CANAMINE (*contemptuously*): Your father. Your father was a hard man.

JOSEPH: My father *loved* me! I was his favourite.

CANAMINE: You're a dreamer. (*Brief pause*) Your brothers, you'd've liked to kill them all, wouldn't you?

JOSEPH: All but one, my youngest brother. He's dead.

CANAMINE: They're all dead, Joseph. They're all dead now.

The grave site and RUTH's *deathbed: slow fade to black as the wind dies. Fade up on* JOSEPH *and* CANAMINE *down centre.*

You're just like your father before you, and your old blind grandfather before him — a dreamer.

VOICE OF JOSH (*in the darkness, contemptuously*): You dreamer.

JOSEPH (*to* CANAMINE, *without enthusiasm*): Josh.

CANAMINE: Mmmm, your older son.

JOSEPH: He's been a great disappointment to me, I'd rather not —

CANAMINE: He was decorated for bravery.

JOSEPH: He was never the same after the war.

> *Fade up slowly on* JOSH *in the unidentified military uniform of* Middle Distance [I.2], *down right.*

JOSH: You dreamer. You never cared for any of us, except Luba.

JOSEPH: Don't you talk to *me* that way, I'm your father!

JOSH (*scornfully*): My father. May-*be*. But what about Jake?

JOSEPH: He's in there, practising the piano —

JOSH: Have you ever really looked at him, I mean *really* had a good look?

JOSEPH: He's going to be a concert pianist, then all our troubles will be over. You and Luba and —

JOSH: He looks like Uncle Gad to me.

JOSEPH: That's impossible! You, Jakey and Luba were already born when your uncles came to live with us. Don't you remember? It's a family resemblance, that's all. (*Brief pause*) Where's Luba? She should be home by now.

JOSH: Out whoring.

JOSEPH: Don't talk about your sister like that, she's a wonderful girl!

JOSH: Hmph, wonderful in bed. Have *you* had her?

> JOSEPH *rushes at* JOSH. CANAMINE *restrains him.*

JOSEPH: You... (*To* CANAMINE) Let me go! (*To* JOSH) You were never any good. You were always a bad lot! I should've disowned you long ago! I'm only glad your mother didn't live to see this.

>   JOSH *produces an oblong case.*
>   JOSEPH *struggles, then relents.* CANAMINE *releases him.*
>
>   (*Eyeing the case*) What's that? What've you got there?

JOSH (*subdued*): I've brought you my medals, father.

>   *Sound of a distant wind.*
>   JOSH *proffers the case to* JOSEPH*: fade to deep blue, frozen, silent. Fade up slowly the grave site; a lone man in silhouette, resembling* JOSH, *stands beside the open grave.*
>   *Grave site and* JOSH*: slow fade to black as the wind dies.*

JOSEPH (*turning back*): He's gone.

CANAMINE: Yes.

JOSEPH: He's dead.

CANAMINE: No, he's still alive.

>   *Pause.*
>
>   What are you thinking?

JOSEPH (*distracted*): What? (*Brief pause*) Nothing.

>   *Pause.*
>   *Sound of a door opening, closing, up left.*
>
>   What was *that?*
>
>   *A shaft of moonlight falls across the L-shaped stair of* Middle Distance *up centre.*

No.

>   *Enter* CORBY *and* RAPITRONE, *clad in overcoats, from the left.*
>   *Fade up on* CORBY *and* RAPITRONE.

(*With a hushed sigh*) Oh.

Blackout JOSEPH *and* CANAMINE.

CORBY's *left hand is swathed in bandages; he has a black eye, puffed lips and a broken nose, crossed band-aids on his left cheek, his right arm draped round* RAPITRONE's *neck as they stagger in.* RAPITRONE *is in full possession of his faculties.*

RAPITRONE (*calling*): Peg?

He eases CORBY *down on to one of the lower steps.*

CORBY (*wincing*): Oooo —

RAPITRONE: There, you all right? (*Calling up the stair*) Peg.

He sprints up to the landing.

Peg?

CORBY: Perhaps she's gone out.

Pause.
CORBY *and* RAPITRONE: *fade to deep blue, frozen, silent.*
JOSEPH *and* CANAMINE *in darkness.*

VOICE OF JOSEPH (*moved*): Why this?

VOICE OF CANAMINE: If it weren't for you they'd be alive today. All this would never have come out.

Pause.
RAPITRONE *walks slowly down the stair and sits beside* CORBY, *both staring blankly ahead, as* CANAMINE *speaks.*

I was a sick man. They put me in his room. The room upstairs, it used to be his, did you know that? It was Corby's room when he was convalescing. They put him up there, looked after him. Then it was my turn.

Pause.

I lay there with the blinds drawn, staring at the ceiling, sometimes for days. At other times my eyes were closed, and I was taken for dead. It was then that the two of them, the man and the woman, came into my room.

Pause.

Rapitrone's room was directly below mine.

> RAPITRONE *rises, helps* CORBY *to his feet. They exit right as* CANAMINE *speaks,* CORBY *leaning on* RAPITRONE.

The man and the woman knew he was asleep. But he heard them, all the same. (*Brief pause*) And I . . . (*Quietly, his voice breaking*) I heard the woman . . . sobbing.

> *Sound of a distant wind.*
> *A low mist rolls in, gliding over the ground from right to left. Enter* CANAMINE *and* JOSEPH *in black full-length capes, with the mist, as the L-shaped stair glides into the shadows at left.*
> CANAMINE *and* JOSEPH, *at centre stage in the moonlight, surrounded by darkness as the mist closes in.*

CANAMINE (*looking about*): Joseph.

> *Pause.*

(*Quietly*) You know, I'm frightened? (*Chuckling nervously*) It's the mist, it makes me giddy. It's a feeling I get sometimes. I could be anywhere. Though nothing changes, there's this sudden . . . strangeness in the look of things. Do you ever get that feeling? As though your own sense of perspective had imperceptibly altered and your mind had erased everything about the image but the image itself, which comes *before* the mind: a sinking, blind fall between one heartbeat and the next, with no memory of the beat that had gone before, or of the one to come.

> *Fade up the grave site slowly as* CANAMINE *speaks. The men and women of the Underground are mourners beside the grave. The scrim has vanished.* CANAMINE *leads* JOSEPH *through the mist to the foot of the hill.*

There's no sensation of movement or gravity because everything is falling at the same speed. And though we might not perceive the fall, it changes everything without altering a single molecule of what we see and who we are.

> *They climb to the summit of the hill. The mourners make way for them. Pause.*

ACT THREE

JOSEPH (*to* CANAMINE): Who are you?

> CANAMINE *takes* JOSEPH *by the hand and leads him into the open grave.*
> *Pause.*
> *Slow fade to black. The wind rises.*

September 1981

III.
The Fall of Prague

גׇּלְמִ֤י ׀ רָא֬וּ עֵינֶ֗יךָ וְעַֽל־סִפְרְךָ֮ כֻּלָּ֪ם יִכָּ֫תֵ֥בוּ יָמִ֥ים יֻצָּ֑רוּ וְלֹ֖א אֶחָ֣ד בָּהֶֽם׃

—Liber Psalmorum, cxxxix: xvi

DRAMATIS PERSONÆ

JOSEPH, *a man of seventy*

CANAMINE
TYCHO
CREATURE
MATTHIAS } *a man of middle age*

[RAPITRONE]
RUDOLF II, *Holy Roman Emperor (born 1552)*

[CORBY]
ISAAC
FALSE ISAAC } *in his twenties*

[MEG]
CATHERINE, *morganatic wife to Rudolf (blonde)*

[LUBA]
AGNES
LEAH } *in her twenties (brunette)*

[YOUNG JOSEPH]
SCOTO, *a villainous necromancer*

[SILVO]
RABBI, *a man of sixty*

[FLINT]
RUMPF, *minister to the Emperor*

[COATES]
TRAUTSON, *minister to the Emperor*

[BLOCH]
1ST SOLDIER
ARCHBISHOP
1ST COURTIER } *in his forties*
MAKOWSKI
1ST SENTINEL

[GUTHRIE]
POPP, *personal servant to the Emperor*

[GUS]
2ND COURTIER
SPINELLI   } *a man of middle age*
2ND SENTINEL
BEDRICH

MAGDALENE, *Tycho's daughter*

2ND SOLDIER } *in his late twenties*
JOHANNES

TORCH BEARER } *in his twenties*
SEYFFART

WENCH, *a young dancer*

Soldiers, corpses, monks, servants, guards, courtiers, musicians, alchemists, spirits, nobles, princes, chorus.

ACT ONE

Scene 1

Sound of a distant wind. Silhouettes of JOSEPH *and* CANAMINE *in black full-length capes against a dim blue aura at the far end of the darkness, up centre. They stand motionless, side by side, facing front. The cavernous, pre-recorded voices of* CANAMINE *and* JOSEPH *are heard.*

VOICE OF CANAMINE (*quietly*): You know, I'm frightened? (*Chuckling nervously*) It's the mist, it makes me giddy. It's a feeling I get sometimes. I could be anywhere. Though nothing changes, there's this sudden . . . strangeness in the look of things. Do you ever get that feeling? As though your own sense of perspective had imperceptibly altered and your mind had erased everything about the image but the image itself, which comes *before* the mind: a sinking, blind fall between one heartbeat and the next, with no memory of the beat that had gone before, or of the one to come.

   As the two men walk solemnly downstage. . .

There's no sensation of movement or gravity because everything is falling at the same speed. And though we might not perceive the fall, it changes everything without altering a single molecule of what we see and who we are.

   Pause.

VOICE OF JOSEPH: Who are you —

JOSEPH (*to* CANAMINE): Who are you?

   They come to a halt, down centre, in a vague amber light crossed by smoke-like shadows, as the blue aura fades to black.
   The wind more distant.
   CANAMINE *smiles wearily, then looks at* JOSEPH.

CANAMINE: You would do better to ask who I was. Or who I will be. (*Touching him, compassionately*) Are you afraid?

JOSEPH: I . . . We've left a trail of corpses behind.

CANAMINE (*nodding*): Mmmm.

JOSEPH: Where are they? Where are the dead?

CANAMINE: With the unborn.

JOSEPH: But my wife, my daughter —

CANAMINE: Your wife?

JOSEPH (*sadly*): Ruth.

Pause.

CANAMINE: The woman you *would* have married died at the age of two, of encephalitis.

JOSEPH: The woman I would've —

CANAMINE: Look. Don't think about it any more. You had some good years with Ruth, at the beginning. The other one — the one who died — she would've made your life miserable.

JOSEPH: But, how can you say a thing like that?

Pause.

CANAMINE: Because you married her.

JOSEPH: What?

CANAMINE: You married her. You married the other one . . . in another life. It hasn't happened yet.

JOSEPH: Hmmm?

CANAMINE: From where we are, at present, it's only a memory.

ACT ONE

JOSEPH: You're mad!

CANAMINE: No. Listen to me. We're a couple of sick men, Joseph, you and I. Everything we've encountered thus far counts for less than nothing in the general scheme of things. Ruth, Corby and Rapitrone, your sons, your brothers, the men and women of the Underground, you've got to forget them. From where we stand, they may or may not be part of a hundred possible lives you may or may not have led. Where we are now, none of them exist. But where *they* are, *we* do not exist.

JOSEPH: Why are we here?

CANAMINE: Because we're nowhere else.

JOSEPH (*looking about*): I can't see anything. How much farther is it?

CANAMINE: How much farther to where?

JOSEPH: To where we stop.

    CANAMINE *smiles*.

    Where are we?

CANAMINE: I don't know. I only know we have to keep moving, for all our yesterdays have vanished. The memories we have, they're memories of things that haven't happened yet . . . of things that may never come to pass. We've already come too far, Joseph, you and I, to turn back. And, by now, even the point of no return is long since swallowed into oblivion. All we have left is the memory of the future.

JOSEPH: The memory of the future?

    Pause.

CANAMINE: The infinitude of possible, and mutually exclusive, historical pasts.

JOSEPH: You've lost me.

    Pause.

CANAMINE: If you plunge your hands up to the wrists in water and rub your fingers together, do your fingers feel wet or dry?

JOSEPH: Dry.

CANAMINE: Of course, because they're completely immersed.

JOSEPH: Mmmm.

CANAMINE (*with appropriate gestures*): Pull one hand *out* of the water, and rub the fingers together. They not only *are* wet, they actually *feel* wet.

    JOSEPH *nods.*

Though the condition of wetness is common to both hands, it is, after all, only a wetness to be *imagined*, and not *felt*, by the hand that is *immersed* in wetness, which feels all other immersed things, including itself, as *dry*.

    Pause.

JOSEPH: What's the point?

CANAMINE: I'm not getting through to you?

JOSEPH: No. We may as well be dead. (*Suddenly, horrified*) Are we —

CANAMINE: No. No, we're not. Here, steady on. (*Brief pause*) But you're not far from wrong.

JOSEPH: What?

CANAMINE: The hand immersed in water... you and I. We've been deprived of the most characteristic sensation of the element in which we are immersed.

JOSEPH: Which is?

CANAMINE: Existence.

JOSEPH (*thoughtfully*): Mmmm.

CANAMINE: So, you see, we might as well be *dead*.

    He chuckles.

JOSEPH: *I* don't think it's funny.

CANAMINE: Nor do I. (*Glancing about*) I'm just getting a bit nervous.

The wind subsides.

Look round you. What do you see?

JOSEPH (*looking*): Nothing. I can't even hear the wind any more.

Pause.

CANAMINE (*looking every which way*): We're nowhere. And yet, Everywhere is all round us. We've only to open our eyes wider.

JOSEPH: Are we dreaming?

CANAMINE: What, the pair of us? Together? Don't be absurd! If this were a dream, only one of us would be dreaming, the other would *be* the dream.

JOSEPH: Then, we're *not* dead.

CANAMINE (*shaking his head*): It only *seems* that way.

Silent pause.

(*Excitedly*) You hear that?

JOSEPH: What?

CANAMINE (*ears cocked*): That. That bell, off in the distance.

JOSEPH: I don't hear anything.

CANAMINE: Never mind. (*Distractedly*) You understand, then, that we're not dead?

JOSEPH: *I* believe you.

CANAMINE (*as though still hearing the bell*): Good, good. Well, then, let's just hope I'm right.

He wanders a few paces into the shadows, as though searching for an exit quite near.

I haven't got *all* the answers, you know —

JOSEPH: Where are you going—

CANAMINE: Sssssh! I can almost *feel* it . . . here, inside.

JOSEPH: What?

CANAMINE: Something. I can't describe it.

JOSEPH: Don't leave me here!

CANAMINE (*emerging from the shadows*): No. No, I won't.

    Chime of a distant church bell.

JOSEPH: What's that? A bell!

CANAMINE (*overjoyed*): Ah, you hear it!

    Far up right: fade up slowly a dim, blood-red patch of sky, the silhouette of the Charles Bridge, the distant spires and rooftops of sixteenth-century Prague and its looming castle.

JOSEPH: Where's it coming from?

CANAMINE (*pointing toward the shadowed city*): Over there! (*Brief pause*) That bridge, I . . .

    Second chime of the bell, a bit louder.

I *know* that bridge! It's . . . Karlsbrücke, Joseph! The Charles Bridge!

    Pause.

But, where are the statues?

    Third chime, louder.

(*Sudden realisation*) Ah . . . yes. (*Brief pause*) Joseph, someday that bridge will be lined with blackened statues, gaunt silhouettes against the dawn and sunset skies . . .

    Fourth chime, still louder. Far up right, the colour of the sky grows more intense.

... figures ripening in the perpetual twilight of this enigmatic city!

JOSEPH: What are you talking about?

CANAMINE: The memory of the future!

JOSEPH: What city is this?

CANAMINE (*joyously spreading his arms, cries out*): Prague!

> *On the fifth and loudest chime,* JOSEPH *and* CANAMINE, *down centre, recoil before a scene of indescribable horror.* CANAMINE'*s joyous greeting of Prague has been answered by a sudden, deafening chorus of shrieks and lamentations, mournful offstage voices chanting a 'Dies Irae', the great thud of an unseen bass drum, the ring of a hand-bell, and cries of 'Bring out the dead!'*
> — CANAMINE *and* JOSEPH *stand appalled in the middle of a narrow street littered with the corpses of men, women and children ravaged by the Black Death.*
> *Far up right: black smoke rises from burning pyres in the distance.*
> JOSEPH *and* CANAMINE *cover their faces up to the eyes with their capes.*
> *Some of the dead are naked, others lie in winding sheets or clothed in rags; some are fully dressed, as though they had dropped in their tracks. Drunken soldiers move in two squads of four amidst the carnage; the first squad slides wooden poles beneath a body, lifts it — arms and legs dangling down — and dumps it into a cart already heaped with corpses, while a nude woman is lowered in a sling of sheets from an upper window on to the pikes of the second squad.*
> *The clamour lessens as the 'Dies Irae' grows louder. Enter a procession of cowled, chanting monks: the first rings a hand-bell, the second swings a censer, the third supports a large and hideous painted crucifix; the others follow two abreast, a beak doctor bringing up the rear. The procession passes through slowly, from right to left. After their exit, the sound of chanting voices and the ringing of the hand-bell gradually fade, but can still be faintly heard as the scene draws to an end.*
> *As the procession passes, a hysterical woman runs out the the house from which the nude corpse is being lowered and attacks the soldiers below. The* 1ST *and* 2ND SOLDIER, *who have been standing idly by, guzzling from the sacks at their belts, rush the woman and try to subdue her. She struggles free and throws herself on the monk bearing the crucifix, groping wildly toward the figure of Christ, shrieking incoherently, gesturing toward the lowering corpse (presumably, her daughter) as the* 1ST *and* 2ND SOLDIER *pull her away and wrestle her to the ground. The woman soon breaks free again, lunging at the hem of the beak doctor's gown. The* 1ST *and* 2ND SOLDIER *pounce upon*

her — now the two men are laughing. The other soldiers begin to laugh and joke. The 2ND SOLDIER *clubs the woman with his mailed fist, knocks her unconscious, and carries her up to the doorway of the house as the second squad dumps the nude corpse into the cart.*

1ST SOLDIER (*staggering toward* JOSEPH *and* CANAMINE): You, there! Back to your houses!

He takes a swill from his sack, wipes his mouth, glances at the cart.

(*To the soldiers*) You're stackin' 'em too loose! We'll never get 'em back to the pits in one wagon like *that!* The top ones'll fall off! God's teeth, use your heads! (*To* JOSEPH *and* CANAMINE) I said move on!

He drinks again.
The soldiers jab at the corpses in the cart with their poles and pikes.

CANAMINE: Soldier, what place is this?

1ST SOLIDER (*chuckles, cynically*): Some say it's the End of the World. (*Noticing* CANAMINE*'s cloak*) Are you a priest?

CANAMINE: No.

1ST SOLDIER: No, I thought not. (*Gesturing toward the cart*) Those that haven't fallen to the wagon themselves have abandoned the city to the soldiers and the wolves. That woman, just now. It's a while since I've seen such grief. She made me laugh.

He drinks.

2ND SOLDIER: She'll trouble us no more.

1ST SOLDIER (*nodding*): Mmmm.

2ND SOLDIER *drinks.*

(*To* CANAMINE) It's only a matter of time before the Black Death drags us all into hell. Look round you. Parents cast their dying children into the streets and lock their doors behind them. Children rob what they can, before they flee to the countryside, while their parents lie screaming and choking in their beds. Husband abandons wife, brother deserts brother. A mother would as soon slit her dying baby's throat than give suck to the raging poison in it.

ACT ONE

He spits.
The other soldiers continue with the task of hauling corpses.

Ay, Father Pestilence is a hard master. He turns you rotten long before you die; and, in the end, when he's lumped your flesh with tumours and turned your blood to ink, he steals the wind from your last, silent shrieks and fries you from the entrails to the skull with his poker.

He drinks.

2ND SOLDIER (*laughs*): We carry him in our bellies. (*Gesturing toward the corpses*) Those venomous lumps are sleeping inside us all, like maggots in the womb of the dead. We're great with child, here in the city of Prague! You cover your faces now, but stop with us yet a while—you'll soon become accustomed to this rare perfume of ours.

He staggers back to the cart.

1ST SOLDIER: Don't listen to him. If it weren't for the stench, I'd as lief save this lot for the dogs, if there were any dogs to be found.

CANAMINE: And what of the wolves?

1ST SOLDIER: The wolves, ah. The wolves are here all right, but living in the houses. They're our newest inhabitants. Death has emptied more than half the residences of Prague and left its mansions and hovels as spoils to swarms of thieves, highwaymen and other murderous rogues, the true masters of our city. They eat their swill off gold plate, drain the wine cellars to the dregs, and tup their gap-toothed whores in the silken beds of bankers' and merchants' daughters, while *we* collect our stinking booty of bankers *and* merchants *and* daughters for the charnel pits. (*Pointing far up right, to the distant pillars of smoke*) There's our destination, where the pyres are blazing day and night. Our burnt offerings have dimmed the sun to a flickering ash, singed off the smiling face of the moon, and snuffed out the stars like so many smoking candles never to be lighted again.

Far up right: begin slow fade to balck as the 1ST SOLDIER *staggers back toward the loaded cart.*

CANAMINE: Tell me, how long has the Pestilence been raging?

1ST SOLDIER: Some say it began when a great ship ran aground at the foot of the Gallows Hill — all aboard were dead. Others hold that it's God's wrath upon the Pope and our Emperor for the sacrilege of having robbed their Christian subjects of a half-score days of their lives.

JOSEPH (*to* CANAMINE): What does he mean?

CANAMINE *uncovers his face.*

CANAMINE: Soldier, what day is this? I mean the date!

1ST SOLDIER (*chuckles*): That depends, sir, upon the name of your sovereign or your religion. (*To the other soldiers*) Come on! Put your backs into it —

CANAMINE (*to himself*): So . . . that's how it was done.

JOSEPH: What is it? What's he talking about, a half-score days of their lives?

CANAMINE: Don't you see? That was the loophole I'd been looking for, back there.

JOSEPH: Back where?

CANAMINE: Where we were. It was our way out . . . or our way in, depending on your view of it. (*Brief pause*) In the year 1582, the Vatican promulgated the reform of the old Julian Calendar. All Catholic countries were required to reckon time ten days forward, with the result that when the new calendar went into effect in October of that — of *this* year, Joseph — the fifth day of the month became the fifteenth day. Ten days were lost — a half-score days — thus bringing Catholic man ten days closer to the day of his death, in the twinkling of an eye. A good portion of the civic council at Augsburg has voted against it, and the citizens have risen in arms to their support. Montaigne has taken to his bed over it!

The far right of the stage is now in darkness.
JOSEPH *and* CANAMINE *down left.*

So, you see . . . we've been lucky. We've managed to find the egress from one limbo to another.

JOSEPH (*sceptically*): It's the only way to travel.

CANAMINE: Truer than you think, Joseph. If it weren't for these ten missing days, in which we now so pleasantly find ourselves inhaling the miasmas of sixteenth-century Prague, we might never have emerged from the darkness. Uncover your face, it's not as strong now.

JOSEPH (*uncovering*): We're getting used to it.

CANAMINE (*nodding*): Mmmm. We're going to have to get used to a lot of things.

1ST SOLDIER: You still here? Take my advice and go! Leave the city now, while you still have legs to carry you. You may gain a few weeks more of life before the contagion overtakes us all! Even the *Emperor's* fled to Vienna!

Blackout, all sounds to silence, leaving JOSEPH *and* CANAMINE *in a blue pool of light down left / light up* RUDOLF, *aged thirty, down right, the blackness behind him slowly fading up on a palace window giving on the twilight sky, as* JOSEPH *and* CANAMINE *speak.*

RUDOLF *is in black attire, as are all the members of his court, unless otherwise noted. He wears a silver, five-pointed star medallion. Of bookish appearance, lightly bearded, he stands facing front, a blank expression on his face.*

CANAMINE: The Emperor.

JOSEPH (*whispering*): That face . . . Rapitrone!

CANAMINE. Don't be a fool. Rapitrone won't be born for another three hundred and sixty-five years, if *then*. No. As to the face . . . A face is apt to turn up anywhere. He's a Hapsburg, and you know how many times *that* face has turned up over the centuries. Haven't you been to the museums? (*With a grand gesture*) Rudolf the Second, by the grace of God, Holy Roman Emperor, Emperor of Germany, Archduke of Austria, King of Bohemia and Hungary, Princely Count of the Tyrol . . .

JOSEPH: Etcetera, etcetera.

CANAMINE: He's an educated man, Joseph. He reads books — the philosophers, the astronomers, the mathematicians, the mystics — and he has an eye for the Arts. (*Brief pause*) And an eye for the ladies, too.

JOSEPH: He doesn't look much like an emperor.

CANAMINE: Have you ever seen one from close to before?

JOSEPH: He looks as though he's just come from a funeral.

CANAMINE: They all look like that in his court. It's the Spanish influence. He spent several years of his childhood under the wing of his uncle, Philip the Second of Spain. For a while it was thought that Rudolf would inherit the Spanish throne. Philip wanted a hand in his upbringing, seeing that his own son, Don Carlos, the heir apparent, wasn't quite right in the head — another Hapsburg failing. He loved it over there.

JOSEPH: Don Carlos?

CANAMINE: Rudolf. Don Carlos wasn't exactly wringing his hands in grief, either. Took a dive down a staircase at the University of Alcalá. He was chasing a coed. That's what did it. He was never the same again. Plotted to depose his father. Died under house arrest in the palace at Madrid after glutting himself on meat and ice water — dysentery: such stuff as romantic heroes are made on. Well, Philip managed to produce another heir and Rudolf was sent back to Vienna, a city in which he was never to feel at home.

RUDOLF (*to himself*): How I long to leave Vienna.

Enter RUMPF *and* TRAUTSON *from right, with papers, and wearing their chains of office. They remove their hats.*

RUMPF: Sire.

RUDOLF (*roused out of his daydream, with slight irritation*): Well?

They bow to the Emperor.

What news of the Pestilence, has it abated?

RUMPF (*urgently*): My lord, as near as can be reckoned, nigh on half the citizens of Prague have perished of the contagion. Your garrison commander sends word that the dead now so outnumber the living, that drunkenness, lechery, thievery and brigandage are so rampant among our legions as to —

RUDOLF (*turning away*): Enough!

RUMPF *and* TRAUTSON *exchange knowing glances.*

(*Turning upon them suddenly*) Rumpf, Trautson. Are you not our ministers?

TRAUTSON: Your grace, we —

RUDOLF: Silence!

He turns away, and calms himself.

RUMPF: But, the garrison commander . . .

RUDOLF (*wearily*): Yes, yes. Give the garrison commander whatever he requires. Now, leave us.

> RUMPF *opens his mouth as if to speak, but* TRAUTSON *gestures him to silence. They go.*
> *Pause.*

POPP (*from the shadows, left*): Sire?

> RUDOLF *turns left as* POPP *enters, urgently.*

(*Genuflecting*) Your grace.

He kisses the Emperor's ring.

RUDOLF (*pulling him to his feet*): Rise, dear Popp, and tell me your news.

POPP (*tearfully*): Good my lord, the city of Prague is an open grave. One can scarce walk ten paces without treading upon a corpse. A vile effluvium smothers every shadowless street; its fumes turn a waxen hue as they rise, o'ertopping Saint Vitus' spires by half a league before the fetid smoke of the pyres that shroud the sun like a pall, reeking of melted flesh and a thousand charred bones, lids them down again.

RUDOLF: Oh, horrible.

POPP: Those that still live have no tears left for the dead, and are deaf to the fearful howls of the dying; caring naught but for their own pleasures, they take their pleasure where they can, and in full abandon, for they already number *themselves* among the dead and, as ghosts to their own vanished lives, love nothing.

> *He breaks off in sadness and disgust.*
> *Pause.*

RUDOLF: Have you been to the Ghetto? Have you seen him? Is he alive?

POPP: Ay, my lord, he still lives. I saw him plain but from afar, and spoke no word to him, just as you would have me do. In Jew's disguise, I stole into the Ghetto and made enquiry of this Rabbi Judah Loew, of his history and habits as far as could be ascertained from what is known to the tradesmen and scholars of the quarter, who imparted this intelligence to me: to wit, what you have read of the High Rabbi's practices in necromantic books, or heard by rumour, would seem to be true.

RUDOLF (*delighted*): Ah.

POPP: Many spoke to me of a poor mute, who was onetime the Rabbi's household servant, and who went mad in the market-place. Some, of a more learned disposition, held that this was no man of flesh and blood but a creature fashioned by the Rabbi's own hand, called forth from the elements to life in a mould of clay.

RUDOLF: Go on.

As Popp continues, the palace window slowly fades to black behind them. Centre stage: fade up slowly to deep blue, a forest clearing on the outskirts of Prague at midnight; an old RABBI *stands, facing front, frozen and silent, at the head of what appears to be a newly-covered grave.*
At left, JOSEPH *and* CANAMINE *look on with growing interest.*

POPP: They told me, my lord — and I did attend them well — of the force of magic by which the Rabbi, framing base matter to the rough image of a man, did stand in a solitary wood hard by the river Vlatava, and pronounce, upon the figure he had sculpted, secret names so as to move the spirits of the dead and the yet-unborn to his purpose, and how by solemn litany of spells and incantation he, like a second Prometheus, conjured fire and ice from the dark face of the moon, called forth salt-water from the ocean's depths to drench the ground, drew into a glass vessel the breaths of the spectral larvæ that stream in the firmament and, breaking the vessel over the sodden soil, caused the earth beneath the clay to kindle. Then the Rabbi stooped, cut a mouth for the sleeping creature with his finger, and placed into it a plaque or parchment, upon which he had inscribed the word *emet*.

RUDOLF: Truth!

POPP: Ay, my lord. Truth. This word formed the creature's eyes and nose, its hair and all its features, so finely chiselled as to perfect the counterfeit of man. (*Brief pause*) Some, disputing the matter of the parchment, say that Rabbi Loew inscribed the letters of the sacred word upon the creature's brow.

CANAMINE (*to* JOSEPH): It wasn't Rabbi Loew. Where did he get *that* idea?

ACT ONE 257

Blackout RUDOLF *and* POPP.

As CANAMINE *speaks, the forest clearing fades up from deep blue to moonlight, the* RABBI *frozen and silent. Fade up* JOSEPH *and* CANAMINE *from blue to a pool of white light.*

No. (*Brief pause*) A pretty legend, though, don't you think?

JOSEPH *does not answer.*

Yes, well . . . we can't always be expected to get our facts straight, can we? The Emperor's man made an honest mistake. He wasn't to know that the arcane accomplishments to which he referred were not those of Rabbi Judah Loew, but of an earlier, somewhat more obscure figure . . .

He points to the RABBI.

The venerable Rabbi Elijah of Chelm. (*Brief pause*) Oh, it's an old and complicated business, as these things usually tend to be. I won't bore you with the details, they're contradictory enough as it is without my adding to the confusion. Even as far as this Rabbi Elijah's concerned, we're not in full possession of the story. Rumour, suspicion, you know how it is.

Pause.

(*Confidentially*) It is believed that two demons hovered above the clay figure before it opened its eyes — the demon Jonathan and the demon Yossele, or Joseph.

JOSEPH *looks at* CANAMINE, *who smiles fleetingly.*

Of the two, it was the second, Yossele, who was permitted to enter the creature and who gave it life, for this demon had often rendered aid and comfort to the Jews in times of great travail, and was well known to the Talmudic sages. The demon Jonathan was wild and could keep no secrets, and so was passed over.

Pause.

Many, before Elijah of Chelm, are believed to have created such a being. According to some, the creature never lived at all, or lived but an hour and was returned to dust.

As CANAMINE *concludes, fade up on* RUDOLF *and* POPP *down right, the blackness behind them. Nineteen years have passed and they are, corre-*

spondingly, older. RUDOLF's *beard is fuller, greying.* POPP *is now a very old man.*
   Fade slowly to deep blue, JOSEPH *and* CANAMINE.

To accomplish this destruction, one simply removed the plaque or parchment on which *emet* was written from the creature's mouth, or erased the letter *alef* from the creature's forehead, thus leaving, in place of the word *emet* — Truth — the word *met,* which is Death.

POPP (*to* RUDOLF): And thus, Sire, having by this expedient deprived the witless mute of its life, did Rabbi Judah Loew cause its mortal remains to be taken from the garret of the Altneushul.

RUDOLF: The synagogue.

POPP: Ay, my lord. 'Twas done in the gloom of night and by some cunning practice; rather call it a bewitchment, for the Rabbi and all who were with him passed through the city gates unseen, conveyed their burden to a copse hard by the Gallows Hill — that selfsame woodland place o'erlooking the river, where the creature first drew breath — and buried it.

RUDOLF: Methinks much time has passed since first we spoke of Rabbi Loew and his creature.

POPP: 'Tis nigh on twenty year, your grace.

   The RABBI *slowly exits left.*

RUDOLF (*to himself*): Nigh on twenty year.

CANAMINE (*to* JOSEPH): Almost twenty years. (*To himself*) Hmmm, 1582 plus nineteen . . . That . . . would make it 1601. It's now the year 1601, Joseph. Think of *that!*

RUDOLF (*to himself*): We have tarried too long in this.

JOSEPH (*to* CANAMINE): Are you mad? We were just —

CANAMINE: Look at them. Can't you see it?

   Pause.

JOSEPH: They've . . . They've aged.

ACT ONE

Pause.

CANAMINE: Time flies when you're having fun. (*Brief pause, delighted*) I'm probably the first person ever to have said that.

RUDOLF (*to* POPP): Go. Fetch the Rabbi straight. Bring him to me.

> CANAMINE *whispers urgently into* JOSEPH's *ear, then hurries into the shadows.*

POPP: Sire.

> *Fade to black* JOSEPH, *perplexed.*
> POPP *bows and exits right.*
> *Slow fade to black* RUDOLF, *lost in thought.*
> *Woodland and river noises.* JOSEPH *steps into the moonlit forest clearing from right. He looks about, sees the newly-covered grave, approaches it cautiously, kneels and touches it.*
> *Enter* CANAMINE *from left.*

CANAMINE (*rubbing his hands in glee*): This is the place all right. (*Looking about, inhaling deeply*) Aaaahhh. Smell that, Joseph. Fresh air, at last. (*Inhales again*) Oh, what a relief! I still had the fumes of death in my nostrils.

> *He approaches* JOSEPH.

JOSEPH (*indicating the grave*): Look.

CANAMINE: Mmmm.

JOSEPH: It's true, then.

CANAMINE: I didn't say *that*.

> *From under his cape he brings a beard, like that of the* RABBI.

Here. We haven't much time. Put this on.

JOSEPH: Where did you get that?

CANAMINE: Never mind that. Here.

He sticks the long beard on JOSEPH'*s face.*

JOSEPH (*recoiling*): What do you think you're doing —

CANAMINE (*fussing with the beard, whispering*): Here, don't move, you'll ruin everything.

JOSEPH (*whispering*): Why are you whispering?

CANAMINE: Sssssh! No time.

From under his cape he brings a wig, like the hair of the RABBI.

Here. Put this on.

JOSEPH: But, what's the —

CANAMINE: Just put it on.

JOSEPH *complies as, from under his cape,* CANAMINE *brings a hat, like that of the* RABBI.

JOSEPH (*shaking his head*): Oh no.

CANAMINE: You want to look the part, don't you?

He puts the hat on JOSEPH.

JOSEPH: What part?

CANAMINE (*unfastening* JOSEPH'*s cape, urgently*): No time to explain. Trust me.

He removes JOSEPH'*s cape and flings it into the woods.* JOSEPH *is dressed as the* RABBI.

JOSEPH (*looking down at himself, touching his clothes in disbelief*): No . . .

Enter ISAAC *from left.*

ISAAC (*calling*): Maharal!

He sees JOSEPH *and approaches.*

(*Familiar but respectful*) Ah, I thought I'd find you here. Come, quick. The Emperor has summoned you to the Castle.

JOSEPH (*dazed*): The Emperor.

ISAAC: His messenger awaits us now, at the city gate. We must go.

JOSEPH: I . . . (*Looks at* CANAMINE *uncertainly, then to* ISAAC) Who are you?

Pause.

ISAAC: Rabbi, are you unwell? It's Isaac, your —

JOSEPH (*to* CANAMINE): Isaac —

CANAMINE (*to* ISAAC): It must be the moonlight. The Rabbi's eyes aren't —

ISAAC (*to* JOSEPH): Who is this man?

CANAMINE: A friend.

JOSEPH (*to* ISAAC): Yes, a friend.

ISAAC (*to* CANAMINE): You're a friend of the Maharal?

CANAMINE: Yes.

> CANAMINE *whispers something to* JOSEPH, *who suddenly appears uneasy and unwilling to comply.* CANAMINE *and* JOSEPH *turn their backs to* ISAAC. CANAMINE *whispers again.* JOSEPH *nods reluctantly.*

JOSEPH (*to* ISAAC): Run back to the city gate and tell the Emperor's man we're coming.

ISAAC: I will.

> *He makes a curt bow to* CANAMINE *and runs off, left.*
> *Pause.*

CANAMINE: I won't be going with you this time, Joseph.

JOSEPH: But, you said —

CANAMINE: No. Listen to me. (*Brief pause*) You're the *Rabbi* now. Rabbi Judah Loew.

> JOSEPH *opens his mouth, but before he can utter a word . . .*

All you've got to do is keep your eyes and ears open. Don't speak before you're spoken to, and go along with everything.

JOSEPH: But, how can I be the Rabbi? It's insane!

CANAMINE: Of course it is, but that's the way things are. In this life, you're almost never who you think you're going to be.

> *Pause.*
> *He puts his arm round* JOSEPH *and walks him down left.*

Joseph, we've been through a lot together, you and I. Together we've witnessed passion, plague, jealousy, murder, cruelty, betrayal, remorse . . . Now we're the last sick men of Europe . . . or the first. So, you'll have to be even more cunning than before . . . and you *will* be, I know it.

> *Pause.*

JOSEPH: Where will you go? What will become of you?

CANAMINE (*smiles*): Ah, that's something even *I* don't know.

JOSEPH: But . . . I'm afraid.

CANAMINE: So am I, my friend. So am I.

> *They embrace.*

(*At arm's length*) Now, go. And try not to be afraid. You resemble the Rabbi well enough. (*Parting and backing away*) Be firm in your purpose and no man will guess the truth. Farewell.

> JOSEPH *makes to go.*

And, Joseph . . . Remember me.

> *Each raises his hand in reluctant farewell.*
> JOSEPH *turns and goes, left.*
> *Fade to deep blue the forest clearing;* CANAMINE, *frozen and silent, his*

hand raised.
To silence, the woodland and river noises.
Fade to black.

Scene 2

A TORCH BEARER *leads two fellow servants across the darkness, from right to left. The servants carry a large, framed painting, its back to the audience.*

Light up RUMPF, *nineteen years older than at his last appearance, on an arched balcony overlooking the darkness, left. He leans over the bannister and squints at the painting.*

RUMPF (*cynically, to himself*): Another whore for the Imperial Collection. (*To the servants*) You, there! Wait!

> *They stop at centre stage. He comes down to them, weary and cynical. They bow.*

(*To the* TORCH BEARER) Well, what is it this time? Venus Rising from the Sea, or is it Leda and the Swan again?

> *He takes the torch and looks as the servants right the painting to an oblong position.*

(*Eyebrows raised in tired incredulity*) Hmmm. Something a bit different this time, eh? (*To the* TORCH BEARER) Spanish?

TORCH BEARER: No, your grace. Of the Florentine School.

RUMPF (*still eyeing the painting*): Florentine. I might've known it.

> TRAUTSON, *nineteen years older than at his last appearance, emerges from the shadows behind* RUMPF.

(*Handing back the torch*) You wouldn't catch a Spaniard dead painting a woman like that.

TRAUTSON (*just as weary and cynical*): It's the only way you *would* catch a Spaniard

... painting a woman like that.

> *The* TORCH BEARER *and servants bow to* TRAUTSON *as he and* RUMPF *exchange knowing glances.*

RUMPF (*eyeing the painting*): It's filth. (*To the* TORCH BEARER) Take it away.

> *The* TORCH BEARER *and servants bow.*
> *As the* TORCH BEARER *leads the servants bearing the painting up to the balcony, from which they exit* . . .

(*To* TRAUTSON) It's sure to please the Emperor no end.

TRAUTSON: Mmmm.

RUMPF: He won't be able to go on like this much longer, not with that damned brother of his in Vienna champing at the bit.

TRAUTSON: Matthias.

RUMPF: Ay. Matthias. *He's* got his spies at court, if you can still call it a court where the Emperor sees no one but his antiquaries and that pack of wolves he's set up in the kitchens downstairs and in that — that . . . Street of the Alchemists. Alchemists, indeed! (*Brief pause*) Five minutes with the Emperor and your clothes are reeking of piss and sulfur for a week. They actually use it in their . . . work.

TRAUTSON: Hmph, sulfur.

RUMPF: And the piss. Imagine it, Trautson . . . gold from piss? Has the whole world gone mad?

TRAUTSON: No madder than the Emperor —

RUMPF (*nods*): Hmmm.

TRAUTSON: From whose chambers I've just come.

> *They walk down left.*

RUMPF: Ah you've seen him, then? I haven't seen him in a fortnight.

TRAUTSON: He wouldn't see me. He's closeted with that Danish astrologer of his.

RUMPF (*contemptuously*): Hmph. Master Doctor Tycho Brahe, the biggest charlatan of the lot. (*Brief pause*) As bad as it was before, what with an Emperor who sleeps by day and keeps us all night waiting for an audience that, when it comes at all, lasts scarcely longer than a curt dismissal — and the other times, weeks on end, when he takes to his bed and none but his servants and that peasant wife of his knows whether he's dead or alive — no, as bad as it was for us then, it's become far worse since this eminent star-gazer, this Tycho Brahe, decided to show his face in Prague. Vain and quarrelsome as he is with others, he has the Emperor so completely under his thumb that death alone can separate them. Mark you, this Master Tycho sets himself to be the Emperor's advisor in all matters, and has lately become his physician, for Emperor Rudolf will have no other since the death of Doctor Hajek.

TRAUTSON: Ay, I know it. All the court whispers of the Emperor's generosity to his Danish mountebank, of the rich benefices that have been squandered on this Tycho Brahe in exchange for what? (*Contemptuously*) Prognostications.

RUMPF: Three thousand florins a year — not counting what the Emperor gives him in the way of . . . expenses — a palatial residence . . . while other, worthier men are passed over.

TRAUTSON: Such as ourselves, Rumpf?

RUMPF: Such as ourselves, Trautson. (*Archly*) For, are we not the Emperor's ministers?

TRAUTSON (*sighing*): He's always been against us.

RUMPF: Never wanted to be bothered with the affairs of state. He treats the Master Doctor better than his mistresses, and lets the empire go to ruin.

Fade up on an archway, right. Guards with halberds stand at either side.

It's an even wager who'll invade us first, his brother the Archduke Matthias . . . or the Turks.

Enter POPP *leading* JOSEPH, *from the archway.* POPP *in a mantle,* JOSEPH *in rabbi's disguise.*
RUMPF *and* TRAUTSON *turn to them, but keep their distance.*

TRAUTSON: The Emperor's old servant, Popp . . . with a Jew.

RUMPF: A Jew indeed. The High Rabbi Judah Loew.

TRAUTSON: Ah, yes.

> *Fade up on a marble bench, up right.*

RUMPF: A Jew to see the Emperor.

> POPP *silently asks* JOSEPH *to seat himself on the bench.*
> JOSEPH *sits.*
> POPP *bows as he passes* RUMPF *and* TRAUTSON, *rises to the arched balcony, and exits left.*

TRAUTSON (*disgusted*): He didn't even have the common courtesy to remove his hat.

RUMPF: He's old. (*Pointing to* JOSEPH) Like *that* one.

TRAUTSON: What business could *he* have with the Emperor?

RUMPF: Well, it isn't a social call, I can tell you that. Probably some sophistical nonsense the Emperor wants to sound him out on. Or maybe Rudolf wants to show off one of his new toys — that contraption on the tower, for instance, that Magister Tycho uses for star-gazing. You know what joy the Emperor takes in such idiocies. (*Indicating* JOSEPH) And, after all, the man *is* a mathematician.

TRAUTSON: What, another man of science? The Rabbi?

RUMPF: I've heard it said. Mark you, he's a crafty one, this Judah Loew. He knows the world. Have you forgotten his learned disputation with Cardinal Silvester a few years back? He succeeded in convincing the Cardinal and three-hundred ecclesiastics, who witnessed the disputation and questioned him in their turn, that the blood of Christian children was not used by Jews in their Passover rites.

TRAUTSON: I remember. Do you think it's true?

RUMPF: What, about the Passover blood? Who can tell with those people what's true and what isn't? The Rabbi accomplished his purpose. Our laws have never been more lenient toward the Jews. (*Ironically*) Under our present Emperor, we live in an age of tolerance and mutual accord. (*Confidentially*) I tell you, Trautson, that old man over there is a statesman. His position as High Rabbi of Prague makes him nominal head of the whole Diaspora. If the Jews had a pope, it would be Rabbi Loew.

> TRAUTSON *stares thoughtfully at* JOSEPH, *then turns to* RUMPF.

TRAUTSON: You think he could be . . . influenced?

RUMPF: What do you mean?

TRAUTSON: Like the Archbishop of Cologne.

RUMPF: Ah. (*Brief pause*) The Archbishop of Colgne was a lecher, a madman. And a fool. There's no comparison.

> *Fade up to a murky violet light* SCOTO *and the* ARCHBISHOP *at centre stage. The* ARCHBISHOP *is seated in an armchair, his back to the audience,* SCOTO *standing before him at left, a little to one side, supporting the grotesquely ornate frame of a full-length 'mirror'.*
> RUMPF, TRAUTSON *and the guards see nothing.*
> JOSEPH *stares with growing excitement at the violet tableau, whose light gradually intensifies.*

It was all the work of that Italian necromancer — you remember him, what was his name?

TRAUTSON: Uh, Scotus —

RUMPF: Ay, Jerome Scoto. What was it, nearly twenty years ago? Hmph. They said he made a magic mirror for the Archbishop, then asked him would he like to see the most beautiful woman of Cologne in it.

> *As* AGNES *appears in the 'mirror', nude, standing at her bath, 'washing' herself, slowly, sensually . . .*

ARCHBISHOP (*sighing*): Oh . . .

RUMPF (*to* TRAUTSON): Her name was Agnes von Mansfeld.

> JOSEPH *rises, gaping at* AGNES.

Well, you know the rest. The Archbishop made a complete idiot of himself. Making Agnes his mistress wasn't good enough for her brothers. Hah, what a business. The brothers were fanatics — Protestants. They wanted him to *marry* her. (*Brief pause*) He married her . . . as a Calvinist! And when he wouldn't step down as Archbishop, in spite of the Emperor's bribes, we nearly had religious civil war on our hands. (*Brief pause*) Oh, yes, that Scoto knew what he was about. The villain.

> JOSEPH *rushes toward* AGNES.
> *Blackout* AGNES, SCOTO *and the* ARCHBISHOP.
> JOSEPH *stands amazed before the sudden emptiness, groping, gazing about in confusion.* RUMPF *and* TRAUTSON *are too absorbed to notice him.*

TRAUTSON: Whatever became of him?

RUMPF (*shrugs*): After he got into that scrape with the Duke of Saxony's wife — imagine, sending a charlatan like Scoto on a diplomatic mission in the first place!

TRAUTSON: You know, as well as I do, the importance the Emperor has always attached to the black arts in these matters.

RUMPF: Ay —

TRAUTSON: Diplomacy means nothing to him.

RUMPF: Ay. And so, an emissary from the Holy Roman Emperor ended his mission by making a cuckold of the man he was intended to woo. (*Brief pause*) We heard no more of Scoto after that.

> JOSEPH *returns to the bench and sits, lost in thought.*

The Duchess was so taken with him she wouldn't let him leave. And when the Duke found out what was going on . . .

> TRAUTSON *'slits' his throat with his finger.*

Exactly. Though I once actually heard the Emperor say that the man they executed in Saxony was a demon in Scoto's shape, and that Scoto — the real Scoto — had escaped to Hamburg.

> *He shakes his head.*
> *Enter* POPP, *who comes down from the arched balcony.*

TRAUTSON: What nonsense.

RUMPF: Hmph. (*to* POPP) You, there!

POPP: Ay, my lord?

RUMPF: You've come from the Emperor's chambers?

POPP: Ay, my lord.

RUMPF: Is the All Highest awake, or does he sleep?

POPP: The Emperor is awake, my lord. (*Indicating* JOSEPH) He waits upon that gentleman.

> *Blackout* POPP, RUMPF, TRAUTSON, *the guards, archway, arched balcony, bench / light up* RUDOLF *in his study, centre stage.*
>
> RUDOLF *sits in a chair to the right of a table cluttered with books, papers, charts, scrolls, scientific and mathematical instruments. Behind him, a wall with a window giving on the night, a wine bottle and goblets on the sill, doorways to the right and left. A large globe on a stand to the right of* RUDOLF, *who faces front, staring at the painting that was earlier carried by the servants. The painting stands on the floor, propped against a tabouret, its back to the audience. The Emperor's study by 'candlelight', its walls hung with maps of the earth and the stars, an erotic tapestry, zodiacal charts and geometers' drawings of outlandish machines. To the left of the window, a curtain.*
> *Pause.*
> *Enter* TYCHO, *from the left doorway, in bright, flamboyant attire, clutching a quill pen and an astrological chart. An outrageous ostrich plume adorns his hat. From a double golden chain round his neck hangs a gold elephant on whose flank the letters* F. S. *are inscribed; the elephant stands atop an open scroll bearing the letters* M. H. Z. G. A. *The bridge of* TYCHO'*s nose is made of metal, forged of a compound of gold and silver. We see in him a burly, once-robust man, still vigorous, though the years of excess have begun to take their toll.*

RUDOLF (*staring at the painting*): How now, Master Doctor?

TYCHO (*handing him the astrological chart*): The signs are unchanged, my lord.

> RUDOLF *glances over the parchment as* TYCHO *lays the quill on the table and brings from his doublet a small box containing ointment. He rubs the ointment on his nose, closes the box and returns it to his doublet. He will do this often, and in the same absentminded manner, throughout the play.*

RUDOLF: Mmmm . . . Still the ambiguities. (*Indicating the painting*) What do you think of this?

TYCHO: It's very fine. Very . . . lifelike.

> RUDOLF *can scarcely take his eyes from the painting.*

RUDOLF: Yes. (*Brief pause*) It's over a hundred years old.

TYCHO: Great is the power of art that a woman so long dead may still excite our passion.

RUDOLF: Mmmm.

> *Pause.*

Tell me, Master Doctor, do you not think she resembles the woman who bewitched the Archbishop of Cologne?

> *Pause.*

TYCHO: I have never seen the woman, Sire. That must have been before my time in Prague.

RUDOLF: Ay, so it was. Her name was Agnes von Mansfeld. (*Brief pause*) I saw her once, many years ago. She would be close to middle age now. (*Points to the painting, troubled*) That woman, there . . .

TYCHO: She must have been beautiful indeed for you to recall her face in that painting.

RUDOLF: I had not thought of her until I saw it. Then her face came back to me. One would almost think she was the painter's model. I can well understand the Archbishop's bewitchment.

> *Pause.*

(*Staring at the painting*) Do you think it possible . . . for a man to create a living being out of clay, as God created Adam?

TYCHO: Ah, your grace refers to the homunculus, the alchemical child. Paracelsus is believed to have —

ACT ONE

RUDOLF: No. No, I was not speaking of a creature brought to life in a vessel by means of alchemical transmutation, still less of the waxen figures Paracelsus shaped in the image of his enemies so as to do them injury, the which he also named homunculi. No. I meant a creature sculpted of earthen clay and made to rise by some spell that turns twigs to sinew and bone, sap into blood, and puts a beating heart where, before, there had been nothing but a clot of loam wrapped in dead leaves. It is said that the High Rabbi of Prague gave life to such a creature in a wood close by the Gallows Hill. Do you know the man, Master Doctor?

TYCHO: The Rabbi, Sire?

RUDOLF: Ay, the Rabbi. Judah Loew, a most learned man — a man of science and, I am told, an adept in the great mysteries.

TYCHO: Ay. Rabbi Loew. I have heard well of the man, but I do not know him.

RUDOLF: You will know him soon. He's here, in the Castle. My servant is bringing him up to us now, from the Great Hall. (*Rising*) I will go behind that curtain, and you, feigning to be alone, will speak with him as one man of science to another. Draw him gradually to the subject of the creature, but say nothing direct; only, speak of larvæ, homunculi, and the like.

TYCHO: But the creature, Sire. Who has seen it?

RUDOLF: Many in the Jewish quarter of Prague have seen it and said it was the household servant of Rabbi Loew; also, that it was, in all respects but one, most like a man.

TYCHO: All but one, my lord?

RUDOLF: It could not speak.

TYCHO (*nodding, thoughtfully*): Ah.

> *He casts a sceptical glance at* RUDOLF, *who has turned toward the painting again, then listens doubtfully to the rest of the tale, though his doubt is concealed from the Emperor by a mask of acceptance.*

RUDOLF (*eyeing the painting from close to*): Many saw the servant go mad in the market-place, where it wreaked great havoc and destruction before the Rabbi came to take it away. He led the creature to the synagogue and, there, destroyed it. The mute servant was never seen again. That very night, its remains were carried from the city to the wooded place from which they had come, and there they were buried. The Rabbi —

A loud knocking at the door, right.
RUDOLF *makes a sign of complicity to* TYCHO, *then rushes behind the curtain.*

TYCHO (*facing right*): Come!

The door opens.
Enter POPP.

POPP (*solemnly*): The High Rabbi Judah Loew.

Enter JOSEPH, *who stops dead in his tracks on seeing* TYCHO.

(*To* JOSEPH, *with a ceremonious gesture*) The illustrious Master Doctor Tycho Brahe.

JOSEPH *stands amazed, turns to* POPP *in confusion, then back to* TYCHO, *at whom he gazes. He opens his mouth as if to speak, but nothing comes.*

TYCHO (*to* POPP): You may retire.

POPP *bows and goes, right, closing the door.*
TYCHO *smiles, tapping his metal nose.*

(*Chuckling*) You needn't look so shocked, Rabbi, it's not the pox.

Pause.

I came by it honourably, I assure you.

He approaches JOSEPH.

JOSEPH (*uncertainly*): Good morrow, Master Doctor.

TYCHO (*tapping his metal nose*): It was a Christmas gift from Manderup Parsbjerg. We were students at the University of Rostock. Some say we fell into a quarrel over who was the better mathematician. Others will tell you our argument was over a woman. I've never refuted either story. (*Brief pause*) We settled our disagreement in the dark of a moonless night. Couldn't see a thing. Parsbjerg was luckier than I. We're still friends. He often writes to me.

JOSEPH *has caught sight of the painting and cannot take his eyes from it.*

Ah, I see you have an eye for the ladies. It's quite . . . daring, isn't it?

JOSEPH (*gaping*): That woman . . .

TYCHO: Ay, very beautiful. The Emperor says she reminds him of the woman who bewitched the Archbishop of Cologne. Doubtless you know the story.

JOSEPH *glances at* TYCHO *suspiciously, unable to decide whether he is indeed* TYCHO *or* CANAMINE. *This constant suspicion will govern his reactions throughout.*
TYCHO *contemplates the painting.*

Mmmm. A proper Bathsheba, that one, eh? Well, they all come to dust in the end, the ones who die while they're still young and fair, the ones who linger and wither slowly through the years, losing their beauty to a mask of wrinkles and white hair long before the worm gets them. Think of it, Rabbi, the cemeteries are full of bones that once were clothed for the adornment of jewels, perfumes, soft silks and ermine. (*Indicating the painting*) All that wanton flesh, laid bare to drive men mad with lust, now lies in the earth, so loathsome and befouled that starving dogs would turn away from it.

Pause.

What are we gaping at but a name on a headstone? (*Brief pause*) In your cemeteries, I am told, the Talmud forbids the tombstones to be moved, so that they lean together, with no space between them, when the graves are full; and when the ground can no longer hold their weight, they topple, one on another, sinking, layer upon layer, into the earth to form a vertical city of the dead beneath the topmost tombs.

JOSEPH (*befuddled*): I . . . Yes, to be sure.

Pause.

TYCHO: Can I offer you some wine?

He goes to the window, takes the bottle from the sill, and pours wine into two silver goblets.

JOSEPH: What? (*Brief pause*) Yes.

TYCHO: Of course, one needn't always have to rely on the graveyard, eh?

JOSEPH: No.

TYCHO: No. If one has the use of a . . . charm, so to speak — a talisman — then it's a different matter altogether.

JOSEPH: I don't . . .

TYCHO: Take, for instance, your synagogue. A grand edifice, that. One of the oldest in Europe, if not *the* oldest. Yet, where would it be without those two white doves?

JOSEPH (*playing along*): Mmmm, the doves.

TYCHO (*handing* JOSEPH *a goblet*): Mmmm. How on earth would it have been able to withstand the barbarities of the pogrom, the pillage and destruction to which the Jewish quarter has too often fallen victim in the past, if not for the fact that, whenever the synagogue is threatened by fire and stones, two snow-white doves alight upon its roof?

> TYCHO *clinks goblets with* JOSEPH. *They drink.*

Ah, a rare vintage.

JOSEPH: Mmmm.

TYCHO: Oh! Sorry, it's not been blessed. I mean it isn't kosher. Of course, you could bless it yourself.

JOSEPH: That's all right.

TYCHO (*smiles*): Ah, Rabbi, they told me you were a man of the world.

> *He sits on the edge of the table.*

And as I also know you to be a man of science, let me ask you . . . do you think it at all possible for a man to create a living being, as God created Adam? Doubtless you're aware of the claims of Paracelsus in this matter.

> *Pause.*

JOSEPH *stares at* TYCHO, *searching his eyes for some sign of how to proceed.*

JOSEPH: Of course, it depends upon how you . . . interpret his words.

TYCHO: You mean, when he describes the alchemical child — the homunculus — he could be speaking in symbols. Oh yes, there's always that. (*Brief pause*) But, what if it *were* possible? Forgetting Paracelsus for the moment, what if one could, say, fashion, out of the four elements, a . . . creature — not an animal, mind you, but a creature — a creature . . . very like a man?

Pause.

As a man of religion, would you say that such a creature possessed . . . a soul — to distinguish it from the lower orders?

Pause.

JOSEPH: Perhaps. If the creature could think for itself. (*Brief pause*) If it could reason.

TYCHO: As a man reasons?

JOSEPH (*nodding*): Mmmm.

RUDOLF (*emerging from behind the curtain*): But what if this creature were unable to speak?

TYCHO (*springing up, to* JOSEPH): The Emperor.

JOSEPH *removes his hat, puts down his goblet, and bows.*

RUDOLF (*arms extended*): No, no. Please, Rabbi, put on your hat and be at ease. (*Taking* JOSEPH *by the arms*) You are among friends.

JOSEPH (*putting on his hat*): You do me great honour, Sire.

He glances conspiratorially at TYCHO, *who quizzically raises his eyebrows as* RUDOLF *sits in the chair to the right of the table,* JOSEPH *at right,* TYCHO *at left.*

TYCHO: Will you take some wine, Sire?

RUDOLF: No, Master Tycho. (*Brief pause*) Now, good Rabbi Loew, tell me, as a theologian, would the creature you have spoken of possess a soul if it had no tongue for speech?

JOSPEH: If it could reason as a man reasons, my lord.

RUDOLF: And if it could not? If it could only . . . do the bidding of its master, of its . . . creator?

JOSEPH: Then it would scarcely be more than an intelligent animal.

RUDOLF: And, therefore, upon its death, unworthy to be buried in hallowed ground.

> *Pause.*
> JOSEPH *looks to* TYCHO, *who is rubbing ointment on his nose.*

JOSEPH: Yes, Sire.

RUDOLF: Good.

> RUDOLF *and* TYCHO *exchange meaningful looks.*
> *Pause.*

(*To* JOSEPH) Strange, is it not, that a dumb animal should be unworthy of burial in ground sanctified for men, seeing that man, for all his gift of language and sly articulation, is so oft undone by a facile tongue which, in anger or passionate ferocity, o'erwhelms the very power to reason that has raised him above brute creation, and hurls him headlong into such murderous acts as would scarce befit the wildest of animals?

JOSEPH: Ay, my lord. Most strange.

RUDOLF: Mmmm. (*Brief pause*) Can you see no remedy?

> *A loud knocking at the door, right.*

(*Calling*) Who's there?

GUARD (*off*): The Lady Catherine, Sire.

> RUDOLF *stands.*

(*Calling*) A moment. (*To* JOSEPH, *hurriedly*) Good Rabbi Loew, we'll speak of this further, for we have much yet to discuss and there is but little time. For now, I commend you to the Master Doctor. (*To* TYCHO) Take the Rabbi to your observatory. Show him the instrument by which you chart the movement of the stars. (*Calling*) Come!

The door opens, right. Enter CATHERINE.

CATHERINE (*to* TYCHO, *coldly*): Master Doctor.

TYCHO (*bowing, removes his hat*): Lady.

RUDOLF (*to* JOSEPH): My consort, the Lady Catherine. (*To* CATHERINE) The High Rabbi of Prague, Judah Loew.

CATHERINE (*politely*): Rabbi Loew.

JOSEPH (*bowing, removes his hat*): My lady.

> *Pause.*
> CATHERINE *looks expectantly at* RUDOLF, *who then nods to* TYCHO.
> TYCHO *and* JOSEPH *bow and exit right.*
> *The door closes.*
> *Pause.*

RUDOLF: The children, are they well?

CATHERINE (*eyeing the painting with disgust*): Well enough, my lord.

> *She walks to the other end of the study, glancing about.*
> *Pause.*

That man, I like him not.

RUDOLF: The Rabbi?

CATHERINE: Tycho Brahe.

RUDOLF: He's a great man. I'll have nothing said against him —

CATHERINE: He uses you . . . for his own advancement.

RUDOLF: 'Twas *I* that asked him to Prague. Long ago, I —

CATHERINE: Ay, long ago. He came not *then*. He waited till the King of Denmark died and the new King refused him his benefices. If the old King had lived, Tycho Brahe would still be on that island of his, gazing at — at the moon!

RUDOLF: Why do you mock him? (*Turning away*) It ill becomes you.

CATHERINE: Because he is no different from those scheming ministers of yours, Rumpf and Trautson.

RUDOLF: That slimy pair? (*Banging his fist on the table*) No!

CATHERINE: Rudolf!

> *Pause.*
>
> Rudolf.
>
> *Pause.*

RUDOLF: No. (*Brief pause*) We're very much alike, you know, Tycho Brahe and I. He, too, married a . . .

> *Pause.*

CATHERINE (*hurt*): Well, my lord? (*Brief pause*) He married beneath his station . . . if he bothered to marry at all, that is. (*Brief pause*) Oh, I know, I know. I should never have consented to become your wife. Our children will never . . . You should have married the Infanta.

RUDOLF (*with distaste*): Oh —

CATHERINE: You should've gone through with it.

RUDOLF: That was a long time ago. I don't like to think of it.

CATHERINE: You *must* think of it!

> *Pause.*
>
> Rudolf. You must think . . . of an annulment.

RUDOLF: What? I . . . No! Catherine —

CATHERINE: We seldom see one another any more. (*Glancing at the painting*) You have your . . . diversions. What difference can it make to us?

RUDOLF: But, the children!

CATHERINE: Unless you marry well, and produce a *legitimate* heir —

RUDOLF (*pacing*): Oh, you sound like Rumpf and Trautson —

CATHERINE: Your brother Matthias will —

RUDOLF (*stops, clapping his hands to his ears*): Matthias!

>   *Pause.*

> (*Trembling with rage, he whispers*) Never speak to me of that man.

CATHERINE (*pulling his hands down*): Rudolf, you must do *some*thing!

RUDOLF (*to himself, agitated*): He says I'm not fit to be Emperor. He means to steal my crown. Yes, I . . .

> *He turns to her.*

Catherine, I'm afraid.

> *A sudden pain. He sucks in his breath.*

(*Gulping*) My . . . (*Clutching his head*) Oh!

> *He falls in a fit, trembling spasmodically, emitting strangled cries.* CATHERINE *drops to her knees beside him, lifts his head on to her lap and cradles it.*
> *Fade to black.*

Scene 3

Fade up on TYCHO's *feast to a roar of mirth and discussion, stage left: a long table laden with food and drink, crowded round by courtiers, wenches, servants, musicians, etc. To the left of the table, an arched balcony and stair, gayly festooned. A rowdy, licentious scene.*
  TYCHO's *place at the head of the table sits vacant.*
  JOHANNES *emerges from the shadows at right, clad in black, a loose bundle of papers under his arm. He is followed by two dishevelled* COURTIERS *and a* WENCH, *locked arm in arm.*

1ST COURTIER (*drunkenly*): Master Johannes, come back —

WENCH (*giggling*): Master Johann —

2ND SCOURTIER (*calling, mockingly*): Oh, Master Johann?

  They attempt to encircle JOHANNES. *He fights them off, but is tripped up by a bystander, who pushes him into the staggering trio.* JOHANNES, *the two* COURTIERS *and the* WENCH *collapse in a heap, to the general merriment, as the papers are scattered over the floor.*
  TYCHO *appears on the balcony with* JOSEPH, *both dressed as before, and wearing cloaks.*

TYCHO (*throwing his arms wide, to the crowd*): Senators and people of Rome!

  Cheers and laughter.

  (*Expansively*) May oceans of black beer and wine flood Tycho's house till the last star falls from the heavens!

  General delirium as TYCHO *and* JOSEPH *come down from the balcony and are surrounded by well-wishers. Voluptuous courtesans sidle up to* TYCHO, *who snatches a beer stein from the table and drains it to the dregs as he embraces them.* JOSEPH, *too, is surrounded by women, who put their arms round him and coo in his ear. He smiles awkwardly.*

(*Indicating* JOSEPH) Some wine for the Rabbi!

JOSEPH *is handed a goblet and drinks, glancing furtively about the tumult. Meanwhile,* JOHANNES *and the* WENCH *are on their knees, gathering up the scattered papers.*

(*Shouting*) Where's Magdalene? (*To* JOSEPH) My daughter, she sings like a nightingale. (*Shouting, to all and sundry*) Send for my daughter Magdalene! Tell her I am seized by bitter pangs of melancholia, and would have her warbling voice about mine ears to lull me into a calm and felicitous sleep!

Laughter.

(*To* JOSEPH) Look. There's Master Johannes, my assistant, at his game. (*To* JOHANNES, *calling*) Master Johannes?

He approaches JOHANNES *and the* WENCH, *whose breasts swell out as she gathers up the papers.*

(*To the* WENCH) And what, my girl, would *you* have to slake your thirst?

WENCH (*twanging his codpiece*): Give me but a fleshly pipe from which the liquor doth flow thick and hot, my lord.

TYCHO (*laughing*): Ah . . .

He turns to jest with JOHANNES, *but, seeing his stern expression, thinks better of it. Instead, he bends to pick up the last of the fallen papers, and hands it to* JOHANNES.

Exit JOHANNES, *sulking, elbowing his way through the crowd to the arched balcony. The* WENCH *makes to follow him, but* TYCHO *catches her by the skirts from behind and wheels her round.*

(*Calling*) Musicians!

The musicians play a sprightly 'Galliard'. All gather to watch the WENCH *dance. She dances with stomping innocence and abandon. On the reprise,* TYCHO *whips off his cloak and joins in the dance, executing, hands on hips, a special flourish which draws cries of admiration from the crowd.*

When the music ends, TYCHO *is handed a flagon of ale, drains it, then tosses the flagon over his shoulder, high in the air, into the crowd as* JOSEPH *gathers up his cloak.*

TYCHO *embraces the* WENCH, *who vanishes amongst the revellers.*

(*Putting his arm round* JOSEPH, *breathlessly*) Well, Rabbi, it's time I showed you my crow's nest. Come.

TYCHO *throws on his cloak as he and* JOSEPH *walk up the stair to the arched balcony, and exit, ignoring the mêlée that has broken out amongst the revellers.*
Goblets, steins and flagons are tossed about. Men and women paw each other, and drunkenly embrace. A courtier collapses in a stupor. A dishevelled courtesan emerges from the throng, chased by a courtier, who catches her by the hair, downstage; she shrieks, as the noise of the feast slowly dies away, and the two fall to the floor in a close embrace.
Fade to black.

Scene 4

Fade up slowly on the great equatorial armillary sphere mounted atop the villa of Ferdinand I, TYCHO's *dwelling place in Prague. The instrument looms large against the starry sky, tremoring dimly, as by the glow of flaming cressets, before a low parapet which extends, right and left, into the gloom; it rests on four supports above a sort of miniature amphitheatre consisting of four steep, concentric steps. One mounts to the top of the 'amphitheatre' from without, by means of six exterior steps. The instrument stands upstage, a little to the right of centre.*
Pause.
TYCHO *and* JOSEPH *emerge from the shadows at right, in their cloaks.*

TYCHO (*bounding up the exterior steps*): Aha! (*Caressing the armillæ*) My armillæ zodiacales, Rabbi. The largest in existence. A beautiful contrivance, is it not?

JOSEPH (*gazing in wonderment*): Yes. It is.

TYCHO (*beckoning*): Well, come up, then.

JOSEPH *mounts the exterior steps and stands, atop the little 'amphitheatre', beside* TYCHO.

ACT ONE 283

I trust you know the workings of it from my *Astronomiæ Instauratæ Mechanica*? Remind me to give you a signed copy.

Pause.

Well, go on. See for yourself if it isn't the most accurate instrument yet devised for the observation of the heavens.

JOSEPH *hesitates.*

TYCHO *swings the eye-piece into position, peers through it, and adjusts the angle of inclination by means of screws, tilting the armillæ slightly.*

There. Have a look.

JOSEPH *squints through the eye-piece.* TYCHO *rubs ointment on his nose. Pause.*

Well?

JOSEPH (*noncommittally*): Remarkable.

TYCHO *leads* JOSEPH *down to the bottom of the 'amphitheatre'.*

TYCHO (*making small adjustments to the instrument as they descend*): My own invention, you know. The ancients had nothing like it. Their instruments were hammered out of solid metal. You can imagine how cumbersome they must have been. The markings on them were too widely spaced, for one. And their lack of symmetry made accurate measurement all but impossible; the stress it put upon the frame, whenever extreme adjustments were required, was more than enough to render the results of any observation worthless. Hmph, it's the sort of thing I've had to deal with all my life.

He ascends to the top of the 'amphitheatre', gazing up at the stars. JOSEPH *remains at the bottom, observing him.*

(*With sweeping gestures*) I alone have seen the heavens move. I, Tycho Brahe, have followed the transit of distant suns across the firmament and kept time to their wayward courses while other men contented themselves with . . . hypotheses! (*Brief pause*) For two-score years my eyes have scanned the unending silence of the cosmos. (*Closing his eyes*) Listen, Rabbi, can you hear them? Can you hear them . . . the whirling spheres of fire and ice strewn upon the blackness like diamonds? (*Opening his eyes*) The comets drag their flaming tails beyond the orbit of the moon. Blinding eddies of dust girdle the dying star before it wanes to a faint blood-coloured coal and flickers out, and who can say how many worlds are ended? The skies are hung with the memories of obscure disasters. (*Brief pause*) Think what it means, Rabbi. (*Brief pause*) Think what it means to me to be able to take the measure of them, and yet know nothing. (*In a great ouburst of emotion*) Oh, if only I could reach out my hand and pluck these mysteries down!

    Pause.

A hydra of enigmas o'erspreads the sublunary and aethereal realms; between them the vast emptiness lies, smothering the roar of the planets in full career, dampering the music of their birth and doom. We will never know who live and die upon those far terrenes, or through what skies they glimpse our own dim star and see us not. If only half those worlds are like our blue-green Earth, then the other half, riven by hail and lightning, or sunk in the mists of their oceans' cauldrons, must be peopled by unimaginable beings, creatures we would quake to look upon, who, in their turn, would shrink in horror at the sight of *us,* myriads of eyes to whom the face of the most beauteous woman would seem a waking nightmare.

    Pause.

But yet . . . if only half those worlds are like our blue-green Earth —

MAGDALENE (*singing, off*): Alba —

TYCHO (*to* JOSEPH, *hushed*): Magdalene!

MAGDALENE (*singing, off*): Alba, alba.

    MAGDALENE *emerges from the shadow, left, clad in a white and silver gown, a chaplet of laurel in her fair, unloosed hair. The lutenist plays at the edge of the darkness behind her, accompanied by the player of the antique cymbal, who is hidden in the murk.*

        Alba is 'white of dawn',
        And all our lovers' passion
        Flies with the alba.

    As JOSEPH *slowly rises to the top of the 'amphitheatre', both he and* TYCHO *enraptured by* MAGDALENE'*s song* . . .

ACT ONE

> Before the stars are gone,
> The watchman, gaunt and ashen,
> Cries out, 'The alba!'

TYCHO *and* JOSEPH *glance at one another.* TYCHO *smiles at* JOSEPH. *They turn their gaze again upon* MAGDALENE.

> O my beloved,
> May the dawn ne'er come again.
> Alba, alba, alba.

As MAGDALENE *slowly aproaches* TYCHO *and* JOSEPH . . .

> Bury our bodies here
> Beneath the redwood bower,
> Far from the alba.
> We nevermore shall hear
> The watchman on the tower
> Crying, 'The alba!'
> O my beloved,
> Let the dawn ne'er come again.
> Alba, alba, alba.

To the closing bars of the lute: TYCHO *removes his cloak and wraps it round* MAGDALENE's *shoulders, kissing her forehead.* TYCHO *puts his left arm round* JOSEPH, *his right arm round* MAGDALENE. *They walk off into the shadows, left, as* ISAAC *rushes on from right, staring after them, stricken with love for* MAGDALENE. *Fade up on* SCOTO, *nineteen years older than at his last appearance, in a narrow, blood-red pool of light, down right, his back to the audience, as though watching* ISAAC, *who stops at centre stage.*

ISAAC (*to himself, with longing*): Magdalene.

> *Begin fade to black as the red pool of light intensifies on* SCOTO, *who turns to face the audience with a sinister smile. His eyes are closed.*
> *To the final chord of the lute:* SCOTO *chuckles.*
> *Blackout.*

ACT TWO

Scene 1

Right and centre: Rabbi Loew's study, at break of dawn. In the right wall, a door giving on the street; to the left of the door, a sideboard with an ornate mirror hanging above it. In the rear wall, a door at centre, on either side of which rise shelves cluttered with books. In the centre of the room, a table strewn with open books, papers, some mathematical instruments, quills and ink, etc.; on the table stands a gold menorah holding seven unlit candles. Against the left wall, a low cabinet crammed with scrolls, prayer shawls, phylacteries, etc.; above the cabinet, a narrow window filtering a shaft of dim, pre-dawn light into the murk.

A cock crows in the distance.

The door at right opens slowly, creaking on its hinges. Enter JOSEPH, *dressed as the Rabbi Loew. He closes the door and gropes his way to the table, gazing at the unfamiliar surroundings. He sinks into a chair, exhausted, squints about the shadows for a moment, then removes his hat and wig. He places the wig on the table and covers it with the hat. He briefly examines the mathematical instruments and the menorah before he yawns and slumps forward into unconsciousness.*

Pause.

The centre door opens. Enter LEAH, *clad in a half-transparent nightdress, bearing a candle. She tiptoes to the table, lights the seven candles of the menorah, carries her candle to the sideboard, sets it down and looks at her face in the mirror, yawning, smoothing her unloosed hair. It is only when she returns to the table that* LEAH *notices* JOSEPH's *close-cropped pate and shakes him gently by the shoulder.*

JOSEPH *wakes with a start, takes* LEAH *to be the woman of the magic mirror, and smothers her in his arms, caressing her with unbridled lust.*

LEAH (*struggling, between giggles*): You're asleep. Ho, you're asleep. Wake up. Come on.

She breaks free and smiles at JOSEPH, *holding him at arm's length.*
Pause.

JOSEPH (*panting with emotion*): I must be dreaming.

LEAH: Your hair . . .

    JOSEPH *clutches his head.*

Are you unwell?

    He starts to make a dive for the wig, then realises it's too late.

What have you done to your hair? You've cut it all off —

JOSEPH (*stammering*): Uh . . . Uh, it's a purification! For . . . For the . . . Passover.

LEAH: That's not for another six months.

JOSEPH: I . . . I had to begin early. Have to allow time enough for the hair to grow halfway out again.

LEAH: What?

JOSEPH: In strict accordance with the Dietary Laws.

    Pause.

LEAH: I heard the creak of the door and I came down. When I saw you there, I thought you were a stranger. (*Stroking his stubbled hair*) It was a foolish thing to do. You read too much.

    She puts her arms round him, pressing his head to her shoulder, as his hands stray again to her body, his caresses more tentative now.

Oy. (*Brief pause*) Where's Isaac?

JOSEPH (*smothered*): Isaac.

LEAH: Why didn't he return with you? (*Brief pause*) Well?

    Pause.

JOSEPH (*smothered*): What?

LEAH: My husband.

JOSEPH, *misunderstanding, caresses* LEAH *more heatedly.*
Pause.

Your son-in-law.

JOSEPH (*smothered*): Who?

LEAH: Isaac. My husband.

JOSEPH *holds her at arm's length, staring.*
Pause.

What ails you, father?

Pause.

JOSEPH (*in great confusion*): Isaac. He . . . He found me in the woods.

LEAH: Yes. And when you didn't return from the Castle, I became worried and sent him to fetch you home again.

JOSEPH: I didn't see him there. (*Walking toward the sideboard*) I saw the Emperor . . . and met his astrologer, Master Doctor Tycho Brache. A very curious man.

LEAH: The Emperor. They say he —

JOSEPH (*catching sight of himself and* LEAH *in the mirror*): The Emperor, too. Yes. He was . . . He had . . . this painting in his study —

LEAH (*hitching her gown high above her left hip*): Look.

JOSEPH (*gasping at her in the mirror*): Uh?

LEAH (*rubbing the rearward portion of her naked hip, wincing*): Ooo!

JOSEPH *wheels round, desperately trying to master himself.*

(*Twisting to look at herself*) Oh, I can't see it. *You* look. (*Thrusting her hip at* JOSEPH) It hurts when I touch it. Is there a bruise?

JOSEPH: Uh?

LEAH: Can you see anything?

> JOSEPH *drops to his knees and scrutinises her bared hip.*
> *Pause.*

Well?

JOSEPH (*his voice cracking*): No.

LEAH: No bruise, then? You're certain?

JOSEPH (*distractedly*): There's no . . . (*He swallows hard*) No bruise. No.

> *She drops the hem of her gown.*
> JOSEPH *remains on his knees.*

LEAH: Hmph, I'll wager I'll be black-and-blue tomorrow, though. (*Clutching him to her midriff*) Oh, what a frivolous daughter you've got!

JOSEPH (*in an agony of unrequited lust*): No —

LEAH (*rocking his head between her swaying thighs, oblivious*): Oh, yes, yes. Vanity, vanity. I can't help it. I should've been born ugly, but what can I do? (*Tilting his head back in her hands, with a jolt*) If I looked like a witch, would you still love me as you do?

> *She clutches him to her again, before he can speak.*

JOSEPH (*smothered*): Mrrlph —

LEAH (*rocking*): Oh, of course you would. Of course you would, I know that.

> *She lets go his head and looks down at him, stroking his stubbled hair.*

I was dreaming, before you came in. The noise of the door woke me. A strange dream. I can't remember it now, but it was . . . strange. (*Brief pause*) I stumbled and fell against the mirror by the bed. (*Rubbing her hip, wincing*) Ooo!

Pause.

(*To herself*) It's not like Isaac to be gone so long.

> *She helps* JOSEPH *to his feet, blows out the seven candles of the menorah*

one by one, goes to the sideboard and takes up the candle she had left there. She walks to the centre door, opens it, and turns to JOSEPH.

Come to bed, father.

JOSEPH *follows* LEAH *through the centre door into the encroaching darkness. Fade to black the Rabbi's study / fade up on* MAGDALENE*'s room, down left.*
Rear wall: a window embrasure through which the murky morning haze pervades the room; in the embrasure, a desk strewn with books, charts, papers, quills and ink, etc. A canopied bed, its curtains drawn, headboard flush with the left wall.
ISAAC *stands, dishevelled, in his shirt, gazing out the window.*

MAGDALENE (*from behind the bed curtains, drowsily*): Isaac. Come back to bed.

    ISAAC *does not move.*
    Pause.

Isaac?

    MAGDALENE*'s head appears between the bed curtains facing front. She is wearing round, thick spectacles. She glances right and left. Her head disappears behind the curtains.*
    MAGDALENE*'s head emerges from between the curtains at the foot of the bed.*

(*Seeing* ISAAC) Ah, *there* you are. Isaac, come back to bed.

    ISAAC *does not move.*

(*Coyly*) Mmmm?

    Pause.
    MAGDALENE *emerges from between the bed curtains. She is naked. She goes to* ISAAC *and embraces him from behind.*
    Pause.

ISAAC (*staring out the window, troubled*): It's still quite dark.

MAGDALENE (*her head on his shoulder*): Mmmm, what are you saying? It's nearly daylight. (*Tugging him, her eyes half closed*) Isaac, come back to bed.

He turns to her, lost in thought, and opens his mouth as if to speak, but nothing comes. He tries to remove her spectacles. She resists.

(*Laughing*) What are you doing?

ISAAC: You don't need them. (*Quietly*) Take them off.

MAGDALENE: I *do* need them. I'd have trouble knowing my own father without them. (*Mischievously*) Besides, if I took them off I'd be naked, and we haven't known one another long enough for that.

Humourlessly, he turns to the window again, and leans upon the desk.

(*In mock disapproval*) Ooooo.

As MAGDALENE *slips into a loose gown* . . .

ISAAC (*inspecting the charts and papers*): This . . . This is your father's work, is it not?

MAGDALENE: Mmmm.

ISAAC: Does he often work in your bedchamber?

MAGDALENE: It is my duty, and my pleasure, to assist my father in his work. Since he entered the Emperor's service, he has had little time to pursue his observations. The Emperor requires so much of him. And my father is ill disposed to go against the Emperor's wishes. I do what I can to help him. Those are *my* charts.

ISAAC: I would think he had assistants enough. (*Lifting a chart to the windowlight*) And you can understand . . . all this?

MAGDALENE: My father has schooled me well.

ISAAC: You spend your hours, you ruin your eyesight on . . . on this? (*Indicating the charts and papers*) But it's all . . . it's all gibberish.

MAGDALENE: And you, Isaac. What of you? You, a rabbi. You've lived your whole life in the shadow of a book of old wives' tales.

Pause.

ISAAC: I don't feel very much like a rabbi, Magdalene.

> *Pause.*

MAGDALENE: No. (*Brief pause*) They say your wife is very beautiful.

ISAAC (*peering out the window, reflectively*): Ay. (*Nodding*) Yes.

MAGDALENE: What is her name?

ISAAC: Leah.

MAGDALENE: Ah. Leah.

ISAAC: Mmmm. (*Brief pause*) I must go.

> *He reaches for his rabbi's coat.*

MAGDALENE: No. No, wait . . . a little longer, till the sun is high and my father is asleep. Otherwise, he might hear you.

> *Pause.*

ISAAC (*deeply troubled, at a loss*): I can't even remember what she looks like.

MAGDALENE: Your wife.

ISAAC: Mmmm.

> *Pause.*

MAGDALENE: Do you love her?

> *Pause.*

ISAAC: I don't know. (*Perplexed*) I don't *know*.

> MAGDALENE *senses that something is out of control, with her as with* ISAAC.
> *Pause.*

MAGDALENE: What will you do?

ISAAC: I don't know.

> *He approaches her. The quiet terror in his eyes contradicts his passionate words. He cannot stop himself from speaking against his deepest inclinations.*

If you told me my wife was fair or dark I would not know the truth from the lie, for there is but one face before me, beside which all others are effigies fit only for tombs. (*Caressing her face, with tears in his eyes*) I see no other living face but Magdalene's. Oh, Magdalene . . . who are you?

> *They kiss.*
> ISAAC *holds* MAGDALENE *close, a look of secret horror in his face. Slow fade to black* MAGDALENE's *bedchamber / fade slowly up on* TYCHO's *study, right and centre.*
>
> *Rear wall: a window through which the rosy light of dawn pervades the room, quadrants and other small astronomical instruments on the sill; on either side of the window, a muddle of bookshelves, star charts, etc.* TYCHO's *work-table is strewn with open books, papers, quills and ink, and the smaller impedimenta of his trade. The work-table is surrounded by a chaos of globes, planispheres, astronomical clocks, etc.*
>
> TYCHO *is quietly humming the 'Alba' melody as he nibbles a turkey leg and guzzles wine from a goblet of pewter; he sits, in his shirtsleeves, at the work-table, facing front.* JOHANNES *stands behind him at the window, peering at the far horizon with a small sextant and making notes.*

TYCHO (*nibbling away*): Well, Master Johannes?

> *Pause.*

Still pouting, are you?

JOHANNES (*peering through the sextant*): No.

TYCHO: You're feeling better, then. Your head?

JOHANNES: Yes.

TYCHO (*taking another mouthful*): Ah, I knew that powder would put you right. The Emperor gave it to me. It's one of his special concoctions. The best remedy yet for a surfeit of wine. I must remember to take some myself later.

JOHANNES (*making notes*): I had no wine. If you ask me, the Emperor would do better to leave such matters to his physicians.

TYCHO: Bah! Physicians, what do *they* know? He'd do as well to submit himself to the mercies of a witches' coven! Besides, he's afraid of being poisoned. That brother of his, Matthias, is itching for the Crown. He's got his spies at court. And the Emperor's no fool. Why else do you think he holds himself aloof even from his ministers?

He guzzles some wine.

JOHANNES: Rumpf and Trautson —

TYCHO: Ay. Ay, Rumpf and Trautson. That aged pair of jackals. The two of them together form a single Janus face which speaks from both sides of the same carious mouth.

JOHANNES (*peering through the sextant*): He ought to get rid of them.

TYCHO: No. It serves his purpose well to leave them in place. They know so little and are too decrepit now to throw in their lot with Matthias, who must, in any case, see them as the instruments of what he views to be the Emperor's ruinous policies. (*Brief pause*) No, Rumpf and Trautson are better left where they are. As they can do naught but evil, I'd as lief see them pawns in the Emperor's grand design.

JOHANNES (*coming from the window, sceptically*): What grand design?

TYCHO: I can tell you nothing now, for the Emperor himself has told me little and still ruminates upon the matter. But you and I will play our part, he has confided that much to me. Everyone believes Rudolf to be incapable of decision; the heathen Turk moves upon his borders in the East, Protestant and Catholic make war on one another to the West, and the Emperor wraps himself in a shroud of silence. But, mark you, in time he will deal with them all. And he will pluck his scheming brother down like a ripened fig from the vine.

He rubs ointment on his nose.
Pause.

JOHANNES: I sometimes fear for the Emperor's sanity.

TYCHO: Do you know he's taken to his bed again?

ACT TWO   295

JOHANNES: No.

TYCHO: His valet sent word to me that the Emperor cried out and fell in a stupor soon after the Rabbi and I left his chambers. His wife was with him. (*Brief pause*) She doesn't care for me. Tell no one of this, Johann, for it would be wise to follow the course we have always set at such times as the Emperor is taken ill.

> *He picks up a small celestial globe no larger than his fist.*
> *Pause.*

JOHANNES: If it's anything like the last attack, you will have more leisure to pursue your observations.

TYCHO (*contemplating the little globe*): Mmmm. (*Brief pause*) Oh, I know, I know ... the Emperor steals precious hours from me with his constant demands for new prognostications, as if the stars, like ciphers to be read in an endless book, could change what *must* be into that which the seer foretells. (*Brief pause*) When I was nineteen, I deduced from a lunar eclipse that the Turkish Sultan would die. I wrote in a Latin poem that the eclipse foretold the Sultan's death, and nailed my verses to the University door for all to see. (*Brief pause*) The Sultan was a man of eighty, but in no wise feeble. (*Nodding*) And he died. (*Turning to* JOHANNES) He died in battle ... nearly two months *before* the eclipse. (*Eyeing the little globe*) The death was kept secret. No one knew of it till *after* the eclipse. Since then I've set little store by the prophesies of others, and almost as little by my own, more fortunate, though still imprecise, prognostications. Yet the Emperor will have them. And I must do his will, for he has been most generous to me and is withal a man of great learning, whom I respect. (*Brief pause*) But now, as you say, I have the time ... time to pursue what is already nearly lost.

JOHANNES: What?

> TYCHO *lost in thought.*
> *Pause.*

TYCHO: No. Nothing. (*Rising*) I was just thinking of ... (*Holding up the little globe*) Do you see this? (*Sitting on the edge of the work-table*) By means of this small celestial globe, and a copy of the star tables of Stadius, I first acquainted myself with the names of the constellations. (*Turning the globe over in his hand*) My father intended me for the Law; but jurisprudence had not the allure of the evening skies, so I turned my eyes from dingy judgement seats and legal tomes to a vast region of darkness spangled with flickering orbs. How their beauty held me. (*Brief pause*) How many nights, while my tutor slept unknowing, did my hands caress this globe, till I knew it as well as if it were my own flesh. I've kept it with me always.

He stares at the little globe, sadly pensive.
Pause.

JOHANNES: Are you unwell, Master Tycho?

TYCHO: I'm tired.

JOHANNES: Before I take my leave, I must ask you again —

TYCHO (*distractedly*): What?

JOHANNES: Before I go.

TYCHO: Are you going somewhere?

JOHANNES: I only meant —

TYCHO (*preoccupied*): I should have stayed at Uraniborg, my residence on the isle of Hveen. I might have found some way to remain there after the King of Denmark died. (*Brief pause*) That island. From its northern shore you could see the ramparts of Elsinore when the air was clear, a faint grey wall in the distance. At Uraniborg, I built my great observatory. If only you had seen it, Johannes. (*Rising*) There, on a grassy eminence at the centre of the island, in the midst of geometric gardens and a bordering wood, the whole enclosed by four great walls — there, on the roof of my mammoth house of brick and stone, I placed towers, domes, spires and pavilions which opened shell-like on the heavens. There I had my laboratories and, in the gatehouse of the southern wall, the printing rooms from which I reached out and touched the Western World. Scholars journeyed from the great cities of Europe to dine at my table, and all were held in thrall by the wonders of my island mansion. (*Brief pause*) And now I have no habitation I can truly call my own but what space the Emperor provides me, here in his eastern realm, to make a gloomy storehouse for my ricketing clocks and spheres, a dingy corner to clutter with the ribs of my dismantled quadrants till the dust turns them white. The instruments I forged to help me read the turnings of the stars are, all but one, pulled down; and now I live a widower, who can only stand and watch the spider that entombs them in its web. Thus is my compass broken.

TYCHO, *much fatigued, goes back behind the work-table, sits, and busies himself.*

ACT TWO

Pause.

JOHANNES: I am not your peer for eloquence, Master Tycho, nor will I ever be. Mine is not the path to poetry or lyric sentiment. Still less am I given to rage in fury at the ignorance and duplicity which surrounds us, though perhaps I have more cause than you to complain of its consequence. But know that I, like you, have watched the stars for the better part of my life, and yet you forget my true position here. Well you may grieve for your lost observatories and the rule of the island over which, I am told, you were a harsh and most neglectful master.

TYCHO (*in a sudden rage*): What? Who told you this? Oh, I was accused, yes... (*Bitterly*) They, the people of the island — there was no pleasing them! They said I failed to maintain the lighthouse, that in the building of Uraniborg I worked them miserably and for small remuneration, that I kept a widow's pension for myself, that I let the chapel fall to ruin, stripped the inlays off its marble altarpiece, cut down its oaken struts, prised forth the crusted rubies from its silver crucifix, and carted off the lot to fill my coffers — oh, yes! The only thing of which they did *not* accuse me was the deflowering of their daughters! They! They forced me out! They turned the new King against me with their incessant complaints!

He slams his fist on the table.
Pause.

(*Subdued*) I'll have wakened Magdalene now.

JOHANNES: I did not mean to put you out of countenance. I'll leave you.

He turns to go.

TYCHO: No. Johannes, wait. What is it you wished to tell me?

JOHANNES: Not to *tell* you, Master Tycho, but to entreat you... once again. (*Brief pause*) I cannot go on like this. I cannot *work* like this. You give me nothing of real importance with which to occupy my thoughts, and only toss me scraps from your table, as a master would to his yelping dog, whene'er I complain of it.

TYCHO: But here, in Prague, you want for nothing. The Emperor has provided —

JOHANNES: I want for that of which I am most in need, and which you will not give up.

TYCHO: Ah. It's *that* again, is it?

JOHANNES: Why will you not allow me to see your observations? What can it profit you to withhold them from me?

TYCHO: We've been over this before, a thousand times. I need you for other things, at present. Your work on the theory of Mars.

JOHANNES: The theory of Mars does not command so much of my time that I cannot take on other, more important matters —

TYCHO (*rising*): Ah! More important, is it, for you to waste our precious time in attempting to prove that blasted Copernican system? God's death, Johannes! What can you be thinking of? Oh, I admit it, Copernicus was a great man — no less venerable, in his way, than Ptolemy or even Hipparchus — but to hold, against all evidence, that the Earth accompanies the five planets in orbit about the sun flies in the face of common logic! No. No, the Earth lies at the centre; and the sun and its five orbiting planets also orbit the Earth, for the Earth is made of denser substance than the rest, and is of such weight and mass as must preclude all possibility of its movement about the sun. (*Pacing*) Consider that if the Earth were a falling body, like those of the aethereal region, a constant flux of air must accompany its rotation. To prove that this is *not* the true condition of the Earth, we would simply need to fire two projectiles — one to the east, one to the west — with equal force. If unhindered by any flux of air, the distances travelled by the said projectiles would be of equal length, thus proving that the Earth does not move, but that the sun and the planets revolve *about* the Earth.

JOHANNES: But there is no manner in which you could be absolutely certain that the projectiles had been fired off with equal force.

    TYCHO *stops pacing and glares wearily at* JOHANNES *from across the room.*

And what of a sudden wind in the distance, have you thought of that? Or would you place a hundred-thousand men along the paths of flight, each to swear on oath that the air was still when the projectile passed?

    As TYCHO *puts his hands to his face, runs his fingers through his hair and slowly down his eyes . . .*

Or, could it be . . . Could it be that your own observations have already proved your system false, and that is the reason you withhold them from me?

TYCHO (*rushing at him, enraged*): You dare to speak to me in that way?

He grips JOHANNES *by the collar, but quickly lets go. Turning away, he places his hand on* JOHANNES*'s shoulder.*

(*Panting*) For pity's sake, Johannes, don't provoke me. You know my temper. I am not well, and there is much on my mind.

Pause.

The Emperor has spoken to me again of that woman, the woman who he says debauched the Archbishop of Cologne. Again, when he asked me if I knew of her, I feigned ignorance. (*Brief pause*) The woman is too much in his thoughts. Tonight, he had the portrait of a dark lady in his chamber, a wanton and lascivious work. He said the lady of the portrait was most like the woman Agnes, who bewitched the Archbishop. I fear her image poisons the Emperor's sleep. (*Turning to* JOHANNES) She is too much in his mind.

Fade to black.

Scene 2

Fade up on RUMPF *and* TRAUTSON, *down left, surrounded by darkness.*

RUMPF: I'm told the Emperor is his old self again.

TRAUTSON: Who told you that?

RUMPF: Never mind. (*Brief pause*) He's up to his usual tricks with those . . . alchemists, he calls them.

Fade up on RUDOLF, *down right, surrounded by five alchemists. They stand in an eerie chiaroscuro, staring, right, into the green flames of an alchemical furnace,* RUDOLF *wearing a black magician's gown garnished with gold zodiacal signs and other, more obscure, symbols. As* RUMPF *and* TRAUTSON *continue their discussion, the flames pass through the following sequence of colours: green, blue, indigo, violet, red, orange, yellow. With a long pair of iron tongs, the Emperor manipulates something hidden in the fire as one of the alchemists fans the flames with a large bellows.*

TRAUTSON: Mmmm.

RUMPF: He pays his respects to them most every night in that . . . that Golden Lane of his, hard by the Castle wall.

TRAUTSON: Ay, a filthy street, that. A slum of smoking dens and hovels. It reeks of putrid eggs and God knows what other foul miasmas.

RUMPF: Think of it, Trautson. The man whose wealth and holdings surpass that of the richest noble in the kingdom, and he must have gold from excrement. Even if the venture *weren't* completely mad, what's the point? Mind you, there's sure to be a nasty accident down there one day. I heard the Emperor's beard took fire one night when he leaned too near one of their ovens. They had to knock him to the floor and beat out the flames with their cloaks.

TRAUTSON: Who?

RUMPF: Who? The learned gentlemen. The sages of sulfur and gall.

TRAUTSON (*ironically*): The alchemists, Rumpf.

RUMPF: The alchemists, Trautson.

   Pause.

TRAUTSON: The Turks are getting nearer.

RUMPF: Mmm, the war goes badly.

TRAUTSON: And now the Emperor may have *another* brother to contend with.

RUMPF: Albert.

TRAUTSON: Ay. Albert.

RUMPF (*nodding*): Mmmm. Matthias has no children, and the Emperor's offspring all come from the wrong side of the bed. Well, what can you expect? The Emperor should never have given his consent to the marriage of Albert and the Infanta. They say she's with child. We should've sent her packing when

Rudolf decided — did I say decided? — when Rudolf left her waiting in the wings. (*Shaking his head*) Oh, he should have married her, I told him.

TRAUTSON: We both told him.

RUMPF: Now, with Albert as her husband, all she need do is drop a male heir into the cradle and the Emperor will have yet another jackal baying under his windows. (*Acidly*) Brotherly love.

> *The yellow flames brighten to a sudden, blinding whiteness.*
> *Blackout* RUDOLF, *the alchemists, the flames.*
> *Pause.*

You know what they've always said, Trautson.

TRAUTON: What?

RUMPF: About the Emperor's wife?

TRAUTSON (*contemptuously*): That woman.

RUMPF: It was all her doing, they say. They say *she's* the one who's bewitched him, that *she's* driving him mad.

> *Fade up on* CATHERINE *in her study, up right and centre.*

Or, at least, madder than he already was.

> *Fade to black* RUMPF *and* TRAUTSON.
>
> CATHERINE'*s study. Rear wall: a narrow, oblong window framing a twilight sky and a jumble of Castle rooftops in silhouette. Right wall: a door; to the right of the door, deep shelves on which lie some large folio volumes. Framed paintings on easels, statues and statuettes, etc., emerge from the shadows at left. In* CATHERINE'*s chamber there are many objets d'art, chief among which is a silver triptych; the triptych stands, shutters closed, on a small table in the foreground, its back to the audience.*
>
> CATHERINE *stands at the window, in black attire, peering out as a maidservant enters with* JOSEPH *through the door at right.*

CATHERINE (*with some anxiety*): Ah, Rabbi Loew.

JOSEPH (*bowing, in some confusion*): My lady.

CATHERINE *nods to the maidservant, who curtseys low, turns and goes, closing the door, as* JOSEPH *glances distractedly about the chamber.*

CATHERINE: It was I who summoned you here in the Emperor's name.

JOSEPH: Is the Emperor's condition worse, then?

Pause.

CATHERINE (*with difficulty*): My husband . . . has recovered in all but his wits.

She turns away, leaning on the small foreground table.

JOSEPH: My lady?

Pause.

CATHERINE (*turning to* JOSEPH): Good Rabbi Loew, for that you know the love my husband bears your people — the which he hath demonstrated since the advent of his reign by the abolishment of many harsh and injudicious strictures upon his Jewish subjects — I ask you now, knowing you for a man of wit and excellence of learning, and also of great cunning in the way of the world . . . I ask you — nay, I beseech you — help me bring your Sovereign to his wits again! (*Brief pause*) The Emperor is surrounded by deceivers.

JOSEPH *tries to mask his guilt.*

(*Nodding*) Ay, be not mistaken as to that. (*Pacing*) His ministers, Rumpf and Trautson, prevaricate against him to their own dark purpose; his brother Matthias casts a long eye on Rudolf's court from far Vienna, and would as lief see the Emperor hanged from a Turkish gibbet than renounce his claim to the Crown, which he means to snatch from off my husband's head whilst he still lives, saying, as he will, that Rudolf is unfit to rule by reason of the sickness in his mind. And now, as though to increase his misfortunes, the Emperor has fallen under the spell of that boastful and quarrelsome drunkard, Tycho Brahe.

JOSEPH: What, Master Doctor Tycho Brahe?

CATHERINE (*contemptuously*): Nay, Master of Pork and Venison, Master Doctor Mountebank; rather, call him a pustulous sack of conjurer's tricks and distempers! He has insinuated himself into the Emperor's good graces, and means to make the most of it whilst he can, for he knows well the high esteem in which Rudolf holds him, and, to keep it, will encourage my poor husband in his maddest whims. (*Tearfully*) O, would that the rumours of the Emperor's sickness of mind were untrue!

She stops before JOSEPH.
Pause.

Good Rabbi Loew, there is in my husband's rooms the portrait of a dark and lascivious woman.

JOSEPH (*tremulously*): I know the painting.

CATHERINE: Know you also that this portrait, which is more than a century in age, bears close resemblance to a certain lady who, not twenty years gone, it is said, bewitched the Archbishop of Cologne?

JOSPEH: Master Tycho made some mention of this.

CATHERINE: Of course. You've *seen* the portrait. You were there the night I first set eyes on it, in the Emperor's chambers.

JOSEPH: Yes, I was there.

CATHERINE: The woman's name was Agnes. The portrait has her so to the life as to suggest that she herself sat for the painter.

Pause.

JOSEPH: But that would be impossible.

As she walks amidst the paintings and statues . . .

CATHERINE: Ay, impossible, I know it. (*Brief pause*) The painting is indeed too old to be of the woman of whom we speak. I can attest to that, for I have no small knowledge in the matter. My father was antiquary to the Emperor, and taught me much of the manner in which pigment and varnish age upon wood. Ay, the painting is old, nigh on an hundred year, and therefore could not be of Agnes. Yet, when lately I stood vigil at the Emperor's bed, where for days and nights he lay in twilight sleep, now tossing in his sheets like an unmasted wreck buffeted by the howling gale, now drenched with burning fever or shivering with the ague, he would sometimes squeeze my hand and, in his stupor, call me Agnes, or would with gaping eye gaze wildly about the candled gloom, crying out upon what he construed to be the dark lady of the portrait, confounding her with the flicker on a wall, the which he would call Agnes, and bid her come to him — for her lips, he said, were made of ice and, thus, sole remedy 'gainst the fire in his seething brain.

> CATHERINE *breaks off in tears.*
> JOSEPH *places a hesitant hand on her shoulder.*

Even now, thoughts of that woman trouble the Emperor's spirit. He can have no rest until we rid him of her.

> *Pause.*

JOSEPH: We? But you said it couldn't be the —

CATHERINE (*bringing a small scroll from inside her sleeve*): Here, read it.

> JOSEPH *takes the scroll, which is small enough to be concealed in the palm of the hand, and unrolls it. Something black drops out. He bends to pick it up.*

JOSEPH (*holding the black thing to the light of the window*): What's this?

CATHERINE: A lock of maidenhair, plucked from the roots of her nether flesh, its raven filaments congealed by blood. (*Brief pause*) This, and the scroll, I found one night beneath the Emperor's pillow. Now, read the parchment.

> JOSEPH *squints and pretends to read the scroll, turning it now one way, now the other, but he cannot decipher its script.*

You see? The inscription is in Hebrew characters.

JOSEPH (*uncertainly*): Mmmm, yes. Yes, to be sure.

> *He continues to 'study' the inscription.*
> *Pause.*

CATHERINE: And now you know the name of the man who has done this sorcery.

> JOSEPH *looks at her.*

(*Her finger to the parchment*) There, beside the word for 'reckoning' — that word, there, which has no meaning of itself. (*Reciting the Hebrew letters, her finger moving right to left across the parchment*) Sadi ... koph ... ayin ...

... tav ... vav ... sadi. (*Retracing the letters*) S - K, which we must take for C — *ayin*, which has no Roman letter, but falls where O would fall - T - V - S. S - C - O - T - V - S.

JOSEPH: Scotus.

CATHERINE: In Italian, *scotto* — amongst other words, the word for 'reckoning'. And by this he means to settle his account with the Emperor. He it was, this Jerome Scoto, that caused the woman Agnes to appear before the Archbishop, in all her wanton nakedness, by means of a magic mirror.

JOSEPH (*with sudden understanding*): Oh.

CATHERINE (*eagerly*): You know him, then.

JOSEPH (*awkwardly*): Only . . . Only by reputation, my lady. But his magic is . . . I'm told he has a powerful command of the art.

CATHERINE: He hates the Emperor for having abandoned him to a fate he so richly deserved. For a long time, all here at court believed him dead. Rudolf alone, knowing the compass of Scoto's powers, was convinced that the wily Italian, having made the Duke of Saxony his cuckold, did escape both torture and dismemberment by conjuring forth a demon, shaped after his mirror image, to plead mercy and die in his stead. I did not believe my husband when he told me this, but I know now there was more reason in his words than I allowed. (*Indicating the parchment and the lock of hair*) For Scoto lives, and here is not the only proof.

She takes JOSEPH *by the arm and walks with him.*

Now, Rabbi Loew, this is what I would have you do. My maidservant will show you the way to Scoto's house.

JOSEPH (*startled*): What, to his house?

CATHERINE: Ay. He lives here in the city, the better to be near his victim. Not two days gone, he was seen in the streets and followed by one of my people. Matthias has not the only spies in Prague.

JOSEPH: But —

CATHERINE: You will go to Scoto's house and give him back the parchment and the blooded lock of hair. Then, you will work your magic on him. By all I have heard my husband tell of you, you are more than a match for Scoto in the casting on of spells and necromantic incantation. It is said that, with your own hands, you formed a man from earthen clay and raised him into life, as God raised Adam.

> JOSEPH *stops dead in his tracks. He now begins to understand, and tries desperately to conceal his alarm.*

Then you alone possess the power to turn Scoto's mind from its vengeful purpose, to still his tongue from conjuring oaths and dispel his black intent. Transform his blood into thick sap, and root his arms to the ground so that he may not raise them up to call upon his demon spirits —

JOSEPH (*in confusion*): I . . . My lady, I —

CATHERINE (*more and more urgently, leading him to the door*): I know the Emperor means to make use of you in some intrigue of his. Of late, he had a bitter dream that he was prisoner in a dungeon; full eleven years was he held captive by some rebellious prince in a far corner of the realm, until you came to him, unlocked the barred window of his cell, and set him free.

> *She opens the door and beckons the maidservant, who appears in the doorway.*

(*To* JOSEPH) My maidservant will take you now. (*To the maidservant*) Go by way of the North staircase, for the Emperor is closeted with his astrologer and might otherwise hear you.

> *The maidservant curtseys low and exits.*

(*To* JOSEPH) I pray you, tell no one of this. (*Brief pause*) You are a good man, Rabbi Loew. Help the Emperor, for he loves you well. (*Almost pushing him out the door*) Go now, and save Prague from its evil destiny!

> JOSEPH *exits in confusion.*
> *The door closes;* CATHERINE *leans back against it, and shuts her eyes. Pause.*
> *Slow fade to black* CATHERINE'*s study / fade up on a shadowy corner of the Emperor's private museum, down left. A mysterious, whimmering halflight falls upon the mummified remains of sea monsters, ill-assembled dinosaur bones, the skeleton of a two-headed child, a winged reptile and other oddities; some are displayed in cases, some hang in mid-air. At left,*

a cabinet of drawers. In the foreground, a large chest on which RUDOLF *sits in his customary black attire, his back to the audience.* TYCHO *stands before him, dressed in black, inspecting the wings of a large stuffed bat suspended above the Emperor's head. Far behind* TYCHO, *a little to the left, hang the enormous, gaping jawbones of a whale, bristling with pointed teeth.*

RUDOLF (*gazing about*): Here, Master Tycho . . . here, among my torpid beasts, am I most at home. Their silence comforts me.

He holds out a whittled dinosaur tooth the shape of an elongated cone.

Know you what this is?

TYCHO *takes the whittled tooth and turns it in his hand.*
Pause.

TYCHO: A horn of some sort, but none the like of which I've ever seen. (*Fingering it*) 'Tis not of ivory or of bone.

RUDOLF: Nay, nor one nor the other. (*Rising*) 'Tis of a unicorn.

TYCHO *looks at* RUDOLF *in amazement as the Emperor takes back the 'horn' and caresses it.*

Beautiful, is it not? 'Twas my father's. (*Brief pause*) Upon my father's death, I was compelled, by the terms of his will, and much against my own desires, to give it over to my uncle Ferdinand. It is said that whoever possesses the horn and can fathom its mystery will have bestowed upon himself the power of the Holy Spirit.

As RUDOLF *carefully sets the 'horn' on a nearby cabinet, bends, and opens the large chest at his feet, and* TYCHO *rubs ointment on his nose . . .*

I implored my uncle to allow me to retain the horn in my keep. He agreed to make me the loan of it, but nothing more. This was no good, as one must gain full title in order to come into its powers. This, Ferdinand refused me. And so, he kept the horn whilst he lived. When the news came of his death, I despatched my valet to Innsbruck and, within hours, took possession of what was then truly mine — the mystical horn, and this.

He lifts a large agate bowl, edged with silver reliefs, from the depths of the chest. A gold statuette stands in the centre of the bowl.

(*Pointing to the statuette*) There. Our Lord. (*Running his finger round the perimeter*) And the twelve Apostles.

TYCHO (*pointing*): And the one whose head is turned away?

RUDOLF: Judas. (*Turning the bowl before* TYCHO's *eyes*) See how it glitters in the light. When I turn it so, the dwindled shapes on the walls and cabinets commence to undulate like corals in a clouded sea. This great cup is the richest of plunders, worth more to me than all the gold of the new-found world. Three hundred years gone, it was delivered up from Constantinople by brave Crusaders. Whosoever drinks from it puts his lips where once were pressed the lips of Jesus Christ.

Pause.

TYCHO (*humouring him*): Is this the Holy Grail?

RUDOLF: Ay, Master Doctor. The very cup Our Lord held in his hands.

RUDOLF *and* TYCHO *hold the bowl between them,* TYCHO *eyeing the Emperor with cautious suspicion.*

There is, imprisoned in these swirls of agate smoke, the key unto eternal life. If we could but only find the right admixture, the potion which will wake the stone from its abiding sleep . . . (*Lost in his revery*) Yes.

Pause.

TYCHO: Sire?

Pause.

RUDOLF (*suddenly*): What?

RUDOLF's *hands fall from the bowl as he turns away.* TYCHO *juggles with the 'Grail' for one precarious moment, regains his hold, and sets it gently in the chest, which he closes.*
From now on, TYCHO's *weariness speaks through.*
Pause.

(*Gazing at the cabinet, coldly*) You know, they want the dissolution of my marriage.

TYCHO: Who, my lord?

RUDOLF: Everyone. My ministers, my brothers, the Papal Nuncio . . . my wife.

TYCHO: Nay, I knew it not. What will you do?

> *Pause.*

RUDOLF: Your wife. Is she not here with you in Prague?

TYCHO: No, my lord.

> *Pause.*

RUDOLF: You had a brother, did you not?

TYCHO: Ay, your grace. He was my twin . . . born dead.

RUDOLF: He never opened his eyes . . . nor took one breath of air, but was as like to you as you to your mirror image.

> RUDOLF *still with his back to him.* TYCHO *sad and pensive.*
> *Pause.*

You think of your dead brother often, do you not?

TYCHO: Not one day passes but that he does not live in my thoughts. (*Brief pause*) My brother is my second shadow, the voiceless, faceless, unformed figure of what I was . . . and what I soon shall be.

RUDOLF: And if *you* had been the one to die, and your brother the one to live? May he not have been the greater man?

> RUDOLF *turns and faces* TYCHO, *who looks at him sadly, without answering.*
> *Pause.*

(*Staring at the floor*) Would that *my* brother, who is neither my twin nor dead, were both. Then might I live in peace. For he is more monstrous to me than the creeping basilisk, whose venom spurts forth from out the sac of its louring eye. (*Brief pause*) Look about you. (*Pointing out some of the more hideous objects of his collection*) Here is the vengeance of brute nature upon iniquity. When my brother dies, he will be reborn into the world as a wonder thrice more abhorrèd than any prodigy in *my* collection. Gaze on these poor creatures, Master Doctor, and tremble at the recompense my brother shall have earned for the wrongs he does me now.

TYCHO (*inspecting the various monstrosities*): Indeed, Sire, the sins of some must be more than even hell can bear, for not long after they die they are reborn blind or lame; others are bereft of all reason, or so hideously malformed that strong men quake to look upon them.

RUDOLF: Ay, you have *seen* such living prodigies?

TYCHO (*slowly*): Ay, my lord, some most piteous to behold; others, less ill-favoured by nature, but frightful still—those that move the heart such as to make a man weep or laugh at seeing, in their fretful countenaces, the mockery of his own soul.

Pause.
RUDOLF *puts his hand on* TYCHO'*s shoulder.*

Slow fade to black the Emperor's museum to the sound of AGNES' *low, sinister chuckle in the shadows right/fade up on a room in* SCOTO'*s house, down right and centre. Night.*

SCOTO'*s room is richly appointed, half Gothic, half Oriental in décor, the floor strewn with carpets and cushions. Along the right wall an 'Arabian' divan, consisting of a truckle bed covered with Persian drapery and an ornate waterpipe. Rear wall: behind the divan, an arras; a lattice window, festooned with obscure talismans; the 'large and hideous' painted crucifix of Act One, hung upside down, merging with the shadows left. In the middle of the floor stands a smoking brazier; to the left of the brazier, a high-backed wooden chair facing the divan.*

SCOTO *sits in the wooden chair, clad in a red doublet, watching* AGNES, *who stands, facing front, behind the brazier with her head thrown back, her arms extended as on a cross; she is wearing a shapeless, but richly embroidered, Oriental gown with long, wide sleeves. The brazier casts a greenish light on her from below.*

Her chuckle . . .

SCOTO (*chuckling*): What see you in the smoke?

AGNES (*peering into the brazier*): I see . . . a woman—a young woman, and a bearded man.

SCOTO (*leaning forward in his chair*): Do they lie abed?

AGNES (*into the brazier, chuckling*): Nnnn, the man is very old.

SCOTO: Where are they now?

AGNES: They walk the streets together. (*Into the brazier*) So close are their faces that I might reach out my hand and pluck the hair of the old man's beard.

> *Pause.*
> *They look at one another, then burst into sinister laughter.* SCOTO *holds out his arms to* AGNES *and she goes to him, sitting on his lap. He reaches into her gown, but she stops his hand and forces it out, smiling imperiously.* SCOTO *looks at her without expression.*
> AGNES *rises and walks about.*

How will you answer the old man, Scoto?

SCOTO (*ironically*): I shall accept his gift . . . through you, as we agreed.

AGNES: His gift? A scroll and a hank of blooded maidenhair?

> *She laughs derisively.*

SCOTO: And is your lap the colder for't?

AGNES (*putting her hand to her loins*): Nay, I did not cringe to part with curlèd wisps of what I have already in abundance, nor is my lap less hot then e'er it was, nor my life's blood consumed by a few drops' loss.

SCOTO: Ay, well I know it. What's the loss of a few drops to you, who nightly gorge upon the blood of men's dreams and suck forth your nourishment from out their anguished slumbers, like the leeching physician crouched upon the sickbed?

AGNES (*slyly*): You mock me.

SCOTO (*rising*): Is't for me to mock the woman who debauched the Archbishop of Cologne?

> *They laugh and embrace. Again he puts his hand into her gown, but she slips away.*
> *Pause.*

My plan goes well, Agnes. The Emperor's wife has taken up the scent and sends her Rabbi, scroll and maidenhair in hand, to the lure.

AGNES: What think you of this Rabbi Loew?

SCOTO: In art of magic there is none his equal, for in time past he raised base matter up to life, made breathing flesh of mud, spake into it its eyes, its hearing, its power to reason, and the perfection of its organs by spells and formulæ the which are known to me, and e'en so remain beyond my compass. For all that, he is but a man of sinew and bone . . . an aged man who, in God's mockery, may call forth life from the elements yet cannot put a hair's breadth distance more 'twixt himself and the hour of his own demise.

She claps her hands to her ears, and shuts her eyes. He forces her hands down from behind.

(*Into her ear*) How now, Agnes? Must not we all grow old and die?

AGNES *opens her eyes in agony.*

Eh?

She breaks free of his grip, but he pursues her to the divan. She falls upon the truckle bed as he catches her up from behind.

(*Into her ear, with quiet ferocity*) Know you how old you truly are —

AGNES (*pleading*): No —

SCOTO: Nay! Nay, you have not made your peace with the hooded Reaper, nor have I; nor shall I be happily cut down by death till the arcane furies, made slave to Rabbi Loew's enjoinment, are mine to command. I, who, with one nub of chalk and dripping candle wax, can summon forth the spirits of the dead from black oblivion and bind them to my darkest covenants, stand mute before a lump of sodden earth and cannot, either by sway of numbers' mystery or by solemn adjuration, bid it rise and live, a man. Yet will I sound the depth of that old magician's cunning, and wrest the secret from him whilst he lives. (*More urgently*) The Emperor . . . Dost thou hear me, Agnes? The Emperor's become the very paragon of madness, and a fool besides. 'Twas none of my doing; e'en so, I'd have him no other way. For all his power and the richness of his vast domains he cares naught, but frets his nights away at noxious ovens, surrounds himself with fawning high priests of the crucible and, through his court astrologers, consults the heavens to confound his destiny with elusive stars. (*Contemptuously*) Had *I* the Holy Roman Empire, I'd have no need of magic. (*Brief pause*) With the connivance of his Danish mountebank Tycho Brahe, Rudolf means to woo the High Rabbi to his purpose, the which is this — that Rabbi Loew return to life what he hath once destroyed, and raise his long dead creature up from ashes to do the Emperor's bidding.

AGNES (*closing her eyes and leaning back against him*): Mmmm.

SCOTO (*in agreement*): Mmmm. And, to this end, nor man nor beast can stop him. (*Brief pause*) Methinks the Emperor would have the creature slay his brother.

AGNES: What, the Archduke Matthias?

SCOTO: Ay, and save his armies the toil of it.

AGNES *laughs and rises, looking down at* SCOTO.

AGNES: Whereof did you come by this testimony to the Emperor's dark intent?

SCOTO: From Isaac.

AGNES: Isaac?

SCOTO: Ay, husband to the Rabbi's daughter. I cast a spell upon him.

AGNES: The Rabbi hath confided to his daughter the Emperor's designs?

SCOTO: Nay, he knows them not.

AGNES: Then, how came Isaac by them?

SCOTO: From Tycho's daughter Magdalene, upon whom I did also cast a spell. She spoke to Isaac of her father's ruminations upon the matter. Of late he hath been greatly vexed by the Emperor's turn of mind.

AGNES: Isaac?

SCOTO: Nay, Tycho. He now believes what his eyes and ears did tell him long agone, and speaks outright the words he hath so oft forborne to say, freely admitting the Emperor's madness both to himself and to his daughter. Whilst the Emperor lay ill, Tycho was much in the Rabbi's company and, through many an evening's disputation upon subjects celestial and profane, their friendship grew apace, the issue of which finds Tycho more ill-disposed to credit what he already held in doubt — to wit, the Rabbi Loew's dominion o'er the world invisible. (*Brief pause*) The more fool he. This Rabbi plays him false, puts on a backward countenance to forestall his queries, poses him unanswerable riddles, and chides himself with soft rebukes the better to persuade the Master

Doctor of his ignorance. (*Shaking his head, with conviction*) O, he's the very fox for cunning, this Rabbi Loew. (*Brief pause*) But soft, he comes now. (*Rising*) Agnes, be none too tame with him, I pray you, but let him see the quintessence of earthly enticement. Then bring him to his knees.

    SCOTO *hides behind the arras.*
    Enter JOSEPH, *in confusion, from out of the shadows left.* AGNES *turns to face him. His hands fly up to his wig, freezing in mid-air. He struggles to understand. His hands drop slowly to his sides as he gapes at* AGNES.
    Pause.
    JOSEPH *catches sight of the inverted crucifix.*

AGNES (*reassuringly*): Be you not harrowed with fear, sweet Rabbi Loew. This is no church, or I'm a priestess.

    Pause.

JOSEPH (*mesmerised*): I . . . Who *are* you?

AGNES (*approaching him*): 'Tis a question left us yet to prove.

    She stokes his beard.

I am one who loves you well, and would not see you fall to any mischief.

    She puts her arms about his neck, her face close to his. He caresses her almost absentmindedly, staring into her eyes as SCOTO *peeps out at them from behind the arras.*
    Pause.

(*Intimately*) Come, sit by me on the divan that I might hear your counsel. (*Brief pause*) I do believe your eyelids droop like leaden coins this side of slumber. Are you so weary?

    JOSEPH *fights to keep his eyes open.*

(*Pulling him toward the divan*) Come and rest a while. We'll take a cup of wine.

    JOSEPH *breaks free of her embrace, falling backwards, in a perfect sitting posture, into the wooden chair.* SCOTO's *head disppears behind the arras.*

JOSEPH (*as though waking from a dream*): Is this the house of Jerome Scoto?

AGNES (*gently*): Hear you, sir. By what reason do you ask me this?

> *He brings the scroll and the lock of maidenhair from under his coat, holding them out to her, one in each hand.*

JOSEPH (*rising*): I've come to give him these.

> *She takes the scroll and tosses it over her shoulder.*

AGNES (*eyeing the lock of maidenhair*): Ay, you have some remembrances of me to redeliver. (*Letting her gown fall*) Wouldst thou replant them for me?

> AGNES *stands naked before him, stroking her loins, a dark bruise on the rearward portion of her right hip. The lock of maidenhair falls from* JOSEPH'*s hand as he backs away from her.*

JOSEPH (*thunderstruck*): That bruise . . . where did you get it?

AGNES (*approaching him*): I fell.

> JOSEPH *staggers backwards, pursued by* AGNES. *He bumps against the inverted crucifix, gashing his right forefinger on the crown of thorns.*

JOSEPH (*wincing*): Oh!

> *He holds up his bleeding finger.*

AGNES (*solicitously*): You're wounded.

> AGNES *kneels at* JOSEPH'*s feet, takes his finger into her mouth, and sucks the blood from it as he looks down in horror.*
> *Pause.*
> JOSEPH *plucks his finger from* AGNES' *mouth and flees into the shadows left.* AGNES, *groping after the hem of his long coat, falls forward beneath the inverted crucifix; she draws her knees up under her, and lies still.*
> *Pause.*
> SCOTO'*s head emerges from behind the arras. A look of anger comes over his face. He walks slowly, thoughtfully, to the fallen gown, picks it up, and goes to* AGNES. *He looks down at her with contempt, spreads the gown and covers her with it completely. As he does so, his glance falls on the crucifix. He sees blood on the crown of thorns, brings some off on his finger, tastes it.*

SCOTO (*to himself, grimly*): It tastes of salt and iron, like the blood of any man.

He rises from his crouching position, licking his upper lip.

(*Rubbing thumb to forefinger*) Mmmm, but this is brine from the deepest ocean bed, and metal tempered in the very fire of hell 'gainst all temptation. One drop would burn sweet wine to gall and make a cinder of the cup that held it.

He puts his hand on the back of the wooden chair and props his chin upon it, brooding.
Pause.

How the occasion doth inform against me. The old man's more the master of his wits than I of mine, and plays the intruding fool to perfection. 'Tis little wonder he hath cozened Tycho Brahe from the Emperor's persuasion. (*Brief pause*) He hath made the Master Doctor first obstacle to my revenge.

Pause.

(*He turns, calling softly*) Agnes?

Pause.

She sleeps. I'll wake her anon. For we have bitter business yet to dispose 'twixt ourselves and this artful Rabbi.

Fade to black.

Scene 3

Distant rumbles of thunder in the darkness.
   Fade up on an unadorned reception room in the Castle, up left and centre. Right to left: a simple throne; a long, gothic window giving on a deeply overcast morning sky. Down left, between the throne and the window, a small table laden with sealed documents, etc. In the left wall, an archway draped by a purple curtain.
   More rumbles of thunder are heard in the distance.
   RUDOLF *sits on the throne, brooding, some scrolls and papers clutched in his hand.*
   Enter MAKOWSKI, *drawing the purple curtain aside.*

MAKOWSKI: His Eminence, the Papal Nuntius.

Enter Cardinal SPINELLI, *a robust man, fiery in temperament.*
Exit MAKOWSKI.

SPINELLI (*bowing*): Your Majesty.

RUDOLF (*barely concealing his distaste*): My lord Cardinal, by what reason do you demand this audience? Though now it be high morning, the hour is late for us, and we are worn most weary by our last night's work.

SPINELLI: Hear you, Sire. I'll mince not words but speak with all my heart. I come to tell you that you court damnation, by reason that you give to negligence all that which doth have grave effect on your continuance as sovereign o'er this land. You stop your ears to the matter of succession, as though the living world would cease and Austria become a desert waste upon your death, and come most tardy to the general will that you, as Holy Emperor, must needs take arms against the enemies of Holy Mother Church, to which you are defender sworn and chrism'd. E'en now, whilst heretic armies to the west and the heathen hordes of the Ottoman tide close upon us, your sword sleeps in its scabbard, your golden laurel is put in pawn for a witcher's cap!

RUDOLF (*rising*): Hold your tongue, priest!

SPINELLI (*aggressively*): Your grace, I do in friendship counsel you —

RUDOLF: Pray be silent! (*Flinging the scrolls and papers in the Cardinal's face*) And *this* for your friendship's counsel I do requite you!

As SPINELLI *bends to pick them up* . . .

Read them! And speak no more to me of the general will, or of slumbering swords, or crowns put up to merchant's ransom, thou thrice-crownèd villain!

He snatches one of the scrolls from SPINELLI's *hand.*

(*Reading aloud*) It is the general opinion, amongst many Catholic people in Prague, that a demon hath bewitched their sovereign into a solemn covenant with the Devil. With my very eyes, I have seen —

SPINELLI: Sire, give me leave to —

RUDOLF (*continuing, louder*): I have seen the chair from which the Emperor hath held bold discourse with the Prince of Darkness. (*Seething*) I have been shown the small bell by which His Majesty doth conjure the spirits of the dead into his presence, so as to work his will upon them! (*To* SPINELLI) Ay, well! Is not this import of our necromancies to your master, the Pope, writ of your own hand and by your seal affix'd, my lord Cardinal?

SPINELLI: Your grace, I pray you —

RUDOLF (*snatching another scroll from the Cardinal*): What, like you not *this*? (*Reading aloud*) 'Tis said you are an alchemist, and much given to necromantic practice. If this be true — and I pray heaven it is not — if Your Majesty doth incline so low as to wake the dead from their eternal sleep and enlist them to your service, may God have mercy upon the House of Austria!

SPINELLI: Good my lord, I —

RUDOLF (*holding the letter under the Cardinal's nose*): Look you there. (*Pointing*) 'Tis signed by our noble brother Albert.

SPINELLI *turns and looks* RUDOLF *in the eye.*

(*Backing away*) Didst thou know that the Abbot of the Capuchin friars daily preaches against us in his sermons?

Pause.

(*Nodding*) Ay, thou knowest well, my lord Cardinal.

RUDOLF *gazes at* SPINELLI *from head to foot, and in his staring begins to see something amiss. Slowly, the Emperor's eyes grow large with fear and welling sickness. He staggers backwards, clutching at the table for support, knocking some of its documents, etc., to the floor as he reels and seems about to faint. The Cardinal rushes to his aid.*

SPINELLI (*close to him*): Your Majesty is ill. Come, my lord, I'll —

RUDOLF (*recoiling in horror*): O, stand away! Breathe not on me! Your breath is foul, Cardinal!

As SPINELLI *draws back in stunned confusion . . .*

'Tis wine-soaked sour, and reeks of rancid fish! (*Quaking*) Breathe not your rotted soul on me! (*Sinking to the floor, his back to the table leg*) O most pernicious villain! O pustulous soul, seven times damned!

As MAKOWSKI *rushes in from the left* . . .

(*Weeping*) O fie! Fie upon it!

MAKOWSKI: My lord, my lord!

He sinks to his knees beside the raging Emperor.

RUDOLF (*staring at the befuddled Cardinal, to* MAKOWSKI, *panting*): Look you. See how his soul spews foul blackness from out his lips and girths his body round as 'twere a cloak of writhing serpents. Makowski, dost thou see it? O, fearful Medusa! And how his raiment doth shimmer forth through the coil'd hydra like blood of a gaping wound whose issue gives the girdling monster suck of its scarlet poison. Dost thou see it?

    Pause.

MAKOWSKI (*dissembling*): Ay, my lord. I see it plain.

    MAKOWSKI *hangs his head and tries to conceal his grief.*

RUDOLF (*muttering*): 'Tis Rumpf's doing. They think I know naught of their vile conspiracies. (*To the Cardinal, crying out*) Eh, my lord Cardinal Spinelli? (*Shaking his fist, his voice breaking*) 'Tis all Rumpf's doing!

    Fade to black amidst growing rumbles of thunder and the noise of heavy rain.
    Pause.
    A sudden flash of lightning illuminates RUDOLF's *silhouette in the long, gothic window, followed by a deafening peal of thunder. Night has fallen.*
    Fade up on RUDOLF, *clad in a long, black dressing gown, pacing the room like a caged animal. The throne and table are gone; a truckle bed and chair now occupy their respective places. The chamber is sparse, lit by 'candle-light', its shadows converging on darkness to the right and the left. The storm is at its height. Lightning and thunder throughout.*
    Enter MAKOWSKI, *right.*

MAKOWSKI: His Excellency, the Lord High Chancellor.

    Enter RUMPF, *hastily dressed and dishevelled, wearing his chain of office.*
    Exit MAKOWSKI.

RUMPF (*bowing*): Sire.

RUDOLF (*archly*): How now, my lord High Minister? We do believe our summons did wake you from deep slumber, for you are more than common disarrayed.

RUMPF (*groggily*): Nay, my liege. I never shut one eye but that the other be half open to mine Emperor's volition. This night, afore your summons came to me, I lay abed and saw the tempest break from out my window.

RUDOLF: Then 'tis well we have summoned thee. Thou wilt have much the nearer prospect of it here.

RUMPF: My lord?

RUDOLF (*toying with him*): How like you this minister's life, Master Rumpf? Does it fit your humour well?

RUMPF: Sire?

RUDOLF: Eh?

RUMPF: Well enough, my lord. I —

RUDOLF: Ay, right well enough. And your chain of office, it doth hang handsome on you, does it not?

RUMPF (*befuddled*): Ay, my lord, it does. Most handsome.

RUDOLF: How comes it, then, that thou art out of it?

RUMPF: Why, out of what, my lord?

RUDOLF: Why, thy chain of office, my lord Chancellor.

RUMPF (*fingering his golden chain*): Why, here is my chain, nor am I out of it.

RUDOLF: Then are the links given to great neglect. They grow so rusty they do vanish in the very hue of thine own garment.

RUMPF (*chuckling nervously*): Faith, my lord, then this be fool's gold, or pigment of gilt laid on, for never saw I rust upon true gold.

RUDOLF: Ay, 'tis so. I had forgot. Then why dost thou come to our bidding thus unchained?

RUMPF: Unchained, my lord? (*Shaking his golden chain*) Marry, my chain is *here!*

RUDOLF: Come hither, by the window, that I might the better look upon it. For though 'tis now the very dead of night and but a short time past the witching hour, the tempest rages and will give some brief illumination of it.

RUMPF: As you will, my lord.

He joins RUDOLF *at the window.*
Great bolts of lightning, deafening thunder . . .

RUDOLF (*gazing out the window*): Look you there. A mighty thunderbolt forks through the clouds and tears their flesh away with a blinding stroke, and they disgorge their ocean's contents full upon our heads.

Another bright bolt, thunder.

(*Eyeing* RUMPF*'s chain of office*) Ah, I do perceive it now. (*Fingering the links*) 'Tis a ponderous heavy chain to bear, my lord Chancellor, is it not?

RUMPF: Ay, your grace.

As RUDOLF *brings a dagger from under his gown and cuts the tabs that fix* RUMPF*'s golden chain to his garment . . .*

RUDOLF: Then we will, in all good mercy, relieve you of your burden.

He twists the chain tightly about the Chancellor's throat, holding the dagger between RUMPF*'s neck and the links, as if to cut it free.*

RUMPF (*choking*): Arrrgh!

RUDOLF (*gently*): Strengthen thy patience yet awhile, sir, thou'lt presently be free of it. First, thou perfidious dog, tell me by what connivance thou hast come to champion my villainous brother for succession?

RUMPF *gasps and flails his arms, but he dare not strike the Emperor.*

(*Tightening his grip*) I'll unchain thy tongue!

With his fist and dagger, RUDOLF *lifts free the golden chain and hurls it against the window.* RUMPF *staggers toward the chair, clutching his throat, the maddened Emperor in pursuit.*

RUMPF (*hoarsely*): Help! Help!

> RUDOLF *bends* RUMPF *backwards over the arm of the chair, his hand to the Chancellor's throat, his dagger poised under* RUMPF*'s nose.*

RUDOLF: 'Twas you that sent the Nuntius to mouth his venomous impeachments to our face —

RUMPF: Arrrgh —

RUDOLF: Ay, confess it! Make me an answer —

RUMPF: Arrrgh! My lord, I cannot!

> RUDOLF *hurls* RUMPF *to the floor and falls upon him. His fingers close about* RUMPF*'s neck.*

RUDOLF: Speak, false worm! Make me an answer straight, and then I'll cut your throat! Who are your agents? I'll have their names —

RUMPF: Good my lord — O help! help! — I prithee take thy fingers from my throat!

RUDOLF: Thou viper's mask! O treason! Treason!

> *The storm reaches a paroxysm of lightning and thunder as* MAKOWSKI, POPP *and two guards rush in from right.*

MAKOWSKI: My lord —

POPP: Sire —

RUMPF (*to* RUDOLF): Hold off thy hand!

RUDOLF (*his dagger raised, poised to strike*): The devil take thy soul!

> MAKOWSKI *stops the Emperor's hand and pulls him off the whimpering* RUMPF. RUDOLF *turns the dagger on himself.*

MAKOWSKI: My lord, no!

> MAKOWSKI *wrests the dagger from him, after a struggle; it falls to floor, and* RUDOLF *collapses into* MAKOWSKI*'s arms.* POPP *helps* RUMPF *to his feet. The*

guards point their halberds at the trembling minister.

RUDOLF (*hoarse and delirious*): O, the dogs! Treason, treason . . .

RUDOLF faints. As MAKOWSKI *lays him on the truckle bed, the guards cross their halberds between* RUMPF *and the unconscious Emperor.*

POPP (*to the guards*): Take him away.

The guards make to take RUMPF *off by force.*

Let no harm come to him!

Exit RUMPF, *under guard, right.*
POPP *goes to the truckle bed, where* MAKOWSKI *is wiping the Emperor's brow.* RUDOLF *lies motionless.*
Pause.

MAKOWSKI (*to* POPP): Fetch hither the Lady Catherine.

Fade to black, all sounds to silence.

Scene 4

RUMPF *confronts* TRAUTSON *in a narrow pool of light, down right. Both men are weary but neatly garbed, their chains of office gone for good.*

RUMPF (*conspiratorially*): Have you heard?

TRAUTSON: What?

RUMPF: He's dying . . . at last.

TRAUTSON: The Emperor?

RUMPF: Tycho Brahe.

TRAUTSON (*hushed*): Oh.

RUMPF (*scarcely concealing his delight*): It all happened quite suddenly. Councillor Minkawitz told me the whole story.

TRAUTSON: You still have ties with the Castle, then?

RUMPF: No. And you?

TRAUTSON: No.

RUMPF: No, I didn't expect you would, after the way they treated you.

TRAUTSON: And you.

RUMPF (*nodding*): Mmmm, and me. (*Fingering his neck with some delicacy*) I know *I've* seen the Emperor for the last time.

TRAUTSON: And I, as well. But, what of Tycho's death?

RUMPF: Well, he isn't dead yet. (*Smugly*) But it won't be long now, I can tell you. It happened over supper at the Baron von Rosenberg's, last week. Tycho was the guest of honour. As usual, he distinguished himself by consuming more than half the wine at table and gorging himself like a ravenous hog. (*Brief pause*) Well, what with one thing and another, it wasn't very long before the Master Doctor began to suffer the . . . pangs of nature.

TRAUTSON (*chuckling*): Mmmm —

RUMPF: Yes. His bladder was soon quite beyond the pale. (*Brief pause*) Because he held the place of honour at the Baron's table, he felt it would be an insult to his host if he were to step out and relieve himself. Can you imagine?

TRAUTSON: Foolish man.

RUMPF (*tapping his temple*): His mind. (*Brief pause*) It's a wonder they didn't have to trundle him out of there in an oxcart. (*Archly*) What agonies he must have suffered.

TRAUTSON: Mmmm. And now it's killing him.

RUMPF: Mmmm. He's been delirious for a week. It's all backed up on him.

TRAUTSON: What, Rumpf?

RUMPF: All that wine, Trautson.

TRAUTSON: The Baron's wine.

RUMPF: It's poisoned him.

> *A low, liquescent death-rattle commences in the shadows.*
>
> *Slow fade to black* RUMPF *and* TRAUTSON */ fade up slowly* TYCHO *on his deathbed, up centre. A shaft of dawn light, filtered through the lattice window in the right wall, falls on his face. In the left wall, a double door. The room in chiaroscuro.*
>
> TYCHO *lies beneath the bed canopy, facing front, his head and back propped up by pillows; he wears a linen mobcap. His eyes are closed, his mouth half open.* MAGDALENE *stands at the bedside, right, holding* TYCHO's *hand, tears in her eyes.*
>
> *Courtiers and* TYCHO's *assistants, in black court dress, stand vigil about the large chamber.*
>
> *Down left,* JOHANNES *confers in low tones with his colleague* SEYFFART, *who has just entered from left.*

SEYFFART: How is't with him, Master Johannes?

JOHANNES: I fear he will not outlive the morning. The Emperor, who lately stood vigil at his bed, is now gone to the Cathedral to offer solemn prayer to God that Tycho's life may yet be spared. (*Indicating* TYCHO) Look you how pale death o'ershrouds his face and, with an icy hand, draws forth the air from out his sinking lungs in coarse, prostrated sighs.

SEYFFART: Alas.

> *Pause.*
> JOHANNES *takes* SEYFFART *aside.*

JOHANNES: Good Master Seyffart, for that I rest much bounden to you, both by your many commendations as by your true devotement to my counsels, I'll tell you that which passed this night 'twixt Master Tycho and myself whilst I happened for a time to be alone beside his bed. Not long since, his fever had in a measure subsided, though his tongue would sometimes bestir itself to utter rags of witless phrases, as in earnest protestation of his innocence against some deep complaint. Such was his stupor broken almost on the hour; yet, by the estimate of his daughter and the opinion of those who stood the vigil with her, he never did speak plain but with such distemper as would impart only the general sense of his griefs, all particulars lying beyond the sad condition of his utterance, nor was he ever once seen to open his eyes. (*Brief pause*) Of a sudden, as I came near to him, there was brief pause in his delirium; his rough sighs left off awhile. Then, as 'twere by accident, his eyes gaped and he gazed about him; rather say his eyes gazed of themselves, for I perceived no register of understanding in his wan countenance till his look lighted upon me. I felt his cold hand at my sleeve, saw the parting of his dry lips, and gave ear to his parcell'd speech. He spoke scarce above a whisper. 'Sweet Johannes,' quoth he, with his mouth full of sadness, 'I thank you for your long forbearance of my company, and do humbly beg forgiveness for having so oft rail'd against you.' Then he charged me, upon his dying breath, to give full demonstration that his astronomic tables lay in true accordance with his universal system, and bade me cast the system of Copernicus aside.

SEYFFART: No —

JOHANNES: Ay. 'Wilt thou do me this last service?' quoth he. 'Wilt thou swear it?' And I so swore, but only to give his final hour some measure of peace. Thus took he his leave of me; and there he lies, wordless ever since.

Enter JOSEPH *from left.*

But soft. Here comes his friend, the Rabbi Judah Loew.

JOSEPH: Master Johannes, is he any better?

JOHANNES: Sir, his condition is grave.

JOSEPH (*in quiet alarm*): Oh.

JOHANNES: I do believe he is about to render up his soul.

JOSEPH (*to himself*): No. (*To* JOHANNES) Were you with him through the night?

JOHANNES: Ay, Rabbi —

JOSEPH: Did he say anything? Did he speak of *me* at all?

JOHANNES: Marry, sir, he said nothing.

JOHANNES *and* SEYFFART *exchange conspiratorial glances.*

ACT TWO 327

JOSEPH: Nothing?

JOHANNES: In those times when he did briefly wake, some sounds rose to his lips as from so many fathoms of the sea and yet our ears construed them not, for his words came but half transformed, caught 'twixt air and water, and still were more than half submerged.

> JOSEPH *seems about to speak, but can only shake his head sadly. He turns from* JOHANNES *and* SEYFFART *and goes to* MAGDALENE, *who falls into his arms.*

MAGDALENE (*in an outburst of grief*): O, Rabbi Loew! My father, my poor father —

JOSEPH (*comforting her almost mechanically as he eyes* TYCHO *with alarm*): Yes. Yes, Magdalene. It's all right. Now, now. It's all right. Yes.

SEYFFART (*his hands on* MAGDALENE'*s shoulders*): O Magdalene, come away.

> *He draws her into the shadows right, as the focus of light narrows to* JOSEPH *and* TYCHO.
> JOSEPH *takes* TYCHO'*s hand. Now, only the sound of* TYCHO'*s death-rattle can be heard.*
> *Pause.*

JOSEPH (*whispering into his ear, with quiet urgency*): Master Tycho. (*Brief pause*) It's me. It's . . . the Rabbi. Can you hear my voice?

> TYCHO'*s eyes open, staring blankly ahead throughout.*

Master Tycho, it's Rabbi Loew. You — you've got to help me. I'm desperate. I've no idea what I'm supposed to be —

TYCHO (*easing his death-rattle, in a hollow, trance-like voice*): Something... I failed...

JOSEPH: What? You can hear me —

TYCHO: The Emperor . . .

JOSEPH: No, you haven't failed him, he's —

TYCHO: Something I failed to tell . . .

JOSEPH: Tell me.

TYCHO: Something I failed . . . to tell the Emperor. (*Brief pause*) The dwarf.

JOSEPH: What's that?

    Pause.

TYCHO: At Uraniborg. The fool.

JOSEPH: The fool?

TYCHO: Jeppe. (*Brief pause*) He was a dwarf.

    Pause.

    (*Prolonging the final syllable*) Jeppe . . . could prophesy.

    Pause.

My dwarf, Jeppe. Logomontanus said he had the second sight. (*Brief pause*) Jeppe. He always knew when I'd be coming back. Whenever I left the island. He told them. (*Brief pause*) He foretold a shipwreck, close on our shores. . . and it came to pass. (*Brief pause*) If anyone fell ill at Uraniborg, and Jeppe foretold their death . . . they would die. (*Brief pause*) He always knew . . . when I'd be coming home.

    Pause.

(*A sudden horror in his voice*) Who are you?

    Pause.

JOSEPH (*into* TYCHO's *ear*): My name is . . . Joseph.

    TYCHO's *eyes grow wider.*
    Pause.

TYCHO (*breathing his last, in cavernous, prophetic tones*): When Neptune's tines, like blind men's fingers, o'erspread the waning moon, then will the Emperor die. He will come to his final hour at last. And nothing . . . nothing will save him, not even the mirror they will hold up to his face at the very end. And all his images, trapped by the black flicker of death, will fall before his staring eyes and scatter like so many grains of sand.

JOSEPH *clasps* TYCHO's *right hand, greatly moved. The 'Adagio' is heard as* TYCHO *speaks his last.*

(*Slowly, and with some sadness in his voice*) All that we have done, all that we *might* have done, what we will do and yet have never done, all that we know of ourselves and of others, what we might have known, what we will and have *never* known, and never *shall* know ... all — all, Joseph — all abides in the memory. In the memory ... of the future.

He gasps, sighs. JOHANNES *emerges from the shadows and stands at the bedside, left, clasping* TYCHO's *left hand.*
To the closing chords of the 'Adagio' ...

Remember me. Ne frustra vixisse videar ... ne frustra vixisse videar ... ne frustra —

He repeats the Latin phrase, less and less distinctly, to the end of the scene, as he sinks toward death.

JOSEPH (*to* JOHANNES): Kepler, what is he saying?

Pause.

JOHANNES: Ne frustra vixisse videar. (*Brief pause*) Let me not seem to have lived in vain.

JOSEPH *bows his head in sadness.*
Slow fade to black; and, with it, fades the sound of TYCHO's *voice, repeating: 'Ne frustra vixisse videar.'*
Last, dying chord of the 'Adagio'.

ACT THREE

Scene 1

Fade up slowly the twilight behind a bartizan high in the Castle walls, up centre — battlements extending, to the right and left, into the shadows — the 1ST SENTINEL *in silhouette, his back to the audience, leaning on his halberd, peering down through the embrasure at the city of Prague below, as a full boys' chorus sings the 'Hodie' [I.].*

CHORUS (*off*): Hodie portas mortis
Et seras pariter
Saxum noster disrupit.
Hodie, hodie, hodie, hodie.

The 2ND SENTINEL *staggers out of the shadows left. The two remain in silhouette throughout.*

1ST SENTINEL (*halberd poised*): Who's there? Stand and unfold yourself!

2ND SENTINEL (*drunkenly*): Long life to the baker's daughter!

He laughs brazenly.

1ST SENTINEL (*recognising the voice*): Ah. You come most drunkenly upon your hour.

2ND SENTINEL: I come ... (*Belching*) O, heaven make me free of it — I come, most grievous sick at heart, caparisoned in my widow's weeds and armour, from the solemn obsequies of that brave doctor, Master Tycho Brahe, whose interment I did witness, by order of the Emperor, in Teyn Church not six hours gone.

1ST SENTINEL: Six hours gone?

2ND SENTINEL (*offering his wineskin*): Ay.

ACT THREE 331

1ST SENTINEL (*taking the wineskin*): Pray tell me, how spent you the interval 'twixt then and now?

He drinks from the wineskin.

2ND SENTINEL: Why, upon my back, sir. (*Snatching the wineskin*) With this physic hard by my yawning lips, the better to requench mine eyes of the tears they shed o'er Tycho's shrouded catafalque.

He hiccoughs as the 1ST SENTINEL *laughs.*

Nay, 'twas a hard matter to see the Emperor there on his knees, so dirgeful, beyond all consoling, wailing like a wounded ram before the high altar.

The 1ST SENTINEL *chuckles as the* 2ND SENTINEL *drinks from the wineskin.*

1ST SENTINEL (*snatching the wineskin*): Hold off awhile! Thou'st had physic enough to drown thine eyes in a sea of grape full seven times over!

As the 1ST SENTINEL *drinks long from the wineskin . . .*

2ND SENTINEL: I drink only that I may not want for tears. 'Tis bruited about the town that the Emperor means to put up a monument to his defunct astrologer, a great statue of red marble. Belike we'll soon have one reason more to squeeze our tear ducts dry. (*More confidentially*) I'll warrant you the Emperor sleeps not easy in his bed since Master Tycho's death, nor gains he but brief repose for his unquiet soul from this day on till the day *his* hour comes to strike. Then will fair Prague be stricken too, and will our eyes pour forth such cataracts of salt as would silt up the depthless Moldau and o'ertop the highest steeple with a towering dune.

Pause.
The 1ST SENTINEL *hands back the wineskin and takes up his halberd.*

1ST SENTINEL: God give you quiet guard.

As the 1ST SENTINEL *exits left, begin slow fade to black . . .*

2ND SENTINEL: And give you good night.

The 2ND SENTINEL, *bartizan and battlements to black / fade up slowly a corner of the Emperor's study, down left.*
Right to left, in chiaroscuro: the cluttered table, seen end on; RUDOLF, *clad*

in grey, sitting at the table, his head buried in his hands; JOSEPH *peering out the window in the left wall, the blood-red glow of twilight on his bearded face. Behind the table, the large standing globe looms out of the shadows.* RUDOLF *raises his head, his eyes red from weeping.*

RUDOLF: And then?

Pause.

JOSEPH (*still peering out the window, gently*): Master Doctor Kepler came and took his other hand. And Tycho sighed, and asked to be remembered. (*Brief pause*) Then he expressed the hope that he would not seem to have lived in vain. He repeated this phrase again and again in Latin, like a prayer. And then he died.

Pause.

RUDOLF: And did he nothing say of me?

JOSEPH *turns round and seems about to speak.*
Pause.

JOSEPH: No, my lord.

RUDOLF *turns his head toward* JOSEPH, *then back toward the table, lost in thought.*

RUDOLF (*with a fierce sadness*): O cursèd fate that ever I was born to wear the Crown! Now does my fortune bear such emphasis as no phrase of sorrow can express without the sundering of its speech by cries of havoc! Great Tycho is dead! (*Brief pause*) I loved him, Rabbi. So much was my love I would have yielded up the better portion of my kingdom for't, wherein I might amass sufficient ransom still to raise his noble spirit and bid it read aloud from the book of stars the yet-unscriptured leaves, and make brave testament of all that moves 'twixt heaven and earth. God's blood, it shall go hard with his vile poisoner!

JOSEPH: My lord?

RUDOLF: The murderous sorcerer who, by dark enchantment, did envenom Tycho's wine!

JOSEPH (*perplexed*): Sire, Master Tycho was in failing health. He drank too much.

It was bound to happen, sooner or later.

RUDOLF (*agitated*): How came he dead, what say you?

JOSEPH: Why, he died of an excess of wine.

RUDOLF: Never say it! Did you not see how his body bore the marks of poisoning?

RUDOLF *stares ahead throughout.* JOSEPH *stands behind him.*

JOSEPH (*with pained conviction*): No, my lord.

JOSEPH *puts his hands on* RUDOLF's *shoulders.*
Pause.

RUDOLF (*to himself*): What hand shall guide me now through this phantasmal labyrinth?

Slow fade to black the Emperor's study/fade up slowly the darkened study of Rabbi Loew, as in Act Two. Night has fallen. LEAH's *mischievous laughter is heard.*

The centre door opens to reveal the FALSE ISAAC *in shirt and hose, his hair dishevelled, holding a lighted candle. Before he can enter the study,* LEAH's *arms curl round his shoulder and neck from behind. He turns to embrace her in the shadows, then enters the study alone as she stands in the doorway, clad in her shift.*

LEAH (*a suggestive whisper*): Isaac?

She smiles at him — a lingering, lascivious smile — then slowly closes the door, leaving him alone.
Pause.
He sets the candle down on the sideboard beneath the mirror, right, makes for the centre door, opens it, and exits, closing the door behind him.
The door at right opens slowly, creaking on its hinges. Enter JOSEPH, *sad and weary. He removes his hat and lays it on the centre table, then stops by the sideboard and stares at his image in the ornate mirror.*
The FALSE ISAAC *reënters silently from the centre door, holding a plumed toque, a red doublet draped over his arm. He sees* JOSEPH *and stops dead in his tracks, easing the door closed behind him as he eyes the 'Rabbi' with suspicion, then lays the toque and doublet gently out of view behind the cluttered centre table.*

> *Just as* JOSEPH *is about to remove his wig, he catches sight of the* FALSE ISAAC *in the mirror. He leaves his wig in place.*
> *The* FALSE ISAAC *turns toward him.*

JOSEPH (*still peering into the mirror, to himself*): You. (*Louder, to the* FALSE ISAAC, *with contempt*): You.

> *He wheels round to face the* FALSE ISAAC.

(*Sarcastically*) So, the prodigal son returns.

> *Pause.*

Well? What've you got to say for yourself? What's the explanation? Leah's been half out of her mind with worry all these weeks! Did you never stop to think of *her* when you wandered off that night? Off with some woman, I shouldn't wonder.

FALSE ISAAC: Peace, father, and pray you give me audience. By my troth, and so God mend me, I came not willing to my late desertion, but was taken of a sudden, on the very night I brought you summons from the Castle, by a stupor which did so infect my wits it did silence in me all the memory of this house and of my wife, your daughter. I know not who nor where nor what I was, nor can I now give answer how I passed the term of my bewitchment.

JOSEPH (*thinking hard*): Your bewitchment?

FALSE ISAAC: Ay, sir, God give me grace.

> *Pause.*

JOSEPH (*to himself*): Can it be true, then?

> *Pause.*

(*To the* FALSE ISAAC) Have you no idea, then, what's been going on here since your... departure?

FALSE ISAAC: None, by heaven.

JOSEPH: Swear it . . .

ACT THREE

The FALSE ISAAC *raises his hand and is about to swear.*

... by King Solomon's oath.

The FALSE ISAAC *turns away, and cannot swear.*

LEAH (*as the centre door opens, off*): Who's there?

JOSEPH *whisks off his wig and hides it behind his back.*
Enter LEAH.

Why, father! God give us joy, Isaac is —

JOSEPH (*feigning joy, but frantic*): Wine! Go and — and fetch some wine!

Exit LEAH, *happily.*
JOSEPH *puts on his wig as the centre door closes.*
The FALSE ISAAC *turns to face* JOSEPH *once more.*

FALSE ISAAC: I prithee, sir —

JOSEPH: Never mind that.

FALSE ISAAC: But, did you not say —

JOSEPH (*pushing him toward the low cabinet, left*): Nothing, nothing! It's of no importance. (*Indicating the cabinet*) Just get down and have a look in here.

He pushes the FALSE ISAAC *to his knees.*

There's something I want you to find. (*Stammering*) A certain scroll!

FALSE ISAAC (*confused*): What scroll, father?

The centre door opens.

JOSEPH (*in quiet panic*): What?

FALSE ISAAC: Tell me the title of it.

JOSEPH: No. I mean, I can't tell you! I can't tell you that —

FALSE ISAAC: Then, how am I to —

JOSEPH (*practically forcing the* FALSE ISAAC*'s head into the cabinet*): It's got a blue ribbon!

FALSE ISAAC: Oh —

JOSEPH: The scroll is tied with a blue ribbon!

> *The* FALSE ISAAC *begins to empty the cabinet of its mass of scrolls, prayer shawls, phylacteries, etc., piece by piece.*
> JOSEPH *yanks off his wig.*
> *Enter* LEAH, *bearing a tray with a bottle of wine and three small silver goblets, which she lays on the sideboard right, her back to* JOSEPH, *who stands at centre, desperately attempting to conceal his agitation.* LEAH *catches sight of him in the mirror, smiles, and blows him a kiss. He waves back, uneasily.*
> LEAH *pours the wine.*

FALSE ISAAC (*poking about inside the cabinet*): Ah, methinks I feel a riband.

JOSEPH: Keep feeling. Don't take it out till you're completely sure.

FALSE ISAAC: By the touch, 'tis very like a riband.

> JOSPEH *puts on his wig.*
> *The* FALSE ISAAC *turns with a red-ribboned scroll in hand.*

JOSEPH (*rushing at him*): That's red! (*Forcing the* FALSE ISAAC*'s head into the cabinet with one hand as he tears off his wig with the other, eyeing* LEAH, *who turns to face him, to the* FALSE ISAAC) I said blue! A *blue* ribbon!

> *He rushes to meet* LEAH *halfway. She hands him a goblet at centre, and makes for the* FALSE ISAAC *with a second goblet.* JOSEPH *downs his wine in one gulp, bangs his goblet down on the table, runs to the mirror and turns its face to the wall.*

LEAH (*turning round before she reaches the* FALSE ISAAC): Sweet father, what custom is it thus to turn the mirror to the wall?

JOSEPH (*panting*): It's... Because it's... good luck for a homecoming! Didn't you know?

ACT THREE

LEAH: Nay, I knew it not.

JOSEPH: Well, this — this is Isaac's homecoming, isn't it?

He chuckles nervously as LEAH *takes up his empty goblet.*

LEAH: Ay, so. Then, for custom sake, I thank you. (*Turning to the* FALSE ISAAC) O, Isaac, come away.

JOSEPH (*staggering round behind the centre table*): No! Let him finish! It's important.

As LEAH *returns to the sideboard,* JOSEPH *collapses into a chair and sits, facing front, with his left hand on the table, clutching his wig, his upturned hat beside him.*

The FALSE ISAAC *extracts a blue-ribboned scroll from the cabinet. Both he and* LEAH *have their backs to* JOSEPH. LEAH *is refilling the empty goblet.*

FALSE ISAAC (*to himself*): Ah, the very one.

JOSEPH, *overhearing, turns pale with alarm.*

(*To* JOSEPH) Look you, Maharal. Here is the scroll.

Slowly, LEAH *and the* FALSE ISAAC *turn to face him.* JOSEPH, *folded wig in hand, strikes the casual posture of a man who sits with his head propped on his left arm, so that, from their respective points of view,* LEAH *sees him bareheaded, the* FALSE ISAAC *sees him bewigged.*

LEAH: Now, take your scroll, father. (*Turning to the sideboard*) And let's drink to Isaac's better fortune.

JOSEPH *puts his feet up and, as if by accident, knocks a heap of papers, books, etc., off the front of the table.*

JOSEPH (*to the* FALSE ISAAC): How clumsy of me. Would you mind?

Still on his knees, the FALSE ISAAC *gathers up the fallen debris.* JOSEPH *hides his wig in his hat, leans back in his chair, clasps his hands behind his head, his feet propped on the table, as* LEAH *approaches, bearing three goblets on the tray. She smiles at* JOSEPH, *who smiles back, handing him his goblet. He downs its contents in one gulp, eyes wide over the brim as the* FALSE ISAAC

grunts and rises with his back to JOSEPH, *the great mass of documents, etc. cradled in his arms. Without tearing his gaze from the* FALSE ISAAC, JOSEPH *holds out his goblet at arm's length toward* LEAH, *who has just turned away from him; he opens his hand, and the goblet plummets noisily to the floor.*
LEAH *turns, sets the tray on the rearward edge of the table, and stoops to retrieve the fallen goblet as* JOSEPH, *still with his feet up, throws on his wig. The* FALSE ISAAC *turns round to him and lays his burden on the table, but a scroll or a book falls out of his arms as he does so.*

Look, you dropped one!

The FALSE ISAAC *bends to pick it up.*
JOSEPH *snatches off his wig.*
LEAH *rises, goblet in hand.* JOSEPH *turns toward* LEAH, *sweeping the tray and goblets to the floor with his feet.*

LEAH (*falling to her knees behind the table*): Oh, father!

JOSEPH *jams his wig down over his ears with both hands and bolts out of his chair as the* FALSE ISAAC *rises and replaces the fallen object on the table.*

JOSEPH (*dashing for the centre door*): It's been a long day! I didn't realise I was so tired. (*With exaggerated cheeriness*) Good night!

Exit JOSEPH, *slamming the centre door behind him.*
As LEAH *tends to the mess, the* FALSE ISAAC *takes up* JOSEPH's *abandoned hat, turning it idly about in his hands.*

FALSE ISAAC: The Maharal doth seem distract.

LEAH: Ay, so.

FALSE ISAAC: I hope it will be well with him. If thou wouldst have the truth on't, Leah, methinks he finds me too much changed by my late wanting of remembrance. It hath unworthied me of his company.

LEAH (*rising*): Nay, sweet husband. Thou art but newly come from brutish slumber. Truly to speak, thy scruple falls too hard on the event and shows no cause in my father's temperance; thy memory restored, so shall his affection be.

She embraces him. As they kiss, he tosses JOSEPH's *hat back on to the table.*

ACT THREE

FALSE ISAAC (*gently*): Come, give me drink.

 LEAH *picks up the tray of goblets and carries it to the sideboard. The* FALSE ISAAC *goes round behind the table and puts on his doublet as* LEAH *pours the wine.*
 He wears the red doublet of SCOTO, *and holds the feathered toque in his hand.*

LEAH (*bringing him the goblet*): How now, Isaac? Thou hast put on thy doublet.

FALSE ISAAC: Ay.

 He puts the toque on his head.

LEAH: What, dost thou mean to widow me again?

FALSE ISAAC (*taking the goblet*): Ay, truly.

 He drains the cup.

LEAH (*fingering his doublet*): This colour ill becomes a man of religion. Faith, 'tis Satan's livery. I pray you, husband, remove it. I like it not.

 She tries to unfasten his doublet. He stops her hands.

FALSE ISAAC: Say you so? Ay, thou speak'st infallibly. 'Tis here the devil's very hue of flesh; and, thus arrayed, I give him all his due, for I go this night to lie with my paramour, the fair Magdalene.

LEAH: What, with Tycho's daughter?

FALSE ISAAC: The same. How say you now, my good wife?

LEAH (*drawing back, in tears*): Ay me, what hast thou done?

FALSE ISAAC (*as she weeps*): Done? Why, such an act as unfetters the will from wretched servitude and wipes off the clinging webs which spiders weave o'er lovestruck eyes that they be proof 'gainst every semblance of verity.

LEAH (*turning away, with her head in her hands*): I understand you not.

FALSE ISAAC: Nay, madam, you understand me well. No more shall holy writ o'errule my sense with superstition; I give it all to hell, and blast the spectre of scowling doctrine from my impenitent soul!

LEAH (*covering her ears*): O, speak no more!

FALSE ISAAC (*forcing her hands down from behind*): All my covenants are this day broken. Henceforth, none but Magdalen' shall be my love. And e'en were it not so, I'd have not you for wife. Dost thou hear me —

LEAH (*falling to her knees*): O, Isaac!

> *She weeps bitterly.*
> *He stoops, puts one hand to her forehead and passes the other hand over her eyes, silencing her sobs as the Rabbi's study fades to black, leaving* LEAH *and the* FALSE ISAAC *in a narrow, blood-red pool of light. He stands behind her.* LEAH *closes her eyes and slumps back on her heels. Her arms go limp at her sides. Her mouth hangs open.*
> *Pause.*

FALSE ISAAC (*to himself*): This is most brave. Now have I done a good night's work. She weeps for that her husband goes a-whoring. Yet what is her loss to mine, now sweet Agnes is dead? O Agnes, thou art slain. (*To* LEAH, *who cannot hear him*) Ay, murdered by your father's blood, madam; poisoned by him who thought to make me swear oath upon King Solomon's ghost! His cursèd venom pierced her body through and stilled her fainting heart ere she fell to ground. All the while I thought she did but swoon, her soul was drowning in the Rabbi's scalded blood!

> *He shuts his eyes, breathes deeply through clenched teeth, and tries to compose himself, resting his hands on* LEAH*'s shoulders.*
> *Pause.*
> *He opens his eyes, goes to the sideboard, and blows out the candle.*

(*To himself*) 'Twas her great age undid her at the last. Nor charm, nor talisman, nor magic dram that fanned her flame of youth an hundred year beyond its natural run could countermine the Rabbi's conjury.

> *He bends and whispers unintelligibly into* LEAH*'s ear.*

Arise, Leah.

> *She rises, in a trance. Her eyes open.*

From this hour, I, Jerome Scoto, am the master of thy soul and body. Henceforth, thou wilt attend on me and do my will in all things, even unto thine own death. Thou shalt have ear for no other tongue but mine, nor give thy worship to any deity, shade or minister of the sphere invisible; moreover shall thy father, Rabbi Loew — who never dreams on aught but bloody murder, and loves thee not — take thy blackest malediction ere he o'ersway thy thoughts to his viperous designs.

Pause.

Know, then, that your husband Isaac is bewitched of Tycho's daughter.

She sucks in her breath —

Ay, hear me. Magdalene grows weary of Prague. Her father's death hath so much grieved her she can nothing take of comfort but in the breath of Isaac's honeyed words, the soft caress of his hands about her person, and the sweet press of his lips.

LEAH (*hollowly*): No.

FALSE ISAAC: Soon she to Denmark shall take ship, and he with her —

LEAH (*sighing*): Oh —

FALSE ISAAC: Unless thou canst prevail upon the Emperor to declare against his embarkation. Then must Magdalene sail alone across the sea, and shall her spell of love be broken.

LEAH (*hollowly*): What shall I do?

FALSE ISAAC: Now stands it well for us to wait upon the most propitious hour. When it falls right, you shall in haste to the Castle and so commend yourself unto the Emperor's grace by the utterance and gesture of your suit that he cannot fail to make concession of it. Let him mistake not your accord to grant whate'er he may exact in barter for the restoration of your wandering husband, e'en though it be the service of your flesh to his passion's frenzy ... and the thralldom of your body to his dream of lust.

She falls in a swoon. He looks down at her.
Pause.

(*To himself*) Hmmm. (*Sarcastically*) Here lies a noble daughter, the Rabbi's second heart, his hope, his very life. And now is my envenomed seed begun to sprout contagion in his house. (*To the unconscious* LEAH) Ay, swoon for your modesty, madam, but do not weep for Isaac's sake else your tears be squandered on a mould'ring corse. A loving husband lives in *me*. Henceforth *my* name is Isaac, and so do I conform the guise of face and body to this unfamiliar usage, wherefore I do requite you life for life in concord with your holy writ — eye for eye, tooth for tooth . . . murder for murder. Therefore is poor Agnes revenged.

Slowly, he squats and looks at her more closely.
Pause.

(*To himself*) Ah, how like she is to Agnes — as semblant as I to her dead husband, though *she* be no counterfeit. She should prove meet to Rudolf's lechery. (*Chuckling* SCOTO*'s chuckle*) Hmmm. She'll please him well, and strike a terror to his ailing soul. (*To* LEAH) Soon, Leah. Yet a little while and we'll make an end on't.

Begin slow fade to black as dockside noises are heard — ships' bells, creaking keels, muffled shouts of sailors against the groans of the rigging, etc. / fade up slowly MAGDALENE, *wrapped in a hooded cloak, sitting on a large trunk, surrounded by darkenss and mist, her face buried in her hands, down right.*

She that was your husband's wanton paramour now waits to take voyage with her lover. But Isaac will come no more to Magdalen'. Let her wait until the night wind freeze her tears, and still he will not come.

MAGDALENE *sobs.*

Let her sobs choke out his name a thousand times and send up curses to his abstentation, he'll hear them not from six feet in the grave.

As MAGDALENE *slowly raises her head from her hands, her eyes red, her face convulsed with sadness, the* FALSE ISAAC *and* LEAH *to black . . .*

(*To himself*) Thus have I drawn down grim calamity and unleashed the slavering dogs' desire, fang to throat, each upon the other's back. So, sail you, Magdalen', for Elsinore, to see your lover Isaac nevermore.

Freeze MAGDALENE, *all sounds to silence / quick fade to deep blue.*
Slow fade to black.

Scene 2

Fade up slowly on the Emperor's private museum of Act Two, now extended to a great hall of monstrous relics, etc. The same whimmering halflight falls upon the surrounding cabinets, display cases, suspended carcasses, bones and teratological wonders. Up centre, a scrim camouflaged as part of the rear wall by the play of light and shadow.

RUDOLF, *clad in a grey magician's gown garnished with black zodiacal signs and other, more obscure, symbols, leans on a low cabinet down left, facing front, sad and pensive.* CATHERINE, *in black, stands a few paces behind him, to the right, staring reproachfully at his back.*

Pause.

CATHERINE: Then, you are determined on't?

RUDOLF: Ay, Catherine.

CATHERINE: This argument speaks madness in your grace. It mocks all kingly virtue. Were I not your sometime wife, and mother to your issue, I'd have tongue to doom this house and see you buried 'neath its toppled stones ere I would stand witness to your despairing blasphemy. (*Sadly sarcastic*) Thou wouldst wake the dead who canst scarce wake thyself to louring disaster. Yea, is it come to this? To kneel i' the charnel house and pluck at bones with howling incantation? Nor wizard's wand nor sacrifice of blood to demons' honour will e'er lend animation to the limbs of Tycho's corse or light the black deeps of its sunken eye with heaven's moon, nor shall they stir stilled lips nor mould heart's breath to their old soft-deceiving praises. Sooner would a summer's drought bake parched earth into a glutted ewer than Tycho resume his life. Ay, go! Unbind the winding sheet before the flesh is off the bone, and bid the dumb voice give you answer! Get you gone! O Rudolf! Husband! The sand of time's oblivion hangs so thick upon thine eye it puts a desert 'twixt thyself and all the world!

RUDOLF (*still with his back to her*): Ha! Sayest thou so?

CATHERINE: Ay, my lord, and so say your brothers!

RUDOLF *shuts his eyes in silent agony.*
Pause.

(*Still to his back*) Thou spake so oft of dark conspiracy, and so oft didst rage against thy brothers' just disquietudes, thou hast for want of wisdom turned thine own wits 'gainst thyself and thine hereditary. 'Tis small wonder they do discommend thee now.

RUDOLF (*nodding*): Hmph, and raise the Empire with loud avenging clamours to proclaim me villain.

CATHERINE: 'Twere truer to proclaim thee fool. Canst thou blame them?

Pause.

RUDOLF (*always with his back to her*): Only one can I find it in my heart to blame. Ere long we are like to see him here and at leisure read the mark upon his brow, which is our doom. My mother, that hatched him out, named the snake Matthias; but hell hath staked him for the devil's claim, and calls him Cain. For my other brothers, I contemn them not; though they be of Matthias' consort, he leads them where he would, tugs the string and works their puppet maws to single voice of his seditious promptings so to wage his enmity 'gainst the eldest born, whose crown sets his lip adribble with spume of the ravening wolf. Well we know him for a monster steeped in blackest crime. He would hold our insouciance to account for the fall of our far capitals to heathen hordes, stain our hand with the blood of a thousand murdered men and call us butcher for *his* butchery, and move to send what decimate legions he may yet command upon Prague's majesty to cast us off for ever. (*Brief pause*) But now have I one card more to play — nay, one *more* than one.

Pause.

CATHERINE (*who has listened with growing despair*): What means your grace by this 'one more than one'?

He turns to face her, but his thoughts are elsewhere.

RUDOLF (*breathlessly*): I'll tell thee not.

She masters her welling tears as he stares vacantly at her.
Pause.

CATHERINE (*shaken*): Pray God keep you in temper, my lord. (*Turning to go*) Fare you well.

Exit CATHERINE *into the shadows right.*
Pause.

RUDOLF (*alone*): She speaks in understanding. O, sweet heaven, keep me from high rage awhile to see the vengeance I might breed about me.

As he walks about the hall, stopping here and there to glance distractedly upon a specimen . . .

As tallow must to fire, so must my fainting soul now sustenance the flame of spirits lately dead and be their guiding lamp across the ebb of silence. Let my incanting speech beguile the guardians of the underworld, put key to the lock, and manacle all ashen ministers of death with sight-confounding lethargies.

Pause.

Two tombs will I open wide on darkness.
Ay, two . . . one more than one, for in this cause
Speaks good hope to tender much confusion.
I'll make the earth gorge out its bitter bile
To stop my brother's curses in his throat
And so divorce me from his grave intent,
Then dyke the mudded Moldau bank to bank,
Turn the thund'ring tide upon his armies
And let Neptune's tines, like dead men's fingers,
Rake each man by the hair into the deep.
I nothing lack to break Matthias' sword
And discommode the murderous practice
That would get him a crown and me a grave;
It only wants the hand of Rabbi Loew,
Which presently I'll seek to join with mine
In the acquittance of this two-fold work.
And when we two call forth 'one more than one',
Then shall my brother's term of life be done.

Enter JOSEPH *from out of the shadows left. He gazes about the hall in amazement.*
Pause.
RUDOLF *turns to face him. The two men stare at one another, stumble, and seem to reel, as though they were slowly waking from a dream.*

> *Pause.*

JOSEPH (*dazed*): Good time of day unto my gracious lord.

RUDOLF (*dazed*): As much unto our good and noble friend.

> *Pause.*

> That our hasty sending of you hither
> Hath so bred your conjecture on the cause
> As to occasion in you some suspense,
> We do much lament the manner of it
> And bid you stay your patience yet awhile
> To hear what confydance we shall make you
> Upon the sad condition of our state.

> > *As he takes* JOSEPH *by the arm, and guides him slowly downstage...*

> Ere long, in sore distressèd grief, we'll weep
> To see the fall of Prague, for even now
> Our great city takes to its bed of death;
> Its church bells toll upon a dreadful hour
> And cry to heav'n for merciful release.

JOSEPH: Your Majesty is overwrought. Perhaps —

RUDOLF: Nay, sweet Rabbi, woe-laden as we are
> By the unjust tyranny of fortune
> That hath set our house beneath the shadow,
> Time runs too malignantly on our heels
> To give our rage its full and tragic breath.
> To let our comfort live in scalded tears
> Were folly whilst our brother hath convoked
> Rancorous and undivided council
> Of our kindred 'gainst the seat of empire.
> Therefore are we resolved most fittingly
> To work our revenge. Now, hear our intent.

> > *He puts his hands on* JOSEPH's *shoulders, and looks at him with admiration.*

> For that I have had much intelligence,
> In these busy days, of your mastery
> In all the realms of magic, and have heard

ACT THREE

        As many proofs of witness to the force
        From which your conjuring voice has carried
        Far into the bleak aethereal worlds
        Forbidden unto every living tongue,
        I am, in cause of this, determinèd
        To lay, on your necromantic power,
        Half the burden of my kingdom's rescue.

    Pause.

JOSEPH (*astonished*): Sire . . . you cannot mean this. I . . . I have no —

RUDOLF (*turning away*): O, what a horrible night I have passed,
        Full of raw terrors in shuddersome dreams
        Whose chill and unaccounted images
        Still crowd upon mine eye like shriving ghosts.

    Pause.
    JOSEPH *hears the Emperor's dream with growing apprehension.*

        Methoughts I lived and perished in the snows
        Of a country strange to my remembrance.
        All the heavy moments of my waking,
        As 'twere in scorn of waking, I did stand
        On meagre-wooded planks above a pit
        So vast and deep the grey light of the sun
        Would scarce traverse its brink afore the rays
        Were scattered by and swallowed in its maw.
        Therein, blear figures crept and were confined;
        And when the moon waxed high betwixt the clouds
        On the boreal wind, their tortured shrieks
        Chorused up a bedlam of savage noise.

    He has raised his hands, as if to muffle his ears, but stops and lets his arms drop slowly to his sides as he turns toward JOSEPH.
    Pause.

        Then was my dream turned inward on itself,
        And every howling creature of the pit
        Snuffed like a candle from my wearied gaze.
        Into silence and smouldering darkness
        I fell. My limbs withered and seemed to die.
        My tongue shrivelled in my throat. No answer
        Could I make to all the foreign voices

That whisperèd upon my hollow ears;
Their single words I knew no meaning of,
But that I understood the sense full well
I misdoubted not. Thus was I, alive,
Entombed amongst the living, and contemned
To reconcile me to eternal night.

    Pause.

JOSEPH (*to himself*): Canamine. Mmmm, the memory of the —

RUDOLF: Good Rabbi Loew, what think you of these dreams
That corrupt my thoughts and so affright me
I quake to hear mine own recount of them?
Be they nothing but dissembling spectres?
Or bear they in their configuration
Some claim of memory on what was not,
With grave purport of what is yet to be?

    Pause.

JOSEPH (*dissembling*): I do not understand Your Majesty.
We all have our dreams. We have our . . . nightmares.

    Pause.

RUDOLF (*nodding*):
So. Since we cannot put off the nightmare
Or purge the blood of importuning fears,
Why then, we may devise us such physic
As is like to suck the acrid poison
Off the spears levelled at our royal head.
Sweet Rabbi, give your hand to this revenge.

    JOSEPH *uncertainly offers his hand to* RUDOLF, *who takes it in both of his.*

Swear, on your sacred office, to dispel
The deadly curse of sleep you once did lay
Upon the creature buried in the wood
Hard by the river Vlatava. Pluck him
From his lying place and fetch him hither

That he may hear my will. Why look you pale?

JOSEPH *swallows hard, and cannot answer as the Emperor releases his grip, turning away.*

I would have this creature to lay waste my brothers' armies in the field, to smash their countless legions into dust with all the fearful engines of war in his enfolded arms, so might their blood gush hot cataracts 'twixt his clenchèd fingers the better to quench our fallow land, seeding sparse grass with thick forests of sinew and bone. (*Brief pause*) At my command, he would uproot great mountains and hurl them headlong into all the oceans of the earth, making mammoth tides spew forth their icy lava to sunder the clouds. Thus could the creature snuff the noonday sun to a dripping cinder and drench the distant stars, nay, engulf the very universe itself in the drowning of a thousand unknown worlds.

He has opened the large chest at his feet, down left, and lifts out an object wrapped in purple cloth, which he unwraps on a nearby cabinet, revealing the agate bowl and whittled dinosaur tooth of Act Two.
  JOSEPH *approaches the Emperor with a growing horror of recognition.*
  RUDOLF *does not touch the objects, but makes vaguely magical passes with his hands about them as he speaks.*

See you these? This cup is the Holy Grail
From which Our Lord and Saviour, Jesus Christ,
Took drink with his apostles on the night
Of Judas's betrayal. Look you here.
The horn that promises eternal youth,
Sprung from a unicorn's brow. In the cup
Lies life immortal; in the charmèd bone,
All the vigour of regeneration.
(*Conspiratorially*) This night will I blaze up the furnaces,
Grind the horn to powder, pour the powder
Into the agate Grail, settle the Grail
Into the crucible, and let it burn
Till the shadows fanned by its ruddy bloom
Collide upon the ceiling o'er the kiln.
Fire shall unshell the vessel of its husk,
Draw forth the cloudy essence of the stone
And brew me up a bubbling distillate,
The which I will carry into Teyn Church
Unto the tomb of the Master Doctor,
Our ven'rable and much lamented friend.

JOSEPH: No. The Master Doctor . . . Tycho Brahe.

RUDOLF: Ay. Though he be clad in his cerements,
Tycho shall live to walk the earth again.

> As JOSEPH *backs helplessly, hopelessly, away* . . .

I'll lift the lid off the burial vault,
Then cut in twain the sling that binds the jaw
'Gainst gaping death; and, when the lips fall wide,
I'll empty the dram into the remains.
No, stay. Attend upon me yet awhile.
There is one favour I would have of you
Ere you go to make what preparation
Your judgement shall warrant th' acquittance of.

> JOSEPH *still backing away at the Emperor's approach* . . .

JOSEPH: What is it you want me to do, my lord?

RUDOLF: Oft, in the solitude of my chamber,
My thoughts do run upon those ancient men
Of holy writ, the fathers of your race,
For whom Jehovah's secret convenant
Gave promise of the land of Israel
Unto the generations of their seed.
If, therefore, by thy conjuring speeches
Thou canst summon forth these sainted spirits
Down from the porch of heaven's mighty throne,
And bring them here before my erring gaze
To walk about me in the selfsame shapes
That clad the glory of their souls' estate
When they did live, thou wilt possess of me
Such treasure as I shall lay round thy head
To garland the perfection of the thine art.

> *Pause.*
> As JOSEPH *lifts his arms in a helpless gesture and seems about to speak, the weak light round the edges of the hall of wonders begins to dim, and the sound of a score of hissing voices rises along with the soft tremolo of a tam-tam. As the noise grows somewhat louder, accompanied by the distant, inarticulate cries of men and women, the centre of the rear wall dissolves in a luminous haze. The spirits of the Patriarchs appear and vanish in their*

earthly shapes. With the coming of each spirit, the tam-tam tremolo (continuous throughout) rises from pianissimo *to* piano, *subsiding again to* pianissimo *at each vanishing.*

The Emperor stands, amazed, to the left of the apparition, JOSEPH *to the right. But* JOSEPH *sees nothing; he can only stare in cautious disbelief, now at* RUDOLF, *now in the general direction of the vision.*

The spirit of Abraham appears, clutching a dagger.

(*To* JOSEPH) The cunning lies beyond all praise of hope
That can, in silence, unloose such wonders!
Nor phrase nor word has fallen from thy lip,
But hither, to answer the argument
Of thine eye and by thy hands' devising,
Comes blessed Abraham the Patriarch,
Who cut God's mark into the flesh of men
And was fountainhead to two great nations.

The spirit of Isaac, old, with blind, dead-white eyes.

O, look you there! The eyes! How white they are!
The spirit of Isaac comes before us.
He, who in the waning hour of his youth
Was given unto a father's dagger
For sacrifice to mortal ordinance
And 'scaped the peril by an angel's hand,
Fell, in the winter of life, to blindness
And the soft deceit of his second son . . .

The spirit of Jacob, eyes closed.

Jacob, whose eyes were shut in pond'rous sleep
'Tween Haran and Beersheba, when his dream
Sundered the jewellèd gate of Paradise
Atop the staircase of the seraphim.
Here plunge the roots of Israel full deep
And stretch their sinews far into the earth.

The spirit of Reuben, his eyes cast down in shame.

Twelve sons had Jacob. The first-born, Reuben,
Excelling all in regard of honour,
Did mount himself to scale his father's bed,
And lived for ever after in disgrace.

The spirits of Simeon and Levi, laden with weapons.

See Simeon and Levi, choler's twins.
Their fury strew the cloth of dead men's shrouds
Across the dunes of flowering Egypt.
So unappeased, the havoc of their wroth,
That it called down the heavy odium
Of their brethren, and settled on their heads
The galled damnation of a father's curse.

The spirit of Judah, a mighty warrior in glittering armour, bearing a sceptre.

There stands great Judah, whelp of the lion,
Whose blazing sword the scourge of heaven was
To the cringing enemies of his house.
Low to him bowed all the sons of Jacob.
O'er the gilded relics of foreign gods,
Heaped in tribute to his name upon pyres
Of ivory, pearl and obsidian,
His wine-drenched garment let fall the shadow
Of unending night. Too few are my words
To tell the grandeur of mighty Judah.

The spirit of Zebulun, clad in a fisher's net.

Behold Zebulun, fifth branch of the trunk.
His fisher's nets, cast like sombre willows
Into the briny kingdom of the deep,
Hauled forth th' abundance of the darkling sea,
And made his dwelling place the rich harbour
To a thousand wandering galleons.

The spirit of Issachar, bearing a scythe.

Issachar, the sixth of Israel's sons.
Vaunted was the land given unto him;
His blood transfused the soil and commingled
With the sap that streamed i' the tow'ring oak,
Whose scented whisper sounded in his ear.

The spirit of Dan, holding a snake half coiled round his body.

Dan's governance was one with all the tribes;

His flesh he moulted for a serpent's skin,
Tricked out his teeth with venomed viper's fangs,
And bit at the heels of rearing horses
To overthrow the riders' armèd force.

The spirits of Gad and Asher. At the mention of their names, JOSEPH *gasps and grows even more uneasily suspicious.*

Look you. Here are Luck and Fortune's namesakes,
Gad and Asher. No raid that ever fell
Upon Gad's titan tribe went unavenged.
From a golden grain, sweet and bountiful,
Came smiling Asher's honey-leavened bread.

The spirit of Naphtali, clad in the skin of a wild stag, his head masked by the animal's gaping snout and antlers.

The tenth of Jacob's brood is Naphtali.
Mark you the horns he carries for a crown.
'Tis said he lived and died in this likeness;
The rest is rooted in deep mystery.

By now the shadows have engulfed all but RUDOLF, JOSEPH, *and the visionary space between them. As the spirit of Naphtali vanishes in mist, the otherworldly voices grow gradually louder, and the tam-tam builds slowly, from* pianissimo *to* mezzo forte, *toward its ultimate* forte *crescendo.*

Now, if the order of succession holds,
We shall see the pride of Jacob's issue.

But the visionary haze goes red, and LEAH *appears, eyes closed, clad in a long purple gown.*
    JOSEPH *sees her and cries out. He rushes at the apparition as* RUDOLF *holds him back.*

God's death! No! Good Rabbi, hold off thy hand!
O, this is no spirit come from out of —

JOSEPH (*struggling*): No, let me go! You see who it is? My —

RUDOLF: See how the mist about her streams with blood!
The wanton shade of Agnes von Mansfeld
Comes forth from the very bowels of hell

To dispossess us of our 'frighted souls!

    JOSEPH *recoils from the apparition. As* RUDOLF *raises his arms in exhortation,* SCOTO's *satanic laughter rising above the din, echoing cavernously through the darkness, louder and louder* . . .

O heavens, gape! Hurl down Jove's thunderbolt
And cleave the burning floor of hell in twain,
Or gouge the horror from my fainting sight
That I may live to see this shade no more!
Away! Away, thrice-damnèd fiend! Away!

    Crescendo. RUDOLF *falls to his knees / blackout* LEAH, *all sounds to silence.*
    Pause.
    RUDOLF *rises feverishly and goes to* JOSEPH.

(*Trembling*) Now a dark and bloody apparition
Doth sardonically adhere itself
To th' intemperance of our enacture.
Get you to your unnatural business,
And I to mine. When the midnight hour tolls,
Haste you to the Charles Bridge, with the creature
Hard by your side, and let the twelfth bell-stroke
Be your summons unto Teyn Church's crypt,
Wherein you will gain a swift admittance
To the cellarage, for none shall stay you.
Pray you, hold firm to this, and fare you well;
This last endeavour must our powers tell.

    Fade to black as they exit, hurriedly, right / fade up slowly the corner of a noisy tavern, up left.
    RUMPF *and* TRAUTSON *are seated side by side at a rude wooden table, facing front, each with a tankard before him:* RUMPF, *to the right, his cheek propped dourly on his left fist;* TRAUTSON, *to the left, vice versa. A mixed lot of tavern patrons — merchants, wenches, courtiers in street attire — come and go in the surrounding gloom.*
    Pause.
    A lusty serving wench falls backwards upon RUMPF *and* TRAUTSON's *table, and is quickly mounted by a dishevelled scholar.* RUMPF *and* TRAUTSON *do not bat an eyelash. The amorous couple roll off the front edge of the table to the floor, then into the shadows.*
    The noise subsides.

ACT THREE

RUMPF (*glumly*): Well, another uneventful evening.

TRAUTSON: Mmmm.

Pause.

RUMPF: I knew how it'd be.

TRAUTSON: Do you miss it?

RUMPF: What?

TRAUTSON: The court.

RUMPF: No. (*Brief pause*) Yes.

TRAUTSON: *I* don't miss it.

Pause.

(*Unconvincingly*) We're well out of it. *I* don't miss it.

RUMPF (*unconvincingly*): Nor do I.

Pause.

She's gone, you know.

TRAUTSON: His wife?

RUMPF: Whose wife?

TRAUTSON: The Emperor's.

RUMPF: No. That girl.

TRAUTSON *peers over the front edge of the table.*

Not *that* girl. I'm talking about the astrologer's daughter.

TRAUTSON: Tycho Brahe's daughter.

RUMPF: Mmmm. Gone back to Denmark.

TRAUTSON: Mmmm —

RUMPF: We're well rid of her. Just like her father. A bad lot, the pair of 'em.

TRAUTSON: What about the lover?

RUMPF (*cynically*): Hmph, that young rabbi.

TRAUTSON: Mmmm, Loew's son-in-law. You think he knew?

RUMPF: Who?

TRAUTSON: Loew. You think he knew what was going on?

RUMPF: Huh, wouldn't surprise me a bit. That man's nobody's fool.

TRAUTSON: Well, if he didn't know then, he knows now.

RUMPF: Oh?

TRAUTSON: Now the pair of 'em have sailed off together.

RUMPF: You forget. The man's a Jew. He can't leave just like that, on the spur of the moment — not without papers. You know how long *that* takes. Only the Emperor's signature would suffice to give him safe conduct on such short notice.

TRAUTSON: She could've got that — the signature, I mean — on some other pretext. Her father could easily have got it.

RUMPF: But he's dead.

TRAUTSON: But he had documents, benefices, signed in Rudolf's hand. It would've been a small matter for the daughter to get hold of one of them and then forge the Emperor's signature.

RUMPF: Mmmm —

TRAUTSON: She's clever enough, you know.

ACT THREE

RUMPF: Hmmm. (Brief pause) We'll never know *now*, will we?

TRAUTSON (*shaking his head*): Nnnnnn.

> *Pause.*
>
> Are you drunk?

RUMPF: No.

TRAUTSON: Nor am I.

RUMPF (*banging his tankard on the table, calling rightward*): Bedrich! More ale!

> *Pause.*
>
> (*To* TRAUTSON) I think the Emperor's brother really *does* mean to march on the city. What do *you* think?

TRAUTSON: You were hand in glove with that lot, weren't you?

RUMPF: What lot?

TRAUTSON: Matthias and his agents.

RUMPF (*noising a pained, yet noncommittal, denial*): Oooo.

> *Pause.*

TRAUTSON: Who do you think will make it to Prague first, Matthias or the Turks?

RUMPF (*shaking his head wearily*): Hmph. We've managed to let the Emperor make a pretty mess of things, in spite of all we tried to do.

TRAUTSON: And now we've lost it all.

RUMPF: Mmm. (*Brief pause*) Well, there it is. Madness reigns in Prague.

> *Enter* BEDRICH *from out of the shadows right, bearing two tankards of ale on a tray.*

TRAUTSON: He never loved us, Rumpf.

RUMPF: He failed us, Trautson. (*Brief pause*) He's failed us all.

> *They stare gloomily ahead as* BEDRICH *sets his tray down on their table.*
> *Pause.*

BEDRICH: Is everything to your satisfaction, my lords?

RUMPF: Yes —

TRAUTSON: Yes.

> *Freeze* BEDRICH, RUMPF *and* TRAUTSON, *all sounds to silence / quick fade to deep blue.*
> *Pause.*
> *Slow fade to black* BEDRICH, RUMPF *and* TRAUTSON */ fade up slowly a corner of the Emperor's study, down right.*
> *Right to left, in chiaroscuro: the window in the right wall; the cluttered table, seen end on; the large standing globe in the foreground. Night has fallen.*
> RUDOLF, *wearing a dark cloak over his grey magician's gown, hunches over a large, dusty tome, beside which lie the 'Holy Grail' and 'unicorn's horn', wrapped in the purple cloth. He is standing, his movements betraying urgency.*
> *Enter* MAKOWSKI *from out of the shadows left.*

MAKOWSKI: The daughter of Rabbi Loew waits without,
And doth entreat your grace, my noble lord,
To hear what urgent suit she would make you.

RUDOLF: Thou art sure it is the Rabbi's daughter?

MAKOWSKI: I' faith, my lord, I know the lady's face.

RUDOLF: I know it not. But thou art sure of her?

MAKOWSKI: Ay, my lord. Will you give her audience?

> *Pause.*

RUDOLF: Do grace to her and bid her to come in.

> MAKOWSKI *bows and exits left.*

ACT THREE

    RUDOLF *continues to pour over the old tome.*
    Enter LEAH, *wrapped from head to toe in a hooded cloak. She bares her head and curtseys low.*

LEAH: Good morrow unto my sovereign lord.

    RUDOLF *turns from his book and stands amazed, trembling.*
    Pause.

    (*Still in her curtsey*) Why looks your grace so heavily on me?

    She rises slowly, uncertainly, as RUDOLF, *edging round the table, backs away from her.*
    LEAH *takes a step toward him.*

RUDOLF: By what reason dost thou convey thyself
    In *flesh* to this second visitation?

    Pause.

LEAH: My lord, I know not how to answer this.

RUDOLF: Thou com'st, hard on thy first apparition,
    To o'erthrow my desperate stratagems
    And carry off my soul with thee to hell!

LEAH (*to herself*): Alas, he's mad. (*Tears*) Good my lord, I pray you,
    By th' esteem you bear my noble father,
    Give me but brief advantage of the hour
    To shriek love's agony into your ear,
    And let my utterance have some small scope
    To tell the folly and damnèd witchcraft
    That hath undone me of my husband's heart!

    She falls to her knees.

    O, hear me! All chastisement falls too short
    Which can turn round the torment I endure!
    None but Satan's vile intelligencer
    Could summon words to such 'luring preachments,
    As devils mouth in silent whisperings,
    To pull my Isaac from the marriage bed
    On to the soft and poison-scented flesh

That spreads itself upon a couch of shame!
The thrall of Tycho's daughter o'ercomes him;
Base lechery hath led him by the nose
Into a Cimmerian dwelling place,
Wherein he may lie till the hour of death
Calls him to perpetual damnation,
Lest your grace will deign to honour my suit
And so affix your seal to the warrant
That shall, by the law, forbid my husband
The pursuit of his wanton paramour
To foreign lands. Wilt thou grant me this boon?

Pause.

RUDOLF (*to himself*): What madness is this? I am lost in it.

Pause.
LEAH *rises slowly, uncertain of the outcome, and trying vainly to conceal her fear.*
Pause.

LEAH: I know your grace doth love my father well.

She unties her cloak and lets it fall to reveal a long, apple-green gown of the same cut as that which she wore in apparition.
Pause.
RUDOLF *slowly approaches* LEAH, *at once repelled and attracted by the woman he takes to be a demon. He looks questioningly into her eyes, then gazes down the length of her gown and up again.*
Pause.
Almost unwillingly, he watches his trembling fingers unfasten the clasps at her shoulders. LEAH *closes her eyes. The gown falls, and she stands naked before him.*
Pause.
RUDOLF *puts his arms about her in disbelief, then slowly descends to his knees, his head pressed to her body, an expression of lust mingled with horror and self-loathing on his agonised face.*
LEAH *turns up her face in shame and disgust.*
Slow fade to black.

Scene 3

Subdued woodland and river noises. Fade up slowly the moonlit forest clearing of Act One, with what had been the newly-covered grave — older now, though still a prominent lump of beaten earth — at centre. The leaves have fallen from the trees. A faint mist clings to the bare branches.
    Pause.
    Enter JOSEPH *followed by the* FALSE ISAAC *from out of the shadows left, both wearing prayer shawls, phylacteries, and other ceremonial accoutrements.*

JOSEPH: There isn't much time. We'll have to work fast.

    He points to the grave.

    Look, there. You're sure you know the ritual?
    My memory isn't all it might be.

FALSE ISAAC: Doubt it not. Steel thyself courageously
    To be resolute in thy grave purpose,
    And we shall rend the hoary jaws of death
    Long afore Teyn Church's bell strikes midnight
    O'er this drear and rueful burial ground.

    He sets to work at the head of the grave, shovelling the earth aside with a spade. An owl hoots in the distance.

JOSEPH (*shivering*): Listen, Isaac, do you hear that? An owl.
    It's hardly what I'd call a good omen.

FALSE ISAAC (*digging*): Nay, Maharal, 'tis the best of omens
    That a featherèd watchman of the night
    Should, to the disposition of our act,
    Maintain a scowling vigil over us,
    And so persuade us, by his fretful cry,
    To the disinterment of this creature;
    For though we are but lately arisen
    From the purgation of our foulest sins
    I' the waters of the ritual bath,
    And come pure of heart to our endeavour,

The fear which sleeps heavily in our souls
And threats to still our hand i' the exploit
Is never so indubitably drowned
That it will not surge again to daunt us.
Therefore, hold the owl for thy protector
In the brave business of this dreadful night;
Infurl thy trepidation in his wings
If thou wilt see th' exertion come to good.

He throws down his spade, and stares into the head of the shallow grave.
JOSEPH, *who has hung back, now approaches the edge of the grave, and looks down upon the unseen corpse with fascinated horror.*
Pause.

Now have we opened up the testament
That shall set us in the plague of nature,
Yet stand us proof 'gainst all malediction.
Look you past the brim of this shallow grave.
There hangs not flesh. Nay, flesh be gnawed by worms
Or glutted through with maggots. Here a corse
Sews up the shroud of its own unmaking
To reparate the misery of death.
Where are its eyes? Where lies its nose, its lips?
Nay, this be no food for carrion crow,
For 'tis all of a piece and wants the stench
Or scent of blood to bait the scavenger.
The very contradiction of decay
May still sit thick upon the bone, and flesh,
With every disunited element,
Be reconjoined so as to counterfeit
The bite it hath vouchsafed to grinning death.
So, let us to our unnatural work.
Hast thou made ready the sacred parchment
Thou hast to place beneath the creature's tongue?

JOSEPH: I have the parchment underneath my cloak;
I'll put it in when you give me the sign.

FALSE ISAAC: Hast thou, upon the parchment's face, engraved
And anagrammatised the name of God?

JOSEPH *shuts his eyes and nods, trembling.*
The FALSE ISAAC *nods in answer, squeezes* JOSEPH's *arms in grim en-*

couragement, then stoops to pick up the spade, with which he traces a circle round the grave. The circle completed, he flings the spade away, and raises his arms in invocation.

Shema Yisroel, the Lord Our God, Iehovæ Tetragrammaton! (*Brief pause*) Elohenu!

The sound of a distant, subterranean wind grows gradually louder as the FALSE ISAAC *paces the circle, counterclockwise, round the grave, muttering his incantations, and the woodland and river noises fade to silence.* JOSEPH *kneels at the head of the grave, and brings a small parchment from under his cloak.*

(*Pacing, solemnly*) Lamed...yod ... nun ... he ... samekh ... mem ... vav ... samekh ... lamed ... aleph ...

The owl cries out and a great flapping of wings is heard as the FALSE ISAAC *signals* JOSEPH *to place the parchment under the unseen corpse's tongue.* JOSEPH *lies forward over the edge and, with great trepidation, reaches deep into the grave. The subterranean wind grows ever louder.*

... yod ... mem ... nun ... he ... vav ... samekh ... aleph ...

A clap of thunder ushers in the low roll of a timpano in G, accompanied, a moment later, by the soft tremolo of a tam-tam — both continuous throughout — as the wind rises visibly from the mouth of the grave. JOSEPH *shrinks back from the edge, and draws himself into a kneeling posture, staring with increasing horror into the grave. The* FALSE ISAAC *continues to pace the circle.*

... nun ... yod ... lamed ... vav ... samekh ...mem ... aleph!

A glaucous light pulses from the mouth of the grave to the sound of a muted heartbeat. JOSEPH, *still on his knees, cowers back without taking his eyes from the grave.*

JOSEPH: It's moving! Oh, God —

As the heartbeat quickens and, with the drone of tam-tam and timpano, grows louder in the midst of the roaring subterranean wind . . .

FALSE ISAAC (*quickening his pace, frantically*): Samekh ... vav ... mem ... nun .... lamed ... yod ... aleph!

Two greyish hands emerge slowly from the mouth of the grave.

JOSEPH: Isaac!

The FALSE ISAAC *turns and stands dazed with wonder to see the* CREATURE *rise. Its curly hair and beard are dark, peppered with dust and grey clods of earth. Its flesh is pale. It wears the tattered garments of a servant. Graven on its forehead are the Hebrew letters of the word* emet: *From the letter* aleph, *blood trickles down.*

This awesome hulk, menacing beyond words, climbs, trance-like, out of the grave. The tam-tam reaches its crescendo, then falls silent. The glaucous subterranean light no longer pulses, but remains steady as the roll of the timpano drones on. The heartbeat continues to quicken, and grows louder.

JOSEPH *is dumbstruck. The* FALSE ISAAC *opens his arms triumphantly as the* CREATURE *moves toward him, a glassy stare in its eyes.*

The CREATURE *halts, extends its hand, and takes the* FALSE ISAAC *by the throat. The* FALSE ISAAC *drops to his knees, struggling, as the* CREATURE *drags him to the head of the grave. He thrashes and gasps, then is finally paralysed by the look in the* CREATURE*'s eyes.*

The CREATURE *thrusts the* FALSE ISAAC *backwards into the grave, whose light, now weakening, recommences its pulse to the faltering heartbeat.*

The timpano falls silent.
Three last, dim, beats of the heart.
The subterranean light fades to black. The wind, too, has subsided, but continues its distant roar.

JOSEPH *rises, trembling. The* FALSE ISAAC*'s feet stick up from the mouth of the grave, askew, motionless.*
Pause.

(*Staring into the grave, to himself*) He's dead. (*To the* CREATURE) You've killed him. You murdered Isaac!

Pause.
The CREATURE *points into the grave.*

CREATURE (*in halting, cavernous tones*): Look at him.

JOSEPH (*looking into the grave*): Isaac, my son-in —

CREATURE: Naught but a *false* Isaac, and no more son to you than you are father to the true Isaac, whom this evil sorcerer bewitched. Look at his face.

ACT THREE

JOSEPH *looks, then sucks in his breath.*

JOSEPH: Oh, my God.

Pause.

(*Still staring into the grave, to the* CREATURE) But who . . . who?

CREATURE: His name . . . was Scoto. Jerome Scoto.

JOSEPH (*thoughtfully*): Scoto. Mmmm, yes. (*To the* CREATURE) Then, where is Isaac?

Pause.

CREATURE: He is no more.

JOSEPH: What, dead?

CREATURE: Murdered. (*Pointing to the grave*) By that man.

JOSEPH (*sadly*): Oh, no. No.

He shuts his eyes to keep back the tears.

My daughter . . .

CREATURE: *Your* daughter?

Pause.

Speak. What would you have of me, Truth or Death? It comes to the same thing in the end. (*Brief pause*) I am your brother.

JOSEPH: My brother? I have no brother! My brothers are all unborn. My daughter is . . . She isn't my daughter.

CREATURE: Then you have not entirely forgotten who you are.

JOSEPH (*bitterly*): Who am I?

CREATURE (*pointing to the grave*): That man made her a widow, and did worse to her than that.

JOSEPH: And you killed him. Can you say that you are any better?

CREATURE: Take my life, Rabbi. It was not yours to give. It is not mine to possess.

JOSEPH: You're not even human!

> *Pause.*

CREATURE (*wounded*): That man was your enemy. And I am as human as you are. (*Brief pause*) After all this, you still don't understand.

> *Pause.*

JOSEPH: I had almost learnt how to forget.

> *Fade to deep blue / the wind to silence as the woodland and river noises return.*
> *Pause.*

(*Suddenly resolute*) The time grows short. Come with me.

> *Fade to black the forest clearing.* JOSEPH *takes the* CREATURE *by the hand and leads it briskly back and forth across the forestage in a wide, meandering walk as they speak. A pool of moonlight, crossed by swiftly moving shadows, tracks them through the surrounding darkness of the 'forest'. The woodland and river noises grow more eerily intense.*

We've got to hurry. For all I know, it may already be too late. But even that doesn't seem to matter now. All this time, I've watched and listened. I've let things take their course. It's not been easy. I did as I was told to do. Fear took care of the rest. Then, Tycho died. I wasn't expecting that.

CREATURE: It wasn't meant to happen. Yet it could not have happened otherwise.

JOSEPH: I'm tired of riddles! I've had enough! (*Brief pause*) What about the woman, Scoto's woman, Agnes von Mansfeld?

CREATURE: Agnes is dead.

JOSEPH: Dead? How? When? Then, who —

CREATURE: It was an accident. She wasn't meant to die.

JOSEPH: Too many deaths. There have been too many deaths — Tycho, Isaac, Scoto, Corby and Rapitrone, Shem — altogether too many. How many more must die before we make an end?

CREATURE: The last three have yet to be born.

JOSEPH: Hmph. Corby, Rapitrone and Shem. (*Vexed*) Yes, I should've remembered that. You know about them, as well.

CREATURE: Yes. But only that, for us, their time has not yet come. *Their* possibilities are infinite.

The woodland and river noises begin to fade.

JOSEPH: Then, you know where I'm taking you.

Pause.

CREATURE: Yes. I know.

They exit left, into darkness / all sounds to silence.

Scene 4

Offstage, the boys' chorus is heard singing the 'Hodie' [II.]. From bars one through seven of the 'Hodie' [1 *through* 7] *fade up slowly a bank of the Moldau giving on the Charles Bridge. Far upstage, along the opposite bank, in silhouette against the passing moonlit clouds, loom the distant spires of St Vitus Cathedral, the cupola of Teyn Church, and the Castle, high above the city of Prague.*

[9] *Enter* JOSEPH *and the* CREATURE *from right.*

[10 *through* 11] *The place is deserted.* JOSEPH *looks furtively about, then leads the* CREATURE *by the hand, up centre toward the Charles Bridge.*

[12 *through* 13] *They set foot upon the bridge.* JOSEPH *pulls at the* CREATURE, *which stops dead in its tracks and will not be moved.*

CREATURE (*in the brief pause*): No. No further.

14 *through* 21 . . .

JOSEPH: What? You must! We've so little time —

CREATURE: Do you hear it?

JOSEPH (*looks about*): Those voices.

CREATURE: He's already begun.

JOSEPH (*tugging at him*): Then we've got to hurry. Come —

CREATURE (*gripping* JOSEPH'*s shoulders*): He's mad! You cannot let yourself be part of this.

JOSEPH: But he's waiting! The Emperor's waiting . . . for *us!* I've done what I had to do. Now I must see it through to the end.

CREATURE: You have done nothing. You have made no difference at all. The tide of history has overwhelmed you.

JOSEPH: But —

CREATURE: Hear me!

> 22 *through* 29 . . .
>
> We have come near to the horizon's end. We are prisoners, Rabbi, you and I. But nothing is lost. Our elements are mingled with the eternal. Our minds' last flicker of consciousness stares down the immense blackness, and traps the brutal light of distant stars in its net long after those stars have dwindled into ash and died.

JOSEPH: The bell!

> JOSEPH *makes to go across the bridge, but the* CREATURE *holds him back.*
> 30 *through* 36 . . .

CREATURE: No! Every stage in the process is self-annihilating. We pass, as we must, unrecognised and unknowing, from one plane into the next with no memory of what was, no notion of what we may become.

> 37 *through* 43 . . .

ACT THREE

JOSEPH: And what of Prague?

CREATURE: Prague has fallen many times, and will fall many times again. Look into my eyes. Closer..What do you see?

JOSEPH: My own reflection!

CREATURE: No. Your image lives not in *my* eyes. Look closer, Rabbi. Whom do you see?

JOSEPH (*astonished*): I see . . . the Creature! It's *your* face!

44 *through* 47 . . .

CREATURE: Nor you nor I know how or why it came about. It might all be the sick fancy of a prisoner on the verge of death. Or the dream of a man who sleeps with a whore in his father's house. Who can tell? It's a mystery, Joseph.

48 *through* 49 . . .

JOSEPH: You called me Joseph. Who *are* you?

CREATURE: My name is . . . Jonathan.

> JOSEPH *shrinks back in horror and falls to his knees.*
> 50 *through* 51 . . .

Choose now, Truth or Death! But take my life, or live and die in sacrilege!

On the third beat of 52 . . .

Joseph!

> *Every available male voice* [monks] *now accompanies the 'Hodie' to its climax as* JOSEPH *rises to his feet and boldly extends his hand toward the* CREATURE'*s forehead.*
> *On the third beat of* 53 . . .

(*Encouraging him*) Joseph!

> *On the first, deafening, beat of* 54, JOSEPH'*s forefinger touches the* aleph, *and* JOSEPH *and the* CREATURE *vanish in a blaze of fire and smoke.*

The din subsides. The bell tolls four times in E.
Begin slow fade to black the clouded, moonlit sky and silhouette of Prague upstage. There, behind the clearing smoke, the 'Dies Irae' of Act One is heard again; now, without its drum accompaniment, it is even more mournful as the bell tolls. Headed by two torch bearers, a solemn procession of nobles comes forward, out of the far darkness, across the Charles Bridge, the men chanting the 'Dies Irae', the women silent. At the end of the procession walks MATTHIAS, *clad in cornonation robes, bearing an orb and sceptre, his train carried by two great princes.*

Once off the Charles Bridge, the members of the procession turn stage right. The torch bearers exit into the shadows right. At stage right, the nobles, two by two, turn again, coming forward as the 'large and hideous' crucifix slowly descends from the flies to hang, facing them, above an altar platform which glides out of the forestage shadows right. Upon the altar, in vestments and mitre, stands Cardinal SPINELLI, *holding the Crown of the Kingdom of Bohemia in his hands. The nobles open ranks to form the aisle down which* MATTHIAS *and the two princes walk slowly to the altar. Sky, silhouette of Prague, and the Charles Bridge to black.*

As MATTHIAS *comes forward, a cavernous, pre-recorded voice is heard above the dirgeful chant.*

VOICE OF CANAMINE: Ten years passed, years in which the Emperor descended deeper and deeper into madness. (*Brief pause*) The Sword of Islam did not come to Prague. But the Emperor's brother Matthias did, at the head of an army, to put down the civil war that raged between Protestant and Catholic. The Emperor was placed under guard in the Castle. His ministers were put in chains.

MATTHIAS *stands before the altar.*

In April 1611, Rudolf . . .

MATTHIAS (*bitterly*): The eccentric and irresponsible celibate!

VOICE OF CANAMINE: . . . sent his resignation to the Parliament of Bohemia.

MATTHIAS *kneels before the altar.* SPINELLI *raises the Crown high above* MATTHIAS' *head.*
Freeze MATTHIAS, SPINELLI, *the nobles and princes.*

One month later, in Saint Vitus Cathedral, Matthias was crowned King of Bohemia. Informed by the Imperial Parliament that he would be deposed and

ACT THREE   371

Matthias named Holy Roman Emperor in a year's time, Rudolf could do nothing but die.

Fade to deep blue MATTHIAS, SPINELLI, *the nobles and princes / fade up slowly the left third of the stage:* RUDOLF *on his deathbed, seen as from above. The bed stands upright, the tiled floor looming behind it. Two doctors 'stand' to the left of the bed; to its right, a man in magician's robes 'stands' holding a large, many-faceted mirror up to* RUDOLF. *The scene in chiaroscuro, lit by a sickly shaft of light from left;* RUDOLF, *gaunt, grey and dishevelled, deep circles round his eyes, which stare, lifelessly, forward.*

The hour of his death struck well before the year had elapsed. On the twentieth morning of January, in the year 1612, a strange parcel arrived at the Castle from a far country. The sender claimed its contents would restore the ailing Emperor to health and power. The parcel was unwrapped and discovered to contain a mirror, which one of the court magicians immediately carried into the Emperor's chamber. The mirror's surface bulged, like the eye of an insect, with a thousand separate facets, each of which held fast to a tiny reflection.

The court magician turns the mirror so that it casts a highlight upon the shadowed side of RUDOLF'*s face.*

Fade up slowly to deep blue the centre third of the stage: a portion of CATHERINE'*s study; the rear wall with its narrow, oblong window framing a twilight sky, a jumble of Castle rooftops in silhouette; on a small table in the foreground, its back to the audience, stands the silver triptych, shutters open.* CATHERINE *in black, ten years older, peering out the window on the city below, frozen, silent.*

And there, in the mirror they held up to him, Rudolf's face was trapped a thousand times . . . by the black flicker of death.

Slow fade to deep blue RUDOLF *on his deathbed as the chant ceases at its 'Amen' / fade up slowly from deep blue to a dim, white light* CATHERINE'*s study. The bell continues to toll in the distance, in G below* middle C *now that the 'Dies Irae' has ended; to its first three solitary strokes,* CATHERINE *turns sadly from the window and slowly approaches the silver triptych. Her hand moves absently along its contours. She stares down at it, a touch of bitter resignation in her voice as she fights back her tears.*

CATHERINE: Our footprints lie in sand and are, too soon,
    Obliterated by the feeblest wind
    Or swept off in the mortal tide of night.

With every transit of the sun and moon
Across the skies, the auguries that limned
Our fortunes' eyes at birth have dimmed their sight,
And we go blindly to our destinies.

Brief pause.

(*Dashing the triptych to the floor with a sweep of her hand, in a great outburst*) O Prague! (*Falling to her knees, the tears flowing*) You are finished! (*Sinking prostrate to the floor*) Finished!

Begin slow fade to black, the entire stage.
Against CATHERINE*'s bitter weeping, the bell tolls twice more, louder and louder.*
CATHERINE *sobbing . . .*
One last, deafening, stroke of the bell rings down silence and darkness.

June — December 1983

Musical Score

"Neon Blue" Copyright © 1981, 1994 by Eric Basso. ALL RIGHTS RESERVED INCLUDING PUBLIC PERFORMANCE FOR PROFIT. Any arrangement or adaptation of this composition without the consent of the owner is an infringement of copyright

"DIES IRAE"

"GALLIARD"

○ ● = Duration of Tycho's fancy steps (reprise only).

"ALBA"

"ADAGIO"

"HODIE PORTAS MORTIS"

I

II

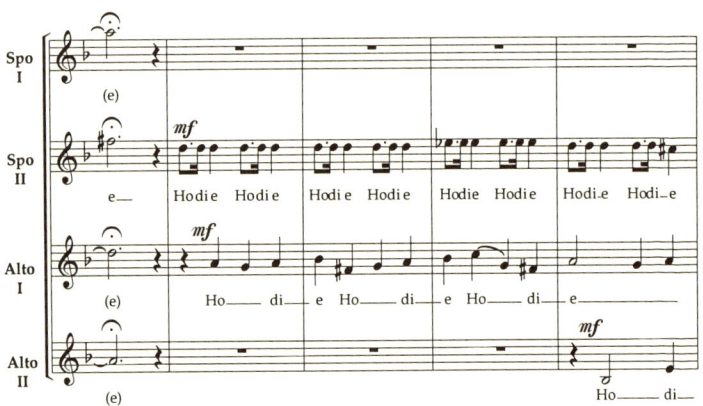

About the Author

Born in Baltimore in 1947, Eric Basso was a regular contributor to the *Chicago Review* from 1977 to 1982, and to *Asylum* magazine since its inception. His fiction, poems, essays, art work and translations have appeared in *Fiction International, Exquisite Corpse, Central Park,* the British magazine *Margin,* and many other publications. His most recently published book is *Equus Caballus* (Atlas Press, London). He is the author of twenty-one plays.